T0354841

10-8
REPORTING
FOR DUTY

SUSAN JURGENS KAMMEN

authorHOUSE®

AuthorHouse™
1663 Liberty Drive
Bloomington, IN 47403
www.authorhouse.com
Phone: 1 (800) 839-8640

Published by AuthorHouse 01/13/2020

ISBN: 978-1-7283-3822-4 (sc)
ISBN: 978-1-7283-3821-7 (e)

"10 – 8 Reporting for Duty" is dedicated to my children, John and Julie, and to all the courageous men and women in law enforcement.

CONTENTS

ACKNOWLEDGMENTS

I am profoundly grateful to the men and women who enthusiastically shared their thoughts and stories with me and those who graciously let me use parts of their books, articles, or letters they had written.

Special thanks to my editor Ruth Kammen Knepper. Her mentoring, insight, and knowledge of the writing business was invaluable. Thanks also to Susan Boulka for helping wrap up some editing on this book.

Only the family of writers understands the unique challenge of living with an author. The process takes a while; we tend to get distracted and work odd hours. No one deserves more appreciation than my husband Ken.

CHAPTER 1

I AM EVERYDAY PEOPLE

It's a summer weekend. Men and women are mowing the yard, working in the garden, planting flowers, and trimming hedges. Inside homes, clothes are in the washing machine, food is being prepared. Someone is using the vacuum and beds are being changed.

They are all doing the usual household chores that ordinary people do. As the weekend comes to a close, men and women are going back to work. One is going to a job as an accountant; another is an attorney, heading for the courtroom. A truck driver starts up his big 18-wheeler and is getting ready for a long haul. A teacher will be driving to a school, and someone else is off to open the library.

One of them is putting on a level 3 bulletproof vest. A camera is attached to the uniform shirt pocket with a magnet. Black leather duty boots are a part of the apparel along with a leather duty belt that holds a .45 caliber H and K semi-automatic handgun, two pair of handcuffs, an ammunition magazine pouch that holds two extra magazines, a key holder, flashlight, Taser, radio, and a can of mace. Uniformed cargo pants are put on which carry latex gloves, alcohol wipes, a tourniquet, and a city-issued cell phone in addition to a personal cell phone. When in full uniform, they are nearly 25 pounds heavier.

These men and women are our protectors. They are expected to be everything for everybody. They need to have tremendous self-control; as they will be spit at, cussed out, and verbally and physically attacked. They need to bring their sense of humor along to work every day, because that will be a part of what keeps them coming to work *every day*.

A sixth sense surrounds them when dealing with people from every walk of life. They have learned through experience to expect the unexpected. Ordinary people wearing a badge to work deal with society's promise and problems. In the end, there are times when they deal with threatened harm and heart-breaking cases of domestic abuse, child abuse, accidental death, suicides, and homicides. Most, however, will state later in their careers that there was no job they would rather have done.

Many young women and men have wanted to be police officers since they were young. They dreamed of wearing the uniform, a badge, and serving their community. They have seen others' tears and also wiped away their own. They have heard laughter and have been a part of tremendous personal joys. The law enforcement community has been given praise and applause for the jobs they do while enduring brutal criticism. Those involved with enforcing the law are required to have empathy, sympathy, incredible control, a sense of humor, and the ability to have that sixth sense about people—what their behavior might be, and, most importantly, to calm situations. They have risen above the call of duty during their law-enforcement careers.

Many have not lived a long life. Family, friends, community members, and officers from across the regions have packed churches to say goodbye to their comrades. Their caskets have been flanked by friends and surrounded by their photographs and flowers as family sat nearby. Every officer should be precious to us. Beyond that uniform, behind that badge, there is a man or woman that is cherished and loved by their family. Beyond that badge, behind that uniform is a person—an ordinary person who wears that uniform, and pins on that badge each workday. He or she has one goal in mind, which is to serve and protect the public. They have our backs—do we have theirs?

> *"With courage you will dare to take risks, have the strength to be compassionate, and the wisdom to be humble. Courage is a foundation of integrity."*

—Mark Twain

Mike Jurgens, July 18, 1944 – September 7, 1999

What you are about to read began as a memoir of my husband Mike's and my family—a record for our children, starting with the last nine months of their father's life. As family and friends shared their stories about Mike, this book has morphed into a story about many others in law enforcement and their families.

When you come to the end of this book, my first hope is that you will see people in law enforcement as just that: people—ordinary people who are sometimes expected to do extraordinary things.

My second hope is that you will understand that people in law enforcement have many of the same worries, expectations, and fears that others have, including yourself.

Their lives are different. Our lives can be as public or as private as we wish, while people in law enforcement are known by most of the people in the communities they serve. They see so many different sides of life. Sometimes they see the day-to-day, normal and happy sides. But, all too often, they are forced to see the seamy, ugly, messy sides that most of us are spared.

Some of the following thoughts and opinions are my own but most are what I have gathered from people involved in the enforcement of our laws. I have researched areas of life to which police, sheriffs, and state troopers are called and have been enlightened by their candid, emotional responses. I am genuinely excited by what they have been willing to share. And hopefully I have correctly put those thoughts, opinions, and emotions into words.

Ultimately, this has evolved into a story of so much more than the last year of a dying man's life. It has become a narrative of many other families, careers, and lives—not just Mike's and mine.

CHAPTER 2

ALL THOSE YEARS AGO

"Do you want to go for a ride?" Those were the first words Mike said to me. I was sitting on the top row of the bleachers at the ball park. Before I could answer, he lifted me off the bleachers and set my feet on the ground. He opened the door to a friend's new cream and bronze Fireflight 1957 Desoto and helped me into the back seat. I didn't know what to think of him. He was handsome with brown curly hair combed into a ducktail and a mischievous look in his eye. I wrote in my diary that night that I had met a boy named Mike Jurgens. He was cute, but I didn't know if I liked him. I saw him a few more times, and then he asked if I would go for a ride with him on a Sunday afternoon. He could have his parents' car, a 1953 two-toned green Studebaker, from 1:00 to 4:00.

As I looked out my upstairs bedroom window the next Sunday, I saw his car drive up. He knocked on the door, and I heard my dad invite him in. "I'd like to take Susan for a ride," he said. "Susan," my dad called while I was standing at the top of the stairs. "Would you like to go for a ride with this young man?" That began the Sunday afternoon rides that we would take together for the next year. My parents liked him. So did I!

"He is clean cut," my mother would say.

5

"Very responsible and reliable," said my dad.

Mike was all of that. He still had the white shirt and dress pants on that he wore to church. His hair was slicked back but it was not an official duck tail. His clothes smelled like the outdoors: clean and crisp, thanks to his mother's lack of a clothes dryer.

I would sit in church on a Sunday morning, worried if the weather looked bad. Too much snow and Mike would not be able to come.

My parents slowly moved past the only-during-the day ride so I was able to see Mike at night. He soon bought his own car, a 1948 Ford. He painted it Fire Engine Red. Buying that car would start a love affair with cars, trucks, and motors in general, that would continue until the last days of his life.

Mike had wanted to be a state trooper since he was in high school. I don't know if he told his friends, but he told me often. We saw the policemen as they patrolled up and down the main street of our town. They were young, although I don't think we realized how young they really were. They seemed almost like friends. When I think back, maybe we thought they *were* friends and that they were just busy doing their jobs, keeping a close eye on young teenagers driving up and down Main Street. They interacted with us: They knew us, and we knew them. We had respect for them, and that helped keep everyone in line.

Weldy, one of the young officers, was the younger brother of my aunt who was married to my dad's brother, so I saw him occasionally at family gatherings.

It's now October 2018 and Weldy is 87 years old. I drove to his home about an hour away to interview him. I knocked on the door and he met me, using a walker to get around. He told me of his lung cancer diagnosis eleven years ago and that it was terminal. He underwent chemo treatments, and his doctors called his survival a miracle.

However, the doctors discovered that his cancer had metastasized and that he had a tumor on his brain. That operation was a success. Although he suffered memory loss, his doctors said his memory should come back in about a year. It did not. He has written a memoir. Weldy started it when he was told he was going to die. He gave it to me and told me all the information that I was asking him was in it and that I could use it in my story.

Mike and I dated off and on for the next four years. All through the other loves in our lives, and there were a few, we remained friends. Even if we weren't dating, I would often find him waiting at my school locker to tell me of the latest escapade that he and his friend Lee had been involved in.

We married while Mike was in the Air Force stationed at an Air Force Base in Florida. We had no money but thought we had the world by the tail, that together we could do anything. We would remind ourselves of that mindset when, thirty-five years later, death strolled into our home, pulled up a chair, and stayed awhile.

Michael and Susan married at an Air Force Base in Florida.

We lived off base in the upstairs of a garage in Florida. It had been converted into two apartments. In the heat of summer, our skin stuck to the green vinyl couch, and the living room was tiny. The couple that lived below us was also in the military and from Georgia. She said she knew we were from the north because we walked fast.

This upstairs of a garage had a shower stall. It was the first bathroom I had with a shower, and I liked it. Bathtubs were the way to bathe in my little home town. No, we certainly did not have a bath every day or twice a day like today. We had a bath Saturday night. We could wash our hair more often, but it was done in the bathroom sink. In the 1950s and 60s we were good stewards of our earth.

Our son John was born while we lived in Florida. He was nine days old when the Air Police came to our apartment to get Mike for duty at an Air Base in Thailand. The Vietnam War was escalating. He had been on alert for a month, with his bags packed and sitting on the bedroom floor. I had just enough money to buy a plane ticket back to Minnesota.

Mike was gone for six months, and I divided my time between my parents and Mike's parents. We kept our apartment in Florida as they were hard to find. Our landlords were wonderful people who charged us little to leave our things there. We had just settled into our little upstairs apartment once again when he was sent overseas again, this time to Vietnam. Again, I would stay with each set of parents until the middle of March when he surprised me by coming home. He had two tours of duty overseas and that qualified him for an early out. I can picture his face today as I write this, walking in the door of his parents' home. We smiled for so many hours our faces hurt.

Mike's home away from home in Vietnam.

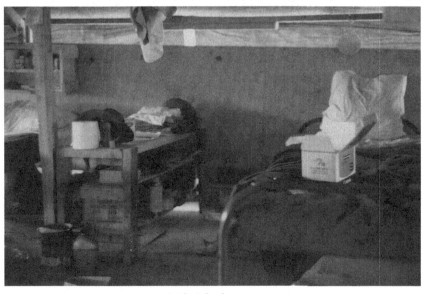

Mike's bedroom.

Mike knew the first thing he needed was a job. His dad was a foreman on a bridge construction crew. Mike had worked for him while he was in high school. His dad had a job for him, even though he did not want Mike to get caught up in that world. Winter layoffs and hard, back-breaking work were not something his dad wanted for his son. My grandma's house sat empty in my home town after her death, and my aunt offered it to us rent free. John and I lived there while Mike was out of town on the construction crew during the week.

At home, I enjoyed the small town life in which I had been reared. When I had difficulty lighting the oil burner in my grandma's house, I told the post master about my dilemma. Before noon, four men from the community had stopped by the house to help. That was the security and care I experienced.

On a snowy day in April 1966, Mike came home from a work site in Minnesota. "There has to be a better way to make a living," Mike said, as he walked in the door unexpectedly in the middle of the week. The weather forced the work to stop and Mike was determined to find a better job. We left for Minneapolis the next day. Staying with my sister and her husband, Mike went out looking for work.

Young men were being drafted for the Vietnam War in record numbers, and workers were needed. Mike had four job offers that first day. A Power company and Telephone company each offered him a job.

My sister's mother-in-law worked for the Minneapolis Police Department. She told him of an opening for a deputy, and also an opening for a policeman in a new suburb. Mike may have been interested in other law enforcement agencies but not in a big city setting.

So, he chose the telephone company. They had an opening in a town in Minnesota, where my parents had purchased a motel two years before. We went back home while my parents looked for a place for us to live. Within a week, we were on our way to a new town and a new job. Mike worked on the line crew, setting poles and running wire for telephones.

The little two-bedroom home we rented on the river road was perfect for us. Our landlords were an elderly couple who looked after us almost like our parents. They owned a farm and raised beef, so we often had fresh meat from them on our table. I would take John with me and have morning coffee with them on my way to help my parents at the motel.

The telephone company was a secure company to work for, with good health insurance and a retirement plan. Just like the job he left; the line crew also worked in all kinds of weather. It was hard work, and Mike wanted more out of a job. He was offered a promotion to install phones and took a transfer to a larger city in Minnesota.

The transfer gave him inside work and that suited him better. Mike was fussy. No one complained about his work as it was always perfect: perfect but slow. He was particular and the installations his boss expected in a day were difficult for him to finish.

After constant complaints about telephone wiring in the walls of new construction, Mike's boss had a job for him. He wired new homes and apartment houses for telephone service. This was the best of both worlds. Mike could be slow and exacting, which he liked. The wiring was done perfectly.

A small newspaper ad caught my eye in the fall of 1968. The Minnesota Highway Patrol was looking for candidates for its class of 1969. There would be forty people accepted. I showed it to Mike. That ad would change our lives forever.

> *"To succeed in life, you need two things: ignorance and confidence."*
>
> —Mark Twain

CHAPTER 3

DREAM A LITTLE DREAM

The ad read:

Highway Patrol Applications Being Sought

St. Paul—*Applications now are being taken by the Minnesota Civil Service Department for positions in the Minnesota Highway Patrol. Interested and qualified persons can apply until Nov. 8 for an examination to be given Nov. 23.*

Qualifications include two years residence in the state, a high school education or its equivalent, sound health and good physical development, ages 21 through 30, height 5-foot-9 to 6-foot-4, and weight proportioned to height.

Those who pass the test and survive a character check, strength and agility test, oral examination and physical examination will be offered an opportunity to attend the Highway Patrol Officer Candidate School next April, May, and June.

There are now several vacancies on the Highway Patrol, and it is expected there will be more before the Candidate School is opened. All graduates of the school last June received immediate appointments to the Patrol.

Officer candidates are provided with room and board, and are paid $200 per month while attending school. Veterans are eligible for additional cash benefits under the G.I. Bill. Upon appointment to the patrol, they work a 40-hour week and are paid $506 per month starting salary, with annual increases. They also receive $3 per day subsistence allowance while on duty.

According to the Minnesota State Patrol web site:

In 1929, the Minnesota State legislature created the Minnesota Highway Patrol in response to the boom in automobiles. The first force was comprised of nine men, including the first chief Earl Brown.

In 1930, Henry Ford's model A was the standard patrol vehicle in the winter. In the spring, summer and early fall, troopers patrolled on Harley-Davidson motorcycles.

Ken Kammen astride the restored to like
condition Harley Davidson motorcycle.

In 1934, the patrol was authorized to enforce speed limits on trunk highways. Many motorists were arrested for driving under the influence of alcohol and these DWI cases were written up as "careless driving." The original trooper uniform was replaced by maroon and gold uniforms. The change was made to honor the University of Minnesota Football National Championship Team.

In 1943, the legislature authorized the purchase of land to erect radio towers to deliver the first voice transmission of calls for service for the Highway Patrol. But for many years (well into the 1950s), troopers would need to call in by phone when signaled, sometimes by a light, flag, etc. At a service station in town, (dispatch would need to know their route) for the call to respond to a crash or other incident.

In 1957, traffic enforcement took to the air with the purchase of two fixed-wing aircraft.

It was 1961 when the patrol units first featured a white door and that tradition continues today.

In 1970 the Department of Public Safety was created, and the Highway Patrol was moved from the Department of Transportation to the newly formed agency.

This was the first year the patrol units were equipped with a "light bar" style rather than the traditional "gumball" (Note both were used during this year.)

In 1974, the Highway Patrol was recognized in the official name changed to "Minnesota State Patrol." Officers were now called "troopers." The official uniform hat was changed from the "peaked hat" style to the "Smoky Bear" style that we know today.

In 1994, first drug detection dog (Pasja) begins work. The patrol currently has 13 K-9s active in the state.

Today, nearly 600 state troopers provide assistance, education and enforcement to people across the state and provide for safe, efficient movement of traffic on Minnesota's roadways. Troopers are supported by 295 civilian personnel.

Troopers also educate Minnesotans about the importance of traffic safety; investigate and reconstruct serious crashes; conduct flight patrols and search and rescue missions; assist other law enforcement agencies; and serve as a vital component of the state's homeland security efforts.

I could hear his footsteps coming down the hall as I cradled Julie, our newborn baby girl in my arms. Mike had a smile that stretched wide across his face and an envelope in his hand. He was not often given to outward expressions of emotions, but this time he could not contain himself. A new baby and a letter from the State of Minnesota were reasons for great joy.

"I passed the test," he said. The letter said they were pleased to inform him that he had passed the first test to become a Minnesota Highway Patrol Officer. Now would begin the process of taking a series of other tests.

The first would be a strength and agility test. It would require him to do a number of physical things such as sit ups, pushups, and other things to determine if he were fit. He had been out of the military for only three years and was twenty-five years old. It did not take him long to get back in shape. We went on a health regimen together: broiled meat and vegetables became our staple foods. We each became mean, lean, and physically fit.

It took more testing: background checks, psychological testing, and oral interviews for Mike to finally be accepted into the Highway Patrol Academy.

This post card was sent to Mike Jan. 30, 1969:

> *Minnesota Civil Service Department*
> *215 State Administration Building*
> *St. Paul, Minnesota 55101*
>
> *Please report to the Highway Department training facilities in Arden Hills for the Minnesota Highway Patrol strength and agility test on Tuesday, February 11, 1969 at 7 a.m.*
>
> *Failure to report will result in elimination from further competition.*

After more testing and interviews Mike received this letter in the mail.

> *State of Minnesota*
> *Department of Highways, St. Paul, MN 55101*
>
> *Dear Sir:*
>
> *You are invited to attend the Highway Patrol training school to be held at the Minnesota highway department – civil defense training center located at 1900 West County Rd. I, New Brighton Minnesota. Report at the school not later than 10:00 PM on Sunday, April 6, 1969*
>
> *Transportation to the school is your responsibility. You may drive a personal car to the school if you wish. There is no bus service to the training facility from the Metropolitan area, so if you use railroad or bus transportation to Minneapolis or St. Paul, it will be necessary to use a taxicab service to the training center.*

A highway patrolman knocked on our door. He had gray hair, and I thought he must be quite old. Thinking back, he was probably in his 40s although I myself at 23 and Mike at 25 thought him elderly.

I poured him a cup of coffee and he joined us at our kitchen table. That *elderly* patrolman talked about the job, what it entailed, what would be expected of Mike, and also the pressure that it would put on his family.

At one point, he spoke directly to me saying it would be up to me if he likes this job. He went on to say that when our children are sick in the middle of the night, he won't be there. When something goes wrong in the house, a problem with plumbing, your lights go out, when things happen, you will have to handle it. He won't be here. Life as you know it will change.

I sat there, stunned. I can't say it hit me at that time...his point of view...his warning, but I certainly mulled it over, remembering those words many times in the next twenty-six years.

Mike and I talked about what he had told us. We hadn't spoken much about what the job would entail, but I'm sure Mike had thought more about it than I.

The actual scope of the job was a mystery to me and, I dare say, to Mike as well. Mike had worked a 9-to-5 job with the phone company. He had, of course, been gone for months at a time while in the Air Force; and he also had been gone Monday through Friday when he worked construction with his dad. I had not minded that time alone because I was prepared for it. I lived with my parents and his while he was in the military stationed overseas. However, for the last couple of years, I was used to his being home every evening and off every weekend.

We were living in southeastern Minnesota at the time and often went either to my parents or to his on weekends. I had no idea how life would change. Even as I thought about everything that patrolman had said, I don't think I grasped the concept. He did not paint a good picture for our ensuing lives, but I didn't think it could possibly be just the way he said it would be. I would learn over the years that, yes, much of what he had said was true and a huge adjustment. It came slowly, not all at once, and I adapted. We adapted. Our son John was just four years old when Mike went on the patrol and our daughter Julie was less than a year old. It was not an adjustment or odd for them. This was their life and they knew no other. Our children viewed their life as other children did no matter what their parents' occupation was. John and Julie did not know or care that their dad drove a squad car or carried a gun.

For Mike to become a patrolman we needed help from our parents. The State of Minnesota paid $200 a month while the men were in school. That amount of money would not pay rent, groceries, and our car payment.

There was no guarantee that Mike would make it through school or that an opening would be available at graduation. So our parents agreed to let us live with them. We would have just enough money to make our car payment and the things the children might need. Mike had been told by the telephone company that he would be welcomed back at any time. This gave us peace of mind. Today's Minnesota State Patrol candidates get full pay while they are in training.

Our parents were patient while two little ones and I brought noise and some amount of chaos into their lives. My parents owned a motel and had three teenagers at home. Their lives were already hectic. Mike's parents, on the other hand, had a relatively quiet life until we moved in. They were wonderful though and took it all in stride.

"Don't wait. The time can never be just right."

—Mark Twain

CHAPTER 4

WORKING FOR THE STATE ON THE HIGHWAY PATROL

I took the bus to Arden Hills for the patrol school graduation—a proud day for the graduates and for their families. Mike's intelligence did not show itself in his high school days. He was there for the social fun; studying was not important. Patrol School was different. He was there to succeed.

1969

Minnesota Highway Patrol

Officer Candidate School

Graduation and Open House

YOU ARE INVITED TO ATTEND AN OPEN HOUSE AND THE GRADUATION CEREMONIES OF THE MINNESOTA HIGHWAY PATROL OFFICER CANDIDATE SCHOOL ON JUNE 27, 1969

OPEN HOUSE FROM 10:00 A.M. TO NOON

GRADUATION CEREMONIES AT 1:30 P.M.

AT THE MINNESOTA HIGHWAY DEPARTMENT-CIVIL DEFENSE TRAINING CENTER

1900 West County Road

New Brighton, Minnesota

Noon Lunch Served
Refreshments following
Graduation Ceremonies

I was full of pride as I watched Mike and the other soon-to-be officers in the Minnesota Highway Patrol take the oath.

MSP OATH

I do solemnly swear, To support the Constitution of the United States, the Constitution and laws of the state of Minnesota, and that I will faithfully and impartially discharge the duties of State Patrol Trooper employed and designated under and pursuant to the provisions of chapter 299D, and all acts amendatory thereto; To serve the state of Minnesota and the United States of America honestly and faithfully and at all times fulfill my oath as State Patrol Trooper; To be loyal to my supervisors and fellow troopers and obey and enforce the law without fear, favor or discrimination as to class, color, race or creed; to help those in danger or distress and, if necessity arise, lay down my life rather than swerve from the path of duty; and to conduct myself at all times in accordance with the highest moral standards and never commit any act that will reflect discredit on the Minnesota State Patrol or any member thereof. All of this I solemnly swear to the best of my knowledge and ability, so help me God.

★ ★ ★

So just what is a policeman? The following poem presents a clear description.

What is a Policeman?

A policeman is a composite of what all men are, a mingling of saint and sinner, dust and deity...

He, of all men, is at once the most needed and, the most unwanted. He's a strangely nameless creature who is "sir" to his face and "fuzz" behind his back.

He must be such a diplomat that he can settle differences between individuals so that each will think he won.

But...

If the policeman is neat, he's conceited; if he's careless, he's a bum. If he's pleasant, he's a flirt; if he's not, he's a grouch.

He must make in an instant, decisions that would require months for a lawyer...A policeman must know everything—and not tell. He must know where all the sin is—and not partake.

A policeman must, from a single human hair, be able to describe the crime, the weapon and the criminal—and tell you where the criminal is hiding.

But...

If he catches the criminal, he's lucky; if he doesn't, he's a dunce.

If he gets promoted, he has political pull; if he doesn't, he's a dullard...

The policeman must be a minister, a social worker, a diplomat, a tough guy and a gentleman.

And, of course, he'll have to be a genius...

For he'll have to feed a family on a policeman's salary.

– Paul Harvey

Mike was in the top ten per cent of his class, so he could state a preference for his first station. His dream of being a Minnesota Highway Patrolman had come true. He could pick three, giving first, second, and third choice. Mike got his first choice. The town was located between my parent's home fifty miles south and Mike's parent's fifty miles north: too far for an impromptu visit and close enough for a day visit. It was perfect.

Michael T. Jurgens, SP 280. Minnesota Highway Patrol.

Mike's first squad car.

We were both excited to hear that he was given his first-choice. The town sat along a river. We enjoyed a touch of woods mixed in with the farmland. It was the same kind of community we had grown up in. It was a laid back, easy going life, with church going people and good work ethics. Our county was "dry" (but you could get an alcoholic drink just across the river.)

We were settled into a rental house in no time. It was an almost new rambler style home. An elderly farmer couple had the home built but one passed away and the other went to a nursing home shortly after moving in. That was, and still is, my favorite style house. We embraced our new community and soon had a large circle of friends.

The law enforcement community gives you instant access to information. You don't have to get to know people to have connections. Who's a good doctor? Dentist? Mechanic? Accountant? Babysitter? These are questions you need answered as soon as you arrive in a new place. We had only to ask other law officers to get whatever information we needed and felt quite secure in getting the right answers.

Mike was a planner and an organizer. I now know how much he worried about doing his job right; however, he did not share those feelings with me until years later.

The first fatality he investigated was on a stormy day in 1969 when the children and I had planned to attend a wedding about a two-hour drive from home that afternoon. It was snowing and visibility was decreasing. I was still deciding if I would go. Mike stopped at home only long enough to tell me, "You're not going!" The accident was no doubt caused by the poor visibility. A man was riding with his brother who had been driving across the railroad track in a small town. They were hit by the train. His death left Mike shaken and impacted his life more than he let on. He paced the floor, stopping at his desk in the dining room to write down eyewitnesses' statements. He felt pressured to draw the layout of the accident where the death occurred just right. There was sure to be a lawsuit involving the train and even perhaps the town.

Later in the week Mike announced, in his matter-of-fact tone, that he believed he had ringworm and that I was to call the doctor and make an appointment for him. What? I had the giggles, and he was not amused. I did not know what ringworm looked like, but I didn't think he had it. The round circles of red flaky patches on his arm were eczema, caused, the doctor said, by stress.

Mike did not agree with the doctor and told me he didn't have any stress. The salve the doctor gave him worked, and the red patches disappeared. I was surprised myself. I did not think he was prone to stress. Since he did not share his worries or his fears with me early in our marriage, I naively didn't think he had any.

As our lives together continued, I would realize that he worried more than most people, certainly more than I. Mike took care of us. I never worried because he was always there to take care of the problems. I took care of the day-to-day grind and small problems that arose within a young family. He was there for the bigger things in life.

In the nine years, we spent in that community, there would be many accidents and of course some resulting in deaths.

"You get used to it," Mike would say. "It's your job, and if you don't look at it as a job, you can't do it right."

I knew he was right; however, shutting down your feelings on the job also means shutting down your feelings for other things as well.

Our town didn't have restaurants that stayed open all night the first years we lived there. The highway patrolman, deputies, and local policeman had no place to stop for coffee or something to eat if they were working after midnight. So, our house became a favorite stopping place. Coffee was quick to make, and I usually had food on hand.

Squad cars in our driveway were a common sight; our children gave no notice of them. Their friends however were always fascinated by them.

Before we had lived there a year, we bought a house. We could qualify for a Veteran's loan, which meant no money down. We had saved $1,000. Most of that would go for the closing costs, deposits for hook-ups, the stove, and refrigerator. We had $150 left when we moved in. I wanted to buy the dryer that was in the basement, but we were just about out of money. There were no credit cards back then. You either had the money or did without.

My dad visited us before the auction the previous homeowner was having. We showed him the house, and he also saw the dryer. "Is that staying?" he asked. "No," I answered. "It's $50, and we've spent a lot so far." "Do you want it?" he questioned. "Yes," I said. Smilingly he took out $50 from his wallet and handed it to me. The dryer lasted for 23 years and was one of the best gifts I have ever received.

Before we had lived there a month, the water heater sprung a leak. A new one would cost $150. We still had money in our checking account for our house payment, food, and our utility bills. However, Mike's comment, after the water heater was installed, was that we were now officially broke. We would, over the years, have newer, nicer homes, but no house would hold the special place in my heart like our first little home on Fifth Street.

Our "new" home was a story and a half; it was built in the late 40s. It had been well cared for and fit our needs and our wallet. It had slanted ceilings upstairs; the second story was our son John's domain. He loved it up there all by himself and would wonder why I ever had to come up.

As of this writing, it has been forty years since I left. I returned to interview old friends. Sitting in the home of a retired sheriff and his wife brought back fond memories. The years had treated them kindly and their welcome brought me close to tears. As the retired sheriff remembered his working days, he told me he had been working at a gas station when the then sheriff asked if he would be interested in being a deputy. It was 1967. He was 24 years old. He had a wife and two children and, yes, would be interested in that job. There was no training; he just started working. The first ticket he wrote was to a local man he knew who didn't speak to him again for years.

The judge in those days often held court in his office. No robe, no formalities, for minor offenses. He simply asked if the person pled Guilty or Not guilty. If the plea was Not guilty, the judge listened to each side and gave his verdict. In more serious cases, he donned his robe, seated the jury, and the trial was held in the courtroom. In the early days, there was one squad car. The sheriff drove his personal car. The squad car had a radio that occasionally worked. Pounding on it usually brought it back to life as it was full of tubes. But there were no dispatchers and no jailers at that time, so chances are there was no one to answer you anyway.

He talked of the advantages and drawbacks of working in a small community. He knew almost everyone. As an officer sworn to uphold the law, he also had to enforce laws broken by friends and relatives.

An officer's watchful eye has to be especially diligent in showing no favoritism. He has lived in the same home and has had the same phone number since starting with the county many years ago. Everyone was welcomed at his home. The public could come to his house or phone him with a complaint or concern any time.

Although sharing many things about work with his wife, he did not share the gory details. In his days of being both a deputy and later the sheriff, he was acutely aware of the problems people faced in their personal lives. It was his county, and he knew well the strengths and weaknesses of the individuals in his community. He was ready to retire after serving as a deputy and, later, five terms as sheriff. It was time to hang it up. Would he want the job today? No!

After the interview, memories flooded my brain as I enjoyed a nostalgic drive around the town I had learned to love so many years ago. Scenes from those wonderful days scrolled through my thoughts. The swimming pool is quite new, built down the road from the old one, but a picture of the old one stays vividly in my mind.

I drove down Fifth Street, savoring the time we had spent in the little house on the corner. Our neighborhood was full of young parents with children in 1970. It was busy, noisy, and a perfect place for us. Our corner lot was a hub of activity. The swimming pool was just a block away. John and Julie would both become excellent swimmers. Julie, at age seven, was allowed in the big pool. The rule was age twelve, but she was a remarkable swimmer and most persistent.

There were three pools at the swimming complex. The smallest one, a baby pool, was shallow and parents were in charge, as there were no lifeguards. The next was the middle pool for ages twelve and under.

A test would then be taken in order to advance to the big pool. That pool had a slide and two diving boards: a low and a high. Julie was a strong swimmer and began to pester the lifeguards in the middle pool to let her go in the big pool. They finally asked my permission to let her test; if she passed, I would have to sign a permission slip for her to be in the big pool.

I watched her in the pool, swimming laps and doing whatever the lifeguards asked of her. The final test was a dive off the high dive. She did a perfect dive and went deep into the water. She seemed to take a long time to come up to the surface. Although the lifeguards were watching her, I was about to jump in myself when she finally surfaced.

With a big smile on her face, she asked, "Did I pass?" She had, and from then on, she could be with the big kids, often sitting in the sun with the pretty young girls during break time.

Our town had a population of about 5,000 people. The river ran close to town and there were beautiful falls in the park on the edge of town. Our children had a tremendous amount of freedom to roam and explore.

Julie, at about age four, marched with the band while they practiced their songs and marching in step. Julie's afternoon naps had often been interrupted as the band marched down our street. She would wake up, screaming. We decided to buy her a baton so she could feel a part of it and less afraid of the noise.

Before long she was twirling the baton as well as the majorette and going everywhere the band went. I didn't worry, as the girls in the band kept a close eye on her. She would always end up back at the school just a block from us.

John and his friend would go tubing down the river. We didn't know this until Mike saw them rolling the tube down the road. They stored it at the gas station, knowing we would not approve. They roamed the area, loving the river and exploring everything. We didn't know half of what they did and also didn't know all the dangerous situations they were involved in. Mike and I could think back to when our parents didn't know all the dangers we faced either.

After seven years in our little home, we bought an almost new three-bedroom rambler. It was in a new development on the edge of town. We left wonderful neighbors in our old neighborhood; but the town was small, and we were never far away from anyone in town. We moved into our long rambler in October 1977.

It was a hard move for our son John. He had enjoyed having the privacy of his upstairs all to himself. There, he and his buddies had a private playroom. I came up occasionally to clean, but John took care of most of that by himself; he didn't want me coming around too often. He brought his laundry down and changed his own bed. He had to give up his room only when we had overnight guests. The walls were made of material similar to ceiling tile but in large sheets. The material was soft and prone to breaking easily.

Posters became a good way to hide the holes he and his friends sometimes put in the walls from aggressive playing. They were mostly hidden from Dad. One in particular comes to mind: A monkey riding a motor cycle covered the biggest hole. Mike didn't see that hole until the day we moved.

John's bedroom in the new house was the first one down the hall just off the dining room. He was twelve years old and had growing pains. He did not like giving up his upstairs hide-away. Even the new bedspread and curtains from Grandma didn't make it better.

Julie loved her new room. It was bigger and brighter than her old one. Grandma gave her a new bedspread and curtains to match. Blue and frilly, they were a huge hit. She loved them.

"Some memories are unforgettable, remaining ever vivid and heartwarming."

—Joseph B. Wirthlin

CHAPTER 5

WHO'S GONNA FILL THEIR SHOES?

What do you want to be when you grow up? That's a question we were often asked when we were kids. I suppose children are asked the same question today. Growing up in the late 50s and 60s, we didn't have the choices there are today. My brother went into the Marines; Mike, into the Air Force.

My first question in my interviews of law enforcement people was, "Did you always want to be in law enforcement?"

The answers varied. A few answered with a simple yes or no. One man said that day he started on the school patrol; he was hooked. He wanted to be a policeman. Another said that he was a mechanic and had never thought much of being a policeman. He was already married with two children. When he told his parents that he was thinking about trying for the highway patrol, they didn't think he had much of a chance. It did, however, become his career with the Minnesota State Patrol—first on the road and later in the sky.

The drive into the North country in September 2017 was another trip down memory lane. The smell of pine trees in the air made me feel like I was on vacation. I had made plans to interview four retired law enforcement men. One of the retired deputies I interviewed has had a stroke and is plagued with other health issues. He told me probation was his first interest, when I asked the question, did he always want to be in law enforcement?

He went on to say there were no openings in that area but he was offered a job as a deputy. He was 23 when he joined the ranks of law enforcement. On his first day, in a hurry to turn around in someone's driveway, he backed over their mailbox. Asking if he was nervous on his first day, he already knew that when you work on the highway, you'd better be nervous.

The gray color mixing with his dark hair and the laugh lines around this retired deputy's eyes remind me that we have each aged. He grew up in the north country and had been in the military. His parents and his wife were not excited about him going into law enforcement. He had also been offered a job to continue in the arena of law enforcement while he was in the military. His wife said if he stayed in she would leave him. A few years later she left him anyway. He applied for the Minnesota State Patrol. They were not hiring but he was hired as a city policeman.

He says the best advice he ever heard was from a police chief. In essence, it was the Golden Rule that many of us learned from our parents and heard often in school. Although the chief's words were just a little different, it was another way of living by the Golden Rule. "Do unto others as you would have them do unto you."

A retired trooper told me he had wanted to be in either law enforcement or the military as long as he could remember. When he was in the third or fourth grade, he wrote to the chief of the Highway Patrol and asked him what he had to do to become a trooper. He did not remember who the chief was at that time but he does remember that he wrote him back. The chief told him to study hard, stay with his dream, and sometimes wishes do come true. He accomplished both of his dreams with 34 years of the Minnesota State Patrol and 30 years in the military.

Officer Weldy had written this:

> *I was a truck driver after the service. One evening, we were invited to a friend's for supper. I mentioned that I was sick of not being home and I hardly knew my kids. He said there was an opening for a policeman where I lived, and he would take me in and introduce me to the mayor. We went right into town and I put in my application.*
>
> *I left on my next run, and over the New Year, I broke down in Trenton, New Jersey. I was a few days late getting home, but when I did, my wife informed me I got the police job. I drove right over and went to the City Hall to see the mayor. He said, "I see you already have a uniform." I still had my gray whipcord driving outfit on. He then handed me some car keys, informed me the police car was parked out back, and said there was a gun on the front seat. I said, "Okay." He went back to work, and I was a cop.*
>
> *I really didn't know anything about being a police officer, so I had to play it by ear. I found out that the police reserve unit in a neighboring town, met on Tuesday nights. I managed to get myself invited and picked up some valuable schooling. I would get off work at 3 a.m. and go to the neighboring town and ride around with the police until 7 a.m. This way I got some practical experience. This went on for months and my knowledge and my confidence both increased.*

After graduating high school, this man had majored in law enforcement, hoping to become a trooper or FBI agent. However, the following year, he changed his major to accounting, as he had heard that the FBI hires CPAs. After his first intermediate accounting course his sophomore year, he soon realized accounting wasn't for him and changed his major again to finance. Out of college he took the first job offered to him at a bank and worked as an analysist.

After about ten years of lukewarm enjoyment in the banking profession, they lost their four-month-old daughter. He became disinterested and changed to another bank for employment, thinking that would make a difference in his discontentment. It did not. However, an event took place that set him on a path for a career change to his first passion, law enforcement.

While working at the bank, he had walked out the door, in full suit and tie and noticed a man sprinting by him. Behind the man was a police officer chasing him. He could see the officer was not getting close, so he took after the man being chased. Thankfully, the runner stumbled a bit and he caught up with him, tackled him to the ground and held him there until the officer came to arrest him.

That was August of 2006. He resigned his position at the bank, went back to school to finish the year he had left of law enforcement credits, and set his sights on the Minnesota State Patrol.

He talked it over with his wife and she was 100% for it. The trooper continued his story remembering how excited he was when he was told he had been hired and invited to attend training at Camp Ripley. However, in January he questioned his career choice when rudely awakened out of a deep sleep at 4:30 a.m. by the sound of a garbage can rolling down the hallway of the billets; his welcome to the first day of the Minnesota State Patrol Academy. He was 35 years old.

The young deputy had told himself when he decided to go into law enforcement that it was either the smartest thing or the dumbest thing. He still has not decided. He had wanted to be a business man. While working at a gas station, he rode along with a friend in law enforcement. He was eighteen when he got a job as a dispatcher and decided he wanted police work. His dad cautioned him, and his wife was not in favor of the idea. He and his wife were both EMTs, and he had shared many of his job-related experiences with her. She knew the danger and everything else that went along with the job. Nevertheless, he enrolled in school, and the job he had as a dispatcher has helped him immensely. As he roared down the road in pursuit of someone, he knew exactly what the person on the other end of the line needed from him.

The retired trooper had never thought of it. While working, five fellows drove from Long Lake to New Brighton. A guy was reading a want ad in the paper and thought his friend should apply for the job of game warden or highway patrol. The patrol hired him.

A Minnesota State Trooper told his story: His first desire for law enforcement started in junior high when he wanted to be a conservation officer. Over time his dad talked him out of that occupation. He signed up for a mechanical course in Vo-Tech after high school but it's not what he wanted. He got married in the fall after graduating high school. During the summer he and his wife discussed his true desire for future work. He withdrew from the mechanical course and applied for the law enforcement course. At that time Alexandria offered an 18-month course straight through and he took that option. He's in year 42 now. The trooper was 20 and couldn't go into a bar off duty.

A Minnesota State Trooper shared her story: Her dad was a policeman years ago but had to quit the job. They just didn't pay enough to support a growing family. She started thinking about a Criminal Justice degree. Her dad thought the Minnesota State Patrol was the best.

Another trooper was a mechanic and worked on squad cars for the Minnesota State Patrol. He remembered seeing a trooper pass through the small town where he grew up. All the young boys were excited.

He was just 23 when he started on the patrol and did not think that was too young.

A man I interviewed said that the idea of entering law enforcement never really occurred to him until his sophomore year of college. He is now a Minneapolis Police Sergeant. He had originally enrolled in college, seeking a business degree. He registered for a Criminal Justice class during his sophomore year to fulfill one of his liberal arts electives. He had a newfound interest in law enforcement, and recalled vividly a conversation he had with Officer Ken Kammen—his future father-in-law. Ken was the inspiration he used to pursue his career in law enforcement and also for pursuing his promotion to sergeant, which he obtained.

An officer went to trade school to be a carpenter, a builder. He came out of school and knew that if he wanted a good wage, he would have to work away from home and family during the week. His mother thought he needed a job with security, benefits, and the ability to be home during the week. His *mom* sent in an application to the Minnesota State Patrol. To appease her, he took the test and passed it. He kept passing the testing until he heard he was being backgrounded. He received an invitation to the academy and the first thing he knew; he was a trooper.

The oldest of seven children talked about his introduction into law enforcement. His dad was a deputy and he saw how much time he missed with his family. He didn't want any part of it. He went to school on a hockey scholarship but did not finish his degree. His friends were making big bucks in the mines. He smiles as he talks about those young days. The money looked good and his friends were buying cars and houses. He decided to join them. After the layoffs at the mines he did some logging. When his father was killed, he took another look at his job. He was 29 when his father was taken. He talked about his father Robert "Beefy" Lawson who was killed, execution style.

Some of his dad's friends said he should think about a job in law enforcement. One day when he was walking down the street, a deputy said that they would like to have him work with them. He started working at the jail. They were called jailers/dispatchers and he didn't have a clue as to what that entailed. He believes he is a better person because of what he has seen in law enforcement. He remembered manual typewriters and that everything was done by telephone. It was the old crow bar motel...like the Gunsmoke jail. He liked that old style. He believed a lot of good people come to jail. He tried to spend time with those who could learn from their mistakes and become better people. The deputy/jailer felt a responsibility to bring the best out in the person.

A New York City Captain was not particularly interested in law enforcement until he was in high school. He goes on to say that he was a bit rebellious at that time in his life, not doing anything in school and on the wrong path.

A young New York State Trooper took him under his wing and became his best friend. He allowed him to ride with him on patrol and the young man became more and more interested in the job. The young man was accepted at a Community College, and into their Police Science (now known as Criminal Justice) program.

A civil service exam was offered for the trainee program at the local police department. He did well and was hired. The program provided a part-time job in the PD while attending college. In the summer he worked full-time, generally in administrative assignment throughout the department. This was normally a three-year program but he took the next civil service exam for police officer and was hired in July 1970.

He also was married that July—they had a lot going on as a young couple. He was 21 years old.

The Academy class hit the streets in late September and he began a rotation of the different sections or precincts for the next several months. His first real assignment was on the midnight shift on the west side of the city. It was a cultural awakening for a skinny young officer from a small town in upstate/northern New York.

The trooper settles in to answer my questions. Sitting in a comfortable chair with his left foot on the floor and the right one tossed across the arm of the chair, he is relaxed. I asked my usual lead off question, "Did you always want to be in law enforcement?" He smiled and told me he had wanted to be a hairdresser. I had a look of disbelief of my face. He acknowledged that look but that is what he had wanted to do.

He was working in the Minneapolis area at the time. He was a small-town boy and didn't like working in the city. A friend told him that they were taking applications for the Minnesota Highway Patrol. He had never thought about law enforcement. He took the test and flunked. Continuing to work in Minneapolis he took the test again the next year and passed. He was nervous on his first day at work mostly because he didn't know what to expect from his supervisors. They were wonderful men and he quickly learned to respect each of them.

The young guy didn't expect to be in law enforcement. He needed a job. Some people were glad to know him; some were apprehensive when they found out he was a police officer. The police officer I am interviewing talked about giving a guy a break if he has a good attitude and if the infraction is fairly minor. Now he laments that everything has to be politically correct. He can't necessarily give the leeway he used to. He has to follow policy.

He started working for a township but had no training as a law officer—no experience at all. He pulled into town with everything he owned in his car. He found a place to live and then went to the Township Board. The board had bought a car from a car lot and had a light bar from the Sheriff's Office. He had a hundred eight square miles to patrol. They gave him a map of the area and a catalog to order his stuff.

He started in July and didn't go to any training for law enforcement until February. He had to learn his area, and it was over three months before he had a radio. He did, however, have a CB radio. Once in a while, he could reach the Patrol Tower if he needed help. The area had never had police protection. When he stopped someone, he had no way to call for backup. He was strictly on his own.

When the officer arrested someone, he had to transport the prisoner about 20 miles away. The people working at the jail asked who he was.

When Mike applied for the Minnesota Highway Patrol, there were over 2,000 applicants. I believe forty were chosen and a few dropped out for various reasons. A former chief of the patrol told me there was a time when over 5,000 applied. Today that has changed. Small towns and suburbs are having a hard time filling the need for police officers. They are also having a harder time keeping them. With the verbal and, more often now, physical attacks on those who swear to protect us, many are asking themselves if it's really worth it.

A college that trains many of Minnesota's officers has seen several students drop out after their families expressed fears for their safety.

Take this job and shove it! If you're still a cop, quit the damn job! Get out while you can! I heard those words many times. Offers of early retirement, which certainly many are going to accept, will also decrease the number of seasoned law enforcement officers. Some departments are already gravely concerned about the absence of women and men ready to step in to what have become perilous occupations.

"This trend is also playing out nationally where the number of applications for police jobs is lower and retaining current officers has become more challenging," said Bill Johnson, Executive Director of the National Association of Police.www.politico.com

These men and women symbolize the same guardians who challenged danger, ran into the buildings, and delivered thousands to safety when terrorists attacked our country on 9/11. People praised their efforts and bravery of the protectors doing their job. Today criticism seems standard practice.

"The undeserved criticism of police, and, from our point of view, the painting of a very broad brush that all officers and police departments are racist or brutal based on a handful of cases, and targeted murders of police officers, are making it difficult to attract and retain qualified officers. There is a growing sense among police that it's not worth it anymore," Johnson said.www.politico.com

The Dallas Police Department, which was also struggling to recruit officers, saw a surge in job applications after the ambush shooting on July 7, 2016, wrote Micah Xavier Johnson of the *New York Times*. "The man fired upon a group of police officers in Dallas, Texas, killing five officers and injuring nine others."

The New York Times goes on to say, "During the 12 days following the July 7 shooting the department said it got 467 job applications, a 344 percent increase compared with 136 at a similar period in June."

Dallas Police Chief David Brown said, "We are hiring, get out of that protest line and put an application in."

Law enforcement agencies are using everything in their arsenal to encourage young people to want the job, wear the shield, and save people often from themselves. Facebook, Twitter, and Instagram are all ways the enforcement arena is trying to connect with the young people of today. I see the Minnesota State Patrol on Facebook with pictures and encouragement to join the ranks of those brave men and women who selflessly serve their communities. October 17, 2018, I saw an invitation on Facebook from the town where I went to school, asking licensed police officers to apply for openings in its department.

Departments want to hire a diverse group of officers. They want officers to come from different races and gender. I asked a Minneapolis officer if he thought more black officers should be involved in patrolling and responding to calls in primarily black neighborhoods. No! He went on to say that black officers in predominately black neighborhoods are even more disrespected than the white officers.

To better understand the job, many recruiters and law enforcement officers recommend volunteering with local police departments or participating in a ride-along with an officer before applying. Recruitment goals aren't just to fill jobs. They are to swear in officers who will serve the community for an entire career.

Officers I spoke to reflected on the day they believed that people liked them. The officers knew us and we knew them, but not anymore.

We knew the policeman in town and the deputies in the county where we would *drag main* mostly on weekends. As we rolled slowly down Main Street, we often met a police car. The men in the car waved. We also, seeing a car full of boys that interested us, rolled our window down and made a hand gesture that meant "meet you in the alley." We'd park in the parking lot to talk and flirt. We often saw police in the squad car also roaming around the alley.

The sheriff of the county used to pick his deputies. He had influence, charisma, and the trust of the people who voted him into office. Now they need at least two years at a school for law enforcement and preferably a four-year college degree in Criminal Justice. Some of the older officers' question whether the college-educated man or woman is prepared to deal with the public. Are they a bit haughty about their newly found authority?

Officers need to present themselves to the people of their community. They must be approachable. The man I interviewed said he often hears from people he has encountered in the jail setting. They tell him they are now doing well and thank him for his interest in them.

Trooper drives by now, I wave, and they don't. I have experienced that and I also heard that from many retired officers. One said he stopped a police officer and told him he'd better stop and talk to people, to be a part of the community. Common sense should tell law enforcement that they need to interact with their community. They know they've lost something.

He spoke of another deputy and of his father, who had also been a deputy. They knew the people in their town. They asked the right questions and knew the shady element.

The officer only has two eyes. The community has thousands.

This officer sees that police expect respect from the community but that respect needs to come from law enforcements' actions with the public as well. He stresses the need for mothers and fathers to participate with their communities and that significant change must come from within communities and neighborhoods themselves. Witnesses to crime must step up and work with their neighborhoods. We need participants in cities, counties, and on the state level to bring real and meaningful changes.

He agrees that officers can give a person a break. If the person screws up again, the officer writes a ticket. You have to be fair, but the public has to know you mean business. Do it again and you're going to suffer the consequences.

This retired deputy/jailer told me that he drives school bus now. He asked the children on the bus what they wanted to be when they grow up? He received the usual answer: nurse, teacher, soldier, cowboy, fireman—but no one said policeman. Didn't any of the children want to be policemen? No! They don't want to get shot.

> *"Do you want to know who you are? Don't ask! Act! Action will delineate and define you."*
>
> —Thomas Jefferson

CHAPTER 6

TAKING CARE OF BUSINESS

Tell me about your first day at work.

A Minneapolis policeman remembered his first day at work very well. June 22, 1997. He was incredibly nervous. Several days prior to starting his first shift he went to the 3rd precinct to get his work schedule and hopefully meet his first month Field Training Officer (FTO). He approached the desk officer and introduced himself, informing him that he was hoping to meet his new training officer. When he told the desk officer who he was looking for, the desk officer laughed out loud and wished him Good Luck!

The stress level was high on his first day of work. After years of schooling and several months in the Minneapolis Police Academy, he was finally ready to hit the streets as an official police officer with real bullets in his gun. The stress level was increased knowing that he was about to start this career in the height of summer in one of the busiest precincts in the city with one of the toughest Field Training Officers.

He felt completely overwhelmed because there was so much to think about. He was a brand-new recruit wearing brand-new shiny leather, meeting veteran officers for the first time in a precinct station that he had never been in before, driving a squad car in an unfamiliar part of the largest city in Minnesota during the busiest time of year.

His head was spinning as he struggled to navigate the unfamiliar streets responding to his first calls as an official police officer. The anxiety level was high knowing that his every move and action were being graded by a salty veteran officer.

The officer recalled that during his first shift, he responded to a report of a "person with a gun" call and he had to pull out his shotgun and point it at the suspect to get him to the ground for handcuffing. He remembers thinking to himself *what the hell have I gotten myself into?*

The first night was both stressful and exciting at the same time. He was so excited about his first day that he shared the experience and stories of the night's events with anyone that was willing to listen.

Mike's first days as a highway patrolman were riding with seasoned patrolmen from his home town area. The two he rode with were patrolling the area when we were dragging Main as teenagers. Mike was only 25 years old and had been gone from that area for seven years. The highway patrolmen in our area were almost celebrities. One of them was gray-haired and as a teenager I thought him old but very handsome. He was probably 40. Another patrolman often parked by a gas station in my town where I turned to go home. Rolling down the window on the squad he would tell me to Slow down! He was still working when Mike started and Mike rode with the two of them for a few days.

Some of the memories of other officers about their first day at work were vivid. A trooper stationed in downtown Minneapolis with heavy traffic told me he knows he was nervous. He had a very busy day. A deputy recalled that he enjoyed his first day on the job. He thought it was different and exciting being a policeman in the town he grew up in. He hadn't smoked for many years but was smoking before the day was over.

The state patrol had trained this officer for over a year, so he felt quite comfortable on his own. He wasn't nervous as much as he was anxious. The trooper didn't like issuing the first ticket and in his first year, issued less tickets than he does now. He still looks for reasons not to give a ticket. If you received one from him, you really must have deserved it.

A deputy tells his story. The Sheriff's office had been relocated from the old downtown part of town over to the newly developed West side of town. He did not get the memo and consequently showed up for his first day of work at the wrong location. Thankfully the chief deputy was very understanding and to this day the deputy considers him one of his favorite administrators at the Sheriff's office.

When he started with the sheriff's office one of the first pieces of advice he got was to keep the map in your lap and don't screw up. It was a lot to take in considering that this deputy was patrolling an area close to 400 square miles with only one or two other deputies on duty with him. Since then his department has incorporated an excellent FTO (Field Training Officer Program). Whether it was the original school of hard knocks (SHK) training or the FTO training he always found that with practice, experience, and technical development he would gain confidence in doing the job.

An officer from the suburbs remembered being somewhat anxious the first couple of months. He recalled his first traffic fatality and added that defense attorneys can sometimes be jerks. He rode along with a seasoned officer and learned how to properly fill out daily reports, accident reports, writing tickets and rendering assistance.

A deputy told me that he was nervous but also having fun the first time he wrote a ticket, wrote a search warrant or took someone into custody. Going to court and having to testify was a bit nerve racking at first, but with experience came confidence.

A trooper recalled his first day at work. He was nervous. And the first ticket he wrote, yes, he was very nervous. A woman had gone through a red traffic light. She said she was sorry and that she got cramps and crabby when she got her period, and was also very sorry she went through the stop sign.

He was proud and nervous on his first day, recalled a retired trooper. He had done some part-time auxiliary work before he started so that helped. He didn't remember who got the honor of his first ticket. The trooper's court experience started in a small town where they had a satellite court in the City Hall. It was very old school and a cozy environment. They would go for coffee with the judge when court was over. Now retired, he works in the courtroom as a Bailiff.

A deputy told me that he wasn't nervous on his first day of work, but he certainly didn't want to look like a fool. He knew that Cops are suspicious and cautious when a new member of their force arrives. It takes a while to break into that circle. He believes he has worked well with his fellow deputies as well as the state patrol and local police. It's a small force with a lot of miles to patrol. They need each other and rely on other agencies for help. The other agencies also count on his department.

The officer took care of an accident on his first day at work. He told about a lady who had rear-ended a car on a ramp from Hwy 36 and I 35 E. She didn't think it was her fault. A ticket was issued and he was nervous when he went to court. The judge found her guilty.

The trooper was a rookie in a small town up north, and chuckled as he remembered the incident. It was a quiet night. There was one stop sign on main street and all of a sudden, one lonely car went speeding through it. The trooper stopped him.

The driver had a little to drink. The trooper asked if he knew where he was. Of course, he did!

The trooper continued with his story. The man thought he was in a town 25 miles away. They didn't have a jail in this little town so he took him to the next town. The police station didn't have a sample bottle, but there was an empty olive jar on the window sill. The officer rinsed it out and the guy gave a urine sample. Later the trooper transferred the urine into an official sample bottle and sent it in to the BCA for testing. The results came back—the sample was over the limit *with a hint of pimento.*

> *"All the worlds a stage, and all the men and women are merely players. They have their exits and their entrances; and one man in his time plays many parts."*
>
> —Shakespeare

CHAPTER 7

TEACH YOUR CHILDREN WELL

Were you—are you—hard on your children?

Men and women working in the arena of law enforcement believed most officers are. They're scared for their children. There's so much out there to hurt them and so many temptations.

A police officer believes he should have been harder. He talked in a sad voice and with an awkward shrug of his shoulders.

A deputy doesn't think he was hard on his children because of his profession. His parents, although not in law enforcement, expected him to be a good kid…to grow up to be a good man. That, he believes, is what we should expect from our children no matter what our career is.

A New York City Officer reflected that he was pretty hard on his kids. He did not feel he was as involved as he should've been mainly because of his night shift work and not being around most of the time. They both turned out great and he has tried to make up for years of being a police officer. His adult children now seem to understand, and both seem to enjoy the difference in him since he retired.

A bitter divorce played a big part in an officer's children's feelings about him. He told me that he was hard on his children and they have not forgiven him.

A police officer believed that he is certainly tougher on his children because of his profession. Because his career is enforcing the law, he trusted that rules and laws were put in place for a reason and that rules should be followed with consequences for those who don't obey them.

He is also aware that being too strict and tough on children can have an unintended, negative consequence. Though not always easy, he tried to do his best to be reasonable and to evaluate the rules and expectations that he has in place for his kids. He has witnessed friends who came from law enforcement families that had rebelled because of the tough, strict, nonnegotiable rules and expectations that had been placed on them. The officer does his best to try to find that happy compromise with raising children that understand the importance of having and following rules without suffocating them and causing resentment by having unrealistic expectations. He finds that that is often a difficult challenge. It's difficult to find that healthy balance. He wants his kids to *be kids,* make mistakes, have fun, and at the same time hold them accountable, teach them valuable life lessons when they mess up, and keep them safe.

A deputy/ jailer thought he was hard on his kids and occasionally when at home, his wife reminded him that he is not at the jail.

When Mike was sick, we took stock of all we had enjoyed over the years as we realized how much God had truly blessed us. We talked of the bad decisions we had made regarding our children and also, that we were proud of the truly great decisions we had made. We asked ourselves how we could have done so well at times and so poorly at others.

Did you know what your dad did for a living?

From his earliest recollections, he knew his dad was a highway patrolman. He continued saying that his father usually went to work after lunch, and in the morning, when he would wake up, his dad was home. He remembered that lunches with dad always seemed special. Then his father would get dressed in his work clothes and drive off in his work car. At first, the young boy had no idea what his dad did. But he was only four or five years old when he began to figure it out. He never picked up back then that his dad's job was potentially dangerous. It sounded to him like his dad had a lot of fun.

Starting to piece things together at a very young age, he knew his dad chased speeders and picked up bad guys. In June 1968, when just five and one-half years old, his dad was home but he kept getting phone calls. After several calls, his dad decided he had better go to work. About that time, the town of Tracy was struck by a devastating tornado and his father was on his way to render aid. He thinks that's when he realized it wasn't all about chasing speeding cars and arresting bad guys. It was about helping people in their time of need. Some years later, he heard recordings of radio traffic from that day. The coordination and cooperation that had been demonstrated left a lasting impression on him.

He realized that his dad had a squad car. They had a second-floor bedroom with a dormer window that faced the front of the house. From that vantage point, he could look out and see the patrol car parked out front: the maroon paint, the white door, the big gold star on the roof. It was topped with a big red *gumball*. Sometimes, if he begged enough, his dad would light up that gumball for just a moment as he was leaving the house to go to work. It would make his day. The first patrol car he has vividly remembered was a 1965 Plymouth. He wasn't quite three when his dad got it. He was barely six when his dad turned it in for a 1968 Ford. He remembered every replacement after that. Those cars always piqued his interest and still do today. Hence, his Website, www.marooncruisers.com.

He never thought his dad was hard on him. Even through his rebellious teens, he doesn't think his dad was ever really hard on him or his siblings.

Were you treated differently?

He doesn't think he was as he continued with his cherished memories. It did seem to him that he received a certain amount of notoriety because of his dad's line of work. He wasn't treated special, and he wasn't shunned, but everyone knew who his dad was and what he did for a living. He was in fourth grade when his father was promoted to Captain. That kind of put his dad in the spotlight in some ways, but he doesn't recall that it ever had an adverse effect on his family.

Were you proud of your parent as you got older, and did he know it?

Yes, his dad knew. He was never afraid to express his love and respect for Dad, the person, or Dad, the captain. In 1983, as a young man, he went to work for the State Patrol, in a civilian role, and was able to work with his dad for the first couple years. As a result, he also went on many ridealongs when his dad would work the road. He said that getting to see his dad in action were some of the best times. His dad was an awesome driver. He saw him do things with cars that he didn't know were possible. He also told me that his dad was tremendous with people and that he could matter of factly *sell* a ticket to an unhappy violator, then part friends. And, when necessary, he could pull a guy from the driver seat and have him hunched over a trunk lid in handcuffs in a matter of seconds, all while remaining polite and respectful.

Did you miss a lot because he was gone much of the time?

He doesn't believe so. When he was born, his dad was already a sergeant. In the Patrol, sergeants at that time were the equivalent of today's lieutenants. They were the field supervisors.

His dad covered 20-some counties until the Mankato district was added in 1966. It seemed to him that his dad worked every holiday. The good thing about that was, as a supervisor, wherever they went for family gatherings, they were always within his dad's territory, and he would always find a way to pop in for an hour or so. Once his dad was promoted to captain, he worked a day shift Monday through Friday. So, generally speaking, his dad was home evenings and weekends. That made it a whole lot easier to make all those ball games, band concerts, and other events.

Did you worry?

He doesn't think he worried about his father. He didn't think anything could hurt his dad. He thought his dad was pretty much invincible.

Did you want to become a law enforcement officer?

There was a time when he thought it would be fun and challenging to be a state trooper. His dad never pushed him. He was hired on to the Minnesota State Patrol as a Commercial Vehicle Inspector. It has served him well for nearly 36 years. He has no regrets.

"Were you proud of your dad?" I asked, when I started my interview with an adult child of a Minnesota State Trooper. Yes, she was so proud of her dad. He was a wonderful father.

"Did he know it? Did you tell him?" Yes. She had told her mom too. She was proud of both of them.

She spoke of sometimes being treated different at school. Her classmates wanted to know what it was like to have a father who was a policeman. It was no different to her. It was the life that she had always had. She did realize that her dad did something dangerous when a deputy was killed. That's when she realized that her dad's job was different from the storeowner, the gas station attendant, or the fellow who worked in the bank. Sometimes she misbehaved just to prove that she wasn't different from anyone else.

Christmas, Thanksgiving, special birthdays, and other important occasions, she remembered him at home, perhaps dressed in his uniform, sitting at the table with a walkie-talkie. He could stop in for a short time and then he was back to work. Did he miss a lot? He made her and her sisters always feel special. Looking back, she realized that, yes, he missed a lot. They all missed a lot but she didn't think of it then. He had tried hard to be there whenever he could.

Her parents divorced when she was ten years old. She never saw them quarrel or argue. Her mother was the disciplinarian. Maybe once or twice her dad actually raised his voice with her, but it was her mom who kept everyone in line.

Giving up her home in a neighborhood full of children was difficult. Giving up her animals was, too. She couldn't have animals in an apartment, and that's where each of her parents lived separately after the divorce. Before the divorce, her father supported them, and her mom was the homemaker, sewing matching dresses for her and her sisters, baking cookies, bread, and being a stay-at-home mom.

Nobody had to take a side. Her parents worked hard to make sure their children had it as easy as possible.

Left alone a lot, with too much time on her hands, she rebelled. She made some poor choices in friends. Her dad made sure he saw her every day, and her mom worked hard to make things run as smoothly as possible.

She could go to her dad whenever she wanted and her mother whenever she wanted. That may have made it more difficult. She didn't want to hurt her mom by being at her dad's nor her dad by being at her mom's. If she would've had an exact schedule it might have been easier.

She was not scared when her parents divorced, but she was sad. The hardest thing was leaving her friends and the safety and comfort of her neighborhood.

Her parents have each married again. Her mom is married to a great guy and her dad is married to a wonderful lady.

Sometimes her dad knew more than she thought, and sometimes he knew less about what she was doing. She always thought he knew everything and especially what she had done the night before. She did get stopped and was told to slow down by another trooper, but he never told her dad, or, if he did, her dad never mentioned it.

This young woman says she's learning life lessons every day, is better than she was in her 20s, and learned more in her 30s. Now in her 40s, she's even wiser. She felt a little smarter because her dad was a Minnesota State Trooper. The tee shirt her father gave her says, "An ounce of common-sense weighs more than your brain." She was young when she got the shirt and it took her a while to figure out what that meant. She knows now.

She hopes the public knows that police are just as human as everyone else. They have feelings like everyone else. They have families they love and worry about. They have up and downs in their lives.

She talked of the anti-police dialogue of today. She wants people to remember that the police are looking out for their safety and their well being. They stand watch, put their life on the line so we can rest peacefully in our beds. It makes her angry that people do not know that police are putting their lives on the line to save us.

A pretty young lady admitted that she was an adventurous, slightly rebellious kid. All she was interested in was hanging out with friends that her dad didn't like. She thinks she was a stubborn kid and probably quite difficult. She understands her dad today, now that she is older and a parent.

One woman said her father, a deputy, worked around the clock at times with investigations. He was able to be home for a special occasion like Christmas dinner, but he would often fall asleep. His children would wake him by calling his car number. He would instantly hear that call and be alert.

A 40-year-old woman remembered in 5th grade that her teacher used to tease her about her dad being a state trooper and asked if she could find him a good "Fuzz Buster," (Like she even knew what a fuzz buster was).

A daughter of a trooper especially remembered her dad's unmarked blue squad car. When her relatives came to visit from out of town, they all wanted to sit in his car and go for a ride if possible.

Her dad was always involved in her extracurricular activities, remembered the daughter of a deceased trooper. She continued that he rarely missed a horse show or a recital. She remembered him taking home videos, loving his family, and being home with them. She thinks she was too young to realize the dangers that came with his job and always believed he was going to work to help people.

Her dad worried, and she knew it. He worried about her safety and also made sure that his children had an education. He also wanted them to be productive and made sure his children had a job so they could take care of themselves. At the time she was young and a little irritated about that, but she is the same way today with her children. She now understands that he wanted to make sure they would survive without him.

When I asked if she had a better understanding of him now that she was older, Yes. The young woman understands her dad more and more the older she gets, especially because she is now raising children of her own.

"Did you want to be in law enforcement?" I asked. She had thought seriously about becoming a police officer when she was in high school. As she got older, she wished she had because she is still interested in law enforcement.

She knew what her dad did and thought he was a hero, realizing his job was different early in elementary school. The squad car in the driveway made her feel safe, and she always thought a burglar would not choose their house to break into.

The kids in school thought it was cool that her dad was a police officer. She went on to say that she was so proud of her dad but doesn't think he knew how truly proud she was. She was only 20 when he died, and started learning about all the things he had to do on the job when he was sick or after he died. She doesn't feel like she missed a lot because he planned family trips and made sure his work did not get in the way of spending time with them.

The adult child of a law enforcement father could tell people treated his family a little differently, knowing that his dad was a trooper. Growing up in a very small town, he only knew of one police officer in town and one state trooper, his dad. It has been almost 40 years since living there, but they still remember the trooper. He thinks people seem to always remember law enforcement. If his dad had been a plumber, or electrician, or a welder, they probably wouldn't remember.

He didn't even think about what his dad did until he was probably in eighth grade, when his friends seemed fascinated with his job and talked about it, remembered the son of a trooper. It was all he knew and was normal to him. He knew his dad wore a gun on a belt around his waist, but that was normal, too, to him—just ordinary. As a teenage boy, when his friends could lie to their parents, he could not. Simple questions like, "What have you been doing?" or "Where have you been?" were not as simple as one might think. He remembered that each question was designed as a slot canyon: the further into the conversation he got, the higher the walls became, and the narrower his options for escape were. Once he was two or three answers into this conversation, there was no turning back or climbing out. He would find no other options but the truth, or suffer the consequences. It made him smile every time he thought about it. This is a great life lesson he thinks everyone should know. When you start any conversation, pay attention and understand early on who you are dealing with.

Through the eyes of a child, those I have talked to did not understand their law enforcement parent—did not comprehend what they dealt with in their job—the fear and worry they had for their children. Adult children of law enforcement officers go easy on their parents. They are older; some are married and have children of their own. They are different. They've changed their thoughts of life and decisions made. They are wiser. The majority said their parent was there when they needed them. Yes, they agreed there were things that they missed, but for the most part they were proud of their parent's occupation and proud of them. Most thought their parent knew of the pride they had in them, but some never actually said the words.

"Through the eyes of your child you are invincible."

—Nadia Tayob

CHAPTER 8

OUTER LIMITS, THE VENTURES, 1967

Each chapter of my mother's book has a song title, each chosen by her for a specific reason. She asked me to give a song title to my chapter. My choice is personal—maybe, to some, not a reflection of the story about my father, but rather a song that resonates pure joy when I think of my father where music is concerned. My father had a wide variety of music genres that he enjoyed. My dad had a motorcycle for the majority of my eighteen years living with them. As a really young girl, I am guessing 5-6 years of age, I remember there being a blue Harley Davidson that sat in the garage. I would play on the swing set that was close to the garage. Every so often, I would jump off that swing set, walk into the garage, and watch him work on his Harley.

Mike's 1968 Harley.

I sat on an old chair that no longer had a back. It was painted light blue. The paint was heavily chipped. And I just watched him. We did not have much of a conversation. I just watched him as he putzed with the bike and waxed any part of it he could shine. Music was always playing on a radio in the garage. (I am someone who remembers life in great detail. I am that person who recalls, from the time I was little, what I wearing, what music was playing in the background, who said and did what. It is a bit uncomfortable for me at times how much detail I remember so vividly. It's the good and the not so good.)

My parents had an expensive Pioneer sound system at the time. I believe it was the late 70s when they got it. Only my parents were allowed to touch or use it. It had many components—the receiver, the record player, the eight-track tape player, then later a cassette player, speakers that, when I was a kid, were almost as tall as I was. Though there were strict rules to using the system, both my brother and I learned quickly how to operate and remember what the volume was set at before we touched it, as well as the station the radio had been on and how to switch the system from stereo to whatever he and I were using. I would sit and go through the many records they had, then eight-track tapes. (That is where I learned about the Beatles and have, from that time, always loved them). There was one tape with a picture of a woman in a gold bikini and long, bleached-blonde hair with a high ponytail. I thought she was stunning but knew it was not for the eyes of a six-year-old. The tape was The Golden Greats by The Ventures 1967. No lyrics, just music—with guitars and drums. Later when cassette tapes came out, my dad turned many records and almost all of his eight tracks to cassette tape copies.

After we had moved to northern Minnesota, my bedroom faced the driveway. We had a tuck-under, two-stall garage. Under my bedroom window is where my dad's truck was parked. He would back the truck out and park the motorcycle in the stall to fuss with it and, of course, wax any part that could shine.

He now had a Honda Gold Wing—a beautiful bike. When he would leave on a ride, I would hear the bike fire up. I, the ever-nosey person, would open my window and see my dad drive away, the music already blaring. He would kick-stand the bike and shut the garage door. Most often the music blaring was either Credence Clearwater Revival or The Ventures Golden Greats 1967. Dad always wore a helmet so he had to blast the volume in order to hear the music.

Mike on his Kawasaki.

Dad was a simple dresser. Fashion was not his thing. However, when it came to his riding attire, he was a cool cat—nothing overstated, no brand flashing (that was the bike's job), the fantastic wax job, the tunes playing for everyone to hear. Blue jeans, black square-toed cowboy boots, a black leather jacket, dark green, gold-framed aviator sunglasses, and a bright white helmet. He looked awesome. He always looked happy, peaceful, and content on that bike. I love the image when I recall it. It makes me smile—smile for him.

As kids, we really do not see our parents as people with a life that did not involve us kids. We lacked the capacity to see our parents with a life together as a couple, a life with independent interests, people that have fun and have a level of suave or coolness. Of course, as we became adults and parents ourselves, all of this comes full circle, and we gain perspective. I love when I think of my parents' *not* being in a parental role, such as a vacation away from the kids on that motorcycle, enjoying themselves and the other couples they traveled with. They had time to nurture a relationship, fall in love again, be romantic with one another, and just be themselves. They could be Michael and Susan, not just mom and dad to my brother and me. I can close my eyes and see them both today as clear as if it were yesterday, climbing on that cycle, filled with excitement, looking forward to their travels, time away from being parents and just being a couple.

My dad was typical when we were growing up. Be it the TV or *our* music in our rooms, we always had the volume too loud. He'd knock on our door, then open it, ask if I needed my hearing checked, then tell me to turn it down. Once we got Walkmans, he lectured me many times on how I was going to have hearing issues one day because of such loud music, in headphones right up against my ears. Once again, he was right. Dad, however, could crank up the volume on the bike. It was blasting when he left the driveway. We had no air conditioning, so from spring to mid-Fall, the windows were open in the house. We could hear dad coming for blocks away (the motorcycle was well mufflered and so quiet) when he was almost home. I still hear The Ventures-Golden Greats 1967.

When I arrived at my parents' home to stay and help care for him, I packed a small suitcase. Basics was all I had. I could do laundry so I had little with me for the five weeks there. I knew I was staying until he died, not leaving until this was over. I always knew there would be a funeral there. I did, however, not bring anything to wear to the funeral. I just couldn't pack funeral clothes, even though I knew he was going to die and I was going to be there: he was not dead yet. So, two days after dad died, I needed to get nicer clothes. I did not have a car there, but Mom offered hers. I was heading to a larger city to shop.

I welcomed the ninety-mile drive one way as an opportunity to be alone. Driving down the highway after of bit of time, finding nothing on the radio worth listening to, I opened a compartment, looking for a cassette tape. Sure enough, there it was, in Dad's handwriting: The Ventures, 1967. I could not believe how random, with all of the cassettes they had, that this was the one there. I listened and cried the rest of the drive. It was my first conversation I had with my dad since passing two days before. Twenty years later we have had thousands.

Through Julie's Eyes

I grew up with a maroon, Minnesota State Patrol squad car in our driveway. My father, Michael T. Jurgens, SP 280, aka Dad, had just passed the first of many tests enabling him to attend patrol school when I was born. Life as a child of law enforcement is all I ever knew.

I can close my eyes and see our little green house, our blue truck in the driveway, and parked next to it, the squad car. At that time, we lived in a small town in a quiet Minnesota farming community. I loved it there. Or maybe what I loved was the innocence of just being a child.

First, a couple stories:

A first memory of my dad and his job is of standing with my Sunday school class in church where we were performing our Christmas program. My guess is that I was four or five years old. I wondered why my mother and brother were seated in the middle of the audience, yet my dad, in uniform, was seated in the last row, closest to the exit door. Like most young children standing in front of so many people, I kept looking for my parents in the audience. I remember looking from my mother, to my dad. My guess is I looked like a parrot with my head in motion back and forth. Then, a man tapped my dad on the shoulder. Dad got up and walked out. I had no idea why he left. As I grew older, I realized that he had been called to an accident.

A second memory about him takes place in kindergarten. While my classmates and I were sitting on a big round rug on the floor, our teacher, a woman, asked us to tell about our weekend. I do not remember what any of the other kids said, but I do remember what she had to say.

My teacher (I am guessing she was young, maybe 25) told us she had learned a valuable lesson over the weekend. Her lesson was not to speed while she was driving, and that she will follow the speed limit, also that Julie's dad, Officer Jurgens, helped her to learn that lesson. At five years of age, I had no idea what she was talking about.

That night at dinner, when asked, "What did you learn today at school, Julie?" I said that I learned that my teacher was going to follow the speed limit and that Dad helped her learn how to follow it.

Dad proceeded to say that she was driving 78 mph and that she'd *better* have learned her lesson.

Still, I did not understand what my dad did with that squad car when he left for work. Conversations about Dad's job were, for the most part, not for young ears. If by any chance I overheard something, I did not have the maturity to understand; and, I was not one who asked many questions.

Moving forward to the age of nine when we had moved to Northern Minnesota, I remember the police scanner that sat in our living room. It was always ON and it *never* stopped *talking*. I learned a lot from its chatter though. Now I was more aware of what Dad did. I paid more attention to the subtle details going on in our home.

My dad's desk sat at the top of our stairway near the kitchen, and it always had a stack of paper work—files and envelopes that contained photos. Close to the desk above the kitchen counter was the phone. At times it was not odd to awake, walk by counter, and see a clipboard with a stranger's driver's license attached to it. Sadly, I would learn that this meant Dad had worked a fatal accident.

Now, about Dad:

Dad was a worrier, a genetic trait that I inherited. As kids, a question about something we wanted to do always seemed to be answered with, "NO." Why, I wondered once again, was I not allowed to do something all of my peers were able to do?

Fear, I would realize many years later, was the reason. He worried about almost everything concerning his children, such as riding our bikes and getting hit by a car. Later he worried about our being passengers in cars driven by teenagers. He had seen enough tragic outcomes over the years. Also, in our teenage years, he worried about peoples' drinking and drug use and the poor choices people made, that one of his own kids could make. He couldn't help himself—he just worried.

He also worried, I am sure, about how the mistakes his kids might make would look to the public. As children of a state trooper, we were under a bit of a microscope, scrutinized much more than I realized.

However, I do believe that his worst worry was that something would hurt or harm one of us. I just thought that he regretted being a parent or that he enjoyed controlling us. How wrong I was!

During one of our many conversations before he died, I asked him, "What would you do different if given the chance?" He said without hesitation, "I would have had more children. Your mother and I should have had at least four, maybe five." He said he should have been a pilot or a farmer. He said he had been selfish, dragging us to Northern Minnesota, that that was one of his biggest regrets. He said that we had made a good life for ourselves in Redwood Falls. We were an hour's drive from each set of grandparents; we lived in a nice, small, farming community; and the people were good.

Dad said he had been selfish and that he was sorry. It hurt me to hear his words, but I realized he needed to talk. Even if I did not agree with everything he said, it did not matter. I needed to listen to him. His need to talk was something I had not experienced with him. Over the month I was there, we spoke of many things. We reminisced about the past. We laughed a lot, and sometimes we cried. I cherished my time with him. I would often put him to bed well after midnight. I was glad I could do that, because my mother needed her sleep. I wanted and enjoyed having Dad all to myself.

In contrast:

My parents had opposite personalities. My father was stoic, stern, controlling, stubborn, quiet, and most often, unemotional. My dad came from a place of *no*. My mother—outgoing, welcoming, freethinking, and talkative—easily shared her emotions. My mother came from a place of *yes*.

Dad also leaned a bit on being dramatic. For example, at the age of five, I stole a pack of gum from the grocery store. I was caught. My mother was standing right there when I did it. After the seemingly hour-long lecture about theft and what it meant to be a criminal, my father told me I would probably, later in life, go to prison for being a thief.

My brother takes after my mother; I take after my dad. Many years after that lecture and shortly before he died, reminiscing, he said, "I knew when you were three years old that you and I were going to lock horns. I saw in you my own stubbornness. Over the years, I realized how much we were alike. You were quiet, like me. It was a wall that kept us apart for so many years. For that, I am so sorry." He did say that because of my mother's genetics, I also had many of her qualities. I will end this part by stating this: In the eyes of an adult, my father sold himself short at times, as did his children.

Back to Dad:

When we were younger, not having the maturity to understand, we only saw life through the eyes of a child. On the surface, Dad seemed to be an unemotional person, which, as a child, I took as uncaring. However, as an adult, I would come to realize that he was probably one of the most compassionate people I would ever know. He did things for so many, quietly helping people in different ways. Just one example is what he did for our wonderful neighbor. We called her Grandma B, and she lived next door in a little log cabin. Dad would blow the snow away from the outside of her house and would caulk the many cracks in the logs to protect her from the winter weather.

Although he could be frugal, it wasn't until years later that we learned of his and mom's generosity to others. We were just unaware.

My dad was a good husband who took care of his family and doted on his mother and grandmother. He was kind to my mother's family, and they loved him. His grandchildren were a joy in his life; and when they were with us, his heart was full of joy. His friends often said they could count on him. We all could.

All in all:

The list could go on and on, but Dad was, without question, reliable and responsible—two qualities for which I am thankful, as both Mom and Dad modeled those qualities for us kids. I was so lucky to have my parents. If I had a life do-over, I would choose them both as my mom and dad. I hope they feel proud of what they accomplished.

> *"In the darkest days, when I feel inadequate, unloved and unworthy, I remember whose daughter I am and I straighten my crown."*
>
> —Unknown

CHAPTER 9

WHERE WERE YOU WHEN I NEEDED YOU?

The name of my chapter asks what one might expect a law enforcement officer's wife to ask, but what I heard from the women was that their husbands were mostly right there, by their sides. Most wives I interviewed were of now retired Minnesota State Troopers. There were no female Minnesota State Troopers at that time. They are happy their husbands chose to be public protectors and felt proud of the community service their husbands provided. They gave their spouses high marks. While the men talked of the many times they were not there for their families, the wives felt differently.

Memories of the Minnesota trooper who came to our door so many years ago flooded back into my thoughts as I listened to the women talk about her husband's job. He had warned me that Mike would probably not be there when he was needed, although I can indeed say that he was.

The women I am talking with are long-time friends. It was close to Christmas when I did this interview, and we enjoyed coffee and holiday goodies. They were smiling, talking, and laughing as we started talking about our husbands and our lives.

The wives felt safer because of their husbands' jobs. They felt close to them even if they were working nights, weekends, and holidays. It also forced them (and I myself agree) to be more independent. We had to make decisions, to know how to handle household and parenting problems.

There was an absolute separation in the role of husband and wife when I married Mike. I liked the idea of a man taking care of me. I wasn't excited about having to be the one in charge. I liked that there was his job and my job. Weekends, nights, and holidays became like every other day of the week. That's what it was all about. I had no quarrel with the conditions of his profession. It was now his job, and my job was to be supportive.

None of the wives believed they were treated differently in a bad way. Many expressed that people were curious and asked a lot of questions. They wanted to hear from the wife of a LEO (a relatively new term for Law Enforcement Officer), to hear what it's like to have a husband who is in police work. Many of the other spouses interviewed did not recall their husbands sharing too much about their own worries or fears. Sometimes they heard about frustrations but not much about their actual feelings. The majority left their work at work, separating their lives on the street or in their cars from life at home.

A few women I interviewed said they missed out on a lot; however, many believed their spouses tried hard to be a part of family life and probably were. Many said their husbands checked in with them regularly. I can't say that Mike ever stopped at home just to say hello. He did occasionally stop by for dinner, especially when we lived in a small town where restaurants weren't open later in the evening during the week. He also stopped long enough to tell me something I really needed to know. Occasionally, I would get a call from the dispatcher, telling me Mike was involved with something and would be late.

One of the women had been a dispatcher for many years, and that job had played a part in the failure of her first marriage. She worked weekends, nights, and holidays. Later she married a state trooper. He understood. They understood each other. Another wife was a nurse; her husband, a trooper. They each worked the night shift and had days off together. They had met when he parked his squad car in her apartment parking space. It didn't take long before they were smitten.

All believed, however, that people who worked in law enforcement did, at times, miss out on holidays, sports events, conferences, and school functions.

HERE'S ONE WIFE'S STORY

A Southern bell who hadn't thought of living in Minnesota, said she hoped she would marry someone who was a little more up in the world. They were poor, poor, poor. Her mother had nothing.

Growing up, she had a lot of love from her family. With a humble devoted momma, eight brothers and sisters, and a caring grandma and auntie, she was not lacking in love, although her dad had died of a cerebral hemorrhage when she was a month old.

Their neighbors shared their food with them, often bringing them vegetables and meat. On her Mamma's way to church one Sunday morning, she found a dime on the road. That was the only money she had, and she put it in the offering plate. On her way home, she found a five-dollar bill. That's her favorite story about Mamma.

As a young girl, she worked at a drive-in on weekends. A man who owned a dry-cleaning business gave her a ride to Panama City, FL, where her job was. She would share her money with her mom so her mother could buy groceries.

She met her future husband at that drive-in. He was a young man from Minnesota in the Air Force. He drove a convertible. She had agreed when he asked her for a date but then stood him up. He had asked her to go boating, but she was scared and embarrassed because she couldn't swim.

She didn't think she was a pretty girl, but was kind of cute. She felt popular in school because people liked her personality. She worked hard to buy clothes to wear to school. Tears filled her eyes as she shared her sadness. She wanted to look decent.

Her Minnesota man was kind to her and may have been a little frightened of her brothers, as he was expected to come to the door to meet the family and let them look him over. He proposed. His mother and grandmother came for the wedding. They wore fancy clothes and hats. Her aunt made her wedding dress, and she felt pretty and special. Her brother walked her down the aisle and reminded her that funerals are cheaper than divorces. They had both laughed.

His family was so good to her. They were amazed that she could cook. She had to help at home, and knew how to do things around the house.

She got her driver's license the day before she left for Minnesota. His grandmother flew down and rode back to Minnesota with her. A flat tire caused some concern, but a Good Samaritan stopped and helped change it.

Cold Minnesota took some getting used to. Her husband went through the patrol training, but the legislature had to appropriate money for additions to the patrol. In the meantime, he worked for a prison and also as a dispatcher. Fortunately, he was soon working for the Minnesota Highway Patrol. They had three daughters; but while the children were still at home, they divorced. Each remarried, and they continue to have a good relationship with each other.

Not every divorce is amicable, ending in friendship. Marriages with law enforcement officers have an abundance of issues working against them. Besides the inevitable lack of time together, their spouses have haunting memories of scenes they have sometimes witnessed during working hours. Unable or unwilling to share their worries and their fears with their spouses, their wives begin to feel left out. However, many wives have said early on that they were too busy with babies and young children to feel left out. A young mom said she often felt disorganized but got through one day at a time.

A DIVORCED WIFE OF AN OFFICER HAD THIS TO SAY

She was married to a gung-ho law enforcement officer and knew something happened in him after he came back from the Academy. He became detached from the kids, their friends, and her. His whole focus was on law enforcement. Everything at home was left to her. The only thing he did was work. He changed his job from police officer to deputy sheriff. They both felt stress during elections because his job depended on what party the sheriff was from. All along, they hoped the current sheriff was able to continue.

She shopped, worked outside the home some, took care of the yard, bills, six kids—all alone. Their only friends were in law enforcement. They were interrupted from a law enforcement function many times because of a fire in the town, an assault, or a drowning. They lived in an area close to a river. There was no search and rescue team at the time, so he created one and trained the divers. She didn't know how to swim, and he never had time to teach her.

They would be out in their boat, and a couple of times, after a drowning, they would troll for a body. One was a friend's five-year-old. Horrible! Then there was the attention from the women who were *attracted* to men in uniform. His wife received consolation gifts from time to time when he would break off a relationship.

The first time she saw him at 13, she knew she would marry him. When he joined the police department, the chief called him by his middle name. She has had a hard time letting go of her childhood sweetheart. She never got to say goodbye. Almost overnight a stranger lived there.

BRIGHT AND AMBITIOUS THIS WOMAN HAD A PLAN FOR LIFE

She had an idea of the type of man she would marry. She knew she would never be happy with someone who was not as smart as she was. After two years of community college, this young woman was on her way to St. Cloud State. Although another state college was closer, she had visited a college in West Central Minnesota and knew that was the place for her.

Graduating with a degree in Elementary Education and Library Science, she quickly found a job in Central Minnesota. She and the man she would eventually marry had gone to school together. Although in a class of 365, she knew who he was, but that was all. Meeting each other a few years later at a mutual friend's party, they connected and married fifteen months later. She already had a job teaching 3rd, 4th, and 5th grade students; and he, a recently discharged Marine MP, soon had a job as a deputy.

With a long-time goal of being on the Minnesota Highway Patrol, passing the patrol test was a dream come true for her husband. They did a juggling act when their children were young: he worked the dogwatch, and she taught part time while living in the Minneapolis area. Her husband would eventually become a captain in the Minnesota State Patrol.

She developed an Adult Basic Education program for the community college when they moved to the North Country. There was a strong move in Minnesota to have a larger, bona fide program—more than just a GED adult education program. The Department of Corrections mandated that local jails provide education programs for the inmates.

It's unbelievable what the teachers have to do. They don't have fun anymore. They have such a regimen. Parents often do not believe that their children can misbehave. She still volunteers one day a week in the third-grade classroom. They are not supposed to hug the children, but if she has a little third grader who wants to give her a hug, she's hugging that child back. Today's parents are spoiled; they have everything they want. But also, she sees good parents who take part in their children's lives.

She was never afraid of any students—not even the adults she taught in jail. She said that people felt better about themselves after leaving jail. She sometimes drove them to the community college to take their GED tests. She didn't sense any physical harm; but, believes she is probably more aware of what's goes on in the world.

CHANGING TRENDS

When Mike went into the patrol, there were no female patrols; spouses of patrolmen were *Women*. Today that has changed. Women *are* in law enforcement, but for us older spouses, we were the *women* who kept the home fires burning. We felt a sense of pride and excitement. Sure, there were risks, but they were minimal, and the career was honorable. I didn't worry about Mike. He had a job to do, and that was that. Today, for those married to people working in law enforcement, feelings have changed.

Spouses and children of law enforcement officers now feel threatened. Names, addresses, and phone numbers can be posted on social media. They fear not only for their own lives but also for the safety of their families. Their loved ones have experienced threats. Bullies find easy prey on social media.

One young woman whose husband has worked nights for a long time said one of the trade-offs was great because they never needed daycare. Her husband was home with the kids from birth through elementary school while she was at work full time. He sacrificed a lot of sleep but he wouldn't change a thing.

ANOTHER RECOUNTS NIGHTTIME VISITORS

One night, around 2 or 3 a.m., when her husband was at work and she and the kids and were all sleeping, the sound of the doorbell woke and startled her. She didn't want to answer the door because she knew it couldn't be good. She didn't know whom to expect on the other side of the door.

The woman slowly walked to the door, and, once she could see that it was two police officers, she was instantly filled with panic. She could hear her heart pounding. She started shaking, fearing the worst, and hesitantly opened the door.

Instead, the officers asked her if so-and-so lived here. No! She wasn't sure if she should be mad or relieved. The people who had lived there before them had that last name.

They explained that they had found a vehicle that had crashed and was abandoned. The plates came back to her address.

She thought her knees would give out. The scared woman almost hit the floor, because in the span of a minute or two, she had gone through such a rollercoaster of emotions.

She explained to the officers that they scared her half to death because her husband is a police officer and that he's at work, telling them in no uncertain words that when two police officers knock on your door in the middle of the night, it is extremely alarming!

They apologized for scaring her and went on their way.

She immediately called her husband. He wondered why she would be calling so late. He was surprised to hear what his wife had just been through.

Patty's story:

Patty's husband, Dick, retired from the Minnesota State Patrol in 1999. He died on Sunday, October 14, 2012, the day after their 41st wedding anniversary. Dick had returned from an elk hunting trip the previous Sunday. Monday, he complained of right jaw pain but refused to go to the doctor. He saw his dentist instead because he thought it was something related to his TMJ. Everything was fine. He seemed better.

Wednesday, his wife had a scheduled trip to South Dakota to go with her cousin to her chemo appointment and to attend a 90th birthday party for a family friend. Dick didn't want to go. She had planned to stay until Sunday.

Thursday evening, Dick called to say he was seeing the doctor the next day to check things out. Patty was unaware that he had also called several friends. He gave all of them instructions on what needed to be done if anything happened. Sunday he felt better, but he didn't want to go out for breakfast, which was their usual routine. Late that afternoon, Dick asked if they could eat supper in the living room to watch the Twins.

Without warning, Dick had a cardiac arrest. Patty attempted to give him CPR as did the local paramedics without success.

Dick was 67 years old.

Susan Jurgens Kammen

A Trooper's Epilog:

Gary took an early retirement from the Minnesota State Patrol and moved his family to Arizona in 1989 to enjoy the sunshine and warmer weather. Life was great. Their family was healthy and comfortable with his pension and their good jobs. He worked security at the Mayo Clinic, and his wife Bonnie was a nurse there. They had no worries. It was a new adventure.

One day, out of the blue, their lives changed. After having a routine physical, Gary was diagnosed with stage IV prostate cancer. There was no cure. He couldn't have surgery as the cancer had spread to his lymph nodes. Medications might put the cancer in remission, but there was no guarantee. His doctor said it was aggressive and would be his demise.

His wife Bonnie wondered; how could this happen? Why? What could have prevented it? They were devastated and had lots of questions but no answers. They began each day as if it was their last, but never gave up hope. In between doctor appointments and scans, they made family time a priority. They started enjoying life like never before. They didn't worry about little things anymore. Life had new meaning. Their children were young adults, going to college and getting married, so they still had expenses but no financial worries.

As time passed Gary began to feel the fatigue and discomfort of cancer. Bonnie soon became his caregiver and realized she was responsible for more than his care. She was also in charge of their finances.

As his health deteriorated, she was sleeping less and worrying more. She wanted to be home where she was needed, but that wasn't an option. They needed the income from her job and the medical insurance. They were blessed, as several family members offered to stay with Gary when she was at work. However, she still felt guilty when she wasn't with him.

76

Before he died, he told Bonnie that she was his guardian angel. She knew he depended on her. She doesn't think it matters how much time you have to prepare for death. Even though they had four years to prepare for losing him, they were so devastated and in disbelief when he died. He was the glue that held them all together. He was the one who always made them comfortable and happy.

Bonnie's expenses didn't change. So, with more time on her hands, she took a second job at a local hospital. Constantly worried about how her children were handling Gary's death and her mounting stress, she decided to have a physical.

Bonnie's doctor, a woman, told her it was time to take care of herself. She had never thought about that before. The doctor explained that if she did, she could improve her health beginning that day.

Today she is married, retired and has lots of grandkids. She has a lot of reasons to live a long and vibrant life.

CHANGING ATTITUDES

The women interviewed spoke often about the disrespectful behaviors they now see towards law enforcement. For example, the emergence of cameras that so many times do not portray an accurate view of what is happening: The recording often starts after the initial meeting with an officer. It does not show what has happened beforehand, but releasing it on social media gives the person breaking the law power and makes a policeman look bad. A young wife reminds us that these guys put their lives on the line every single day. The media is quick to criticize and shows the video over and over; but once the entire story is told and the officer is exonerated, there's hardly a word about it.

What follows is an article written by Chaplain Brook LeClaire. She has graciously given her permission to share it.

Susan Jurgens Kammen

Law Enforcement Officer Wives
By Chaplain Brooke LeClaire

As the leader of 1,000 law enforcement officer wives (LEOWs) throughout the state of Minnesota in the organization Backing the Blue Line, I asked, "what would you say, from a LEOWs perspective regarding the recent shootings of officers if you could?" I asked, thinking I could generate some ideas, but as their answers came in, so did my tears. I continued to cry as I read their answers and viscerally felt the pain of their words in my heart.

These are my girls, my sisters in blue, and the burdens of their hearts are daunting. Their pain is my pain, and it feels like we're the only ones who understand it.

Being a LEOW today feels very lonely. This wasn't what I expected in 2004 when my then construction worker husband told me he was going to become a police officer. I felt pride at the time; I felt excitement; and I felt honor. Sure, I knew there were risks with the job, but they were minimal, and the career was honorable.

Fast-forward 12 years and those feelings of pride and honor are still there, but the excitement on most days has been replaced with feelings of anger, feelings of fear, and the thought I'd try to convince even myself isn't there, "I wonder if he's next..."

A young woman never thought she was next when her husband, graduated just three months prior from the police department. But he was. He was shot in cold blood when someone drove over 12 hours just to kill a cop.

Knowing that there are people in this world with that level of hatred for a profession makes sending my husband, the father of my baby girls, out the door to do his "dream job" harder and harder every day. It used to be that you got into law enforcement (LE) for the retirement. Now with LE ambushes up 300 percent, we pray they'll make it to retirement. As a fellow LEOW put it, "Each day they walked back in the door after their shift is celebrated with silent prayers and grateful hearts." I don't think many other professions can fully *understand that, which makes this life feel very isolated. No one else knows what it's like to plan your hero's funeral long before it happens or discuss who you would prefer to be the bearer of that news. No one else has a plan for where you'll go when your home is no longer safe.*

It's not just the fear of his loss of life that I believe no one understands. I worry that someday he may not have his life taken, but that he's the one who has to do the taking. Then what? What happens if he becomes the next "racist cop," because it was him or them? Those who know him think I have nothing to worry about because "He's one of the good cops!"

There've been plenty of good cops who had to make a split second decision, resulting in their being the victim of the media's latest obsession of stirring the racial-hatred pot. I think about having to explain to confused little girls why people want to hurt their daddy.

As I let the dog out at 11 p.m. the other night, I stared out into the pitch black, and I caught the thought running through my head, "What if someone's out there? What if someone saw our blue line flag and is now out there, waiting to harm me?" It was then that I realized the fear that I tried to suppress is closer to the surface than I thought. This was the fear I never considered and certainly never signed up for. I never thought that loving a police officer would ultimately put my whole family at risk. A fellow LEOW summed it up well: "I agreed to send my husband (my heart, my soul, my everything) out into this scary world every day to do what he believes in...and I believe in him. I just never thought there would come a day when he would bring that scary world home to me." The quote that keeps me going is "If they're brave enough to suit up, you have to be brave enough to let them." Because of that we will continue to stand behind him as he holds that thin blue line.

"We promise forever in a world where even life is temporary."

—Anonymous

CHAPTER 10

HERE WE GO AGAIN

The Boston Tea Party was the first protest in the United States of America. 342 chests of tea belonging to the British East India Company were thrown from ships into the Boston Harbor by American patriots disguised as Mohawk Indians Dec 16th. Americans were protesting both the tax on tea and the monopoly of the East India Company. — www.history.com

The right to assemble is recognized as a human right and protected in the First Amendment to the US Constitution under the clause "Congress shall make no law respecting an establishment of religion or prohibiting the free exercise thereof; or abridging the freedom of speech, or of the press; or the right of the people peaceably to assemble, and to petition the Government for a redress of grievances. —HTTPS//constitiution.com. (Peaceably is, of course, the key word.)

A power line controversy was raging in January of 1978 on the farmland of Minnesota. Our local television stations reported on the protest along with newspapers. I got most of my information first hand from Mike who stood in the cold, trying to keep things civil and, mostly, keep everyone safe. "It was a Dog and Pony show," he said with a big grin on his face. He had said the same thing about many instances but especially once the cameras were rolling. He would say that when the cameras were turned off, it wasn't as much fun for the protesters to *perform.*

Farmers chased power line crews with their tractors, protesters took part of a tower down, and some complained that their skin itched, tractors lost power, radios crackled, TVs were snowy, and one woman said she felt like spiders were crawling on her.

Our Minnesota governor ordered what was, at the time, the largest mobilization of state troopers in Minnesota history. National and international news reporters began arriving in Lowry, Minnesota, to cover the protest.

On January 9, 1978, 200 protesters marched across a survey site to hand each trooper a plastic carnation. (Mike's was pink and he saved the carnation for a long time). Protesters offered troopers coffee and cookies.

On February 15, 1978, farmers sprayed troopers with anhydrous ammonia, a fertilizer that can cause serious burns. Media reaction to this act was negative and protesters became divided.

A few militants had caused the power line problem. Many did not live in the area but came to protest and be a part of the *show*. Protesters who lived in the area had their fifteen minutes of fame.

The real cost was to the Minnesota taxpayers. The overtime pay Mike received paid for central air in our home, a new washer, and a Yamaha trail bike. Today, thirty years later, the power line is working well. The cows still give milk. The crops still grow. The losers in this were those of us who work for a living and don't destroy property, that is, the American tax payers.

The Minnesota State Patrol received praise for their outstanding service from Governor Rudy Perpich. He commended the patrol for their superb performance. He praised them for bringing the State of Minnesota and the public through two exceedingly difficult and dangerous months. He applauded them for finding the difficult balance between firmness and restraint.

As I researched the cost of protests that turn violent and are called a riot, I was dismayed at the cost to taxpayers. *The Washington Times* Oct. 20, 2014, reported that the Ferguson riot had cost $5 million and counting. It could easily cost 10 million. *The Baltimore Sun,* May 26, 2016, reported that the riots in their streets cost the tax payers $204 million.

Protests have been a part of our nation's history. The 1960s turmoil came to my mind. However, not everyone in the 1960s was battling against the war in Vietnam or advocating free love. The majority of young people were beginning their families. They were law abiding and for the most part working hard to provide food, clothing, and shelter for their families. Mike returned from the Vietnam War in 1965. There was no fanfare for anyone coming home in uniform. The Vietnam War was not popular. Much of the turmoil in the 60s was college students protesting that war. Although there was a draft, college students were exempt.

President Kennedy continued our descent into the quagmire of that impossible war, although they never called it a war. President Johnson walked us deeper into the quicksand. Watching a special on PBS about American presidents, I saw Johnson sitting at the table with his joint chiefs of staff. When the truth was finally told, when he heard from his staff the failure and futility of continuing the military action that was never a "war," he said, "Someone has poisoned the well."

I was a history buff beginning early in my youth. But at 16, with the election of John Kennedy, I was officially hooked. Enamored by his small children, beautiful wife, his charm, and good looks, I watched and read everything I could about the popular family. I remember vividly his assassination, the swearing-in of Lyndon Johnson, and the televised funeral.

In a televised speech on March 31, 1968, Johnson sat at the desk in the Oval Office with a sad look on his face and said, "I shall not seek, nor will I accept, the nomination of my party for another term as your President." I thought it was very sad. I can't say I knew anything about politics. But I already loved history, and government seemed interesting as well. Johnson was our president, and, even as a young girl, I held that office in high regard. I now consider myself an independent and have voted for both Republicans who have won and lost and Democrats who have won and lost since I turned 21.

Governor Mark Dayton did not mind protesters camping outside his official residence 24 hours a day but said interstate shutdowns are dangerous. "It is against the law," the governor said on television station and newspapers. "It creates a very dangerous situation."

Protesters shut down a major route into downtown Minneapolis July 14, 2016, during morning rush hour, demanding that police be demilitarized. Local television stations— ABC, CBS, NBC, — showed the chaos and anger of not only the protesters but disgust felt by the people whose lives were disrupted by not being able to get to their destinations.

Their highway actions have gained a sarcastic and angry response from truckers. The activists believe that taking over highways is an effective way of getting attention. Truck drivers are paid by the mile, not the hour. Protesters screamed at, threatened, and terrorized drivers as they stopped traffic on Interstate 35 in Minnesota.

Truck cabs are often home for much of truckers' lives, and the drivers are responsible for what's in the tractor and trailer. Truckers feel they are innocent targets and wonder why their goods, security, and income should be forfeited because protesters are dissatisfied. Whatever sympathies might have been felt by the haulers were replaced with fear, anger, and resentment. The feeling of many truckers was that they'd like to just drive right over them.

Television stations were again filled with the news of protesters for a second time July 13, 2016. Twin Cities protesters blocked parts of Interstate 94 for a second time during rush hour in the aftermath of the July 6, 2016 fatal police shooting of a Philando Castile in Falcon Heights. The governor said, "Protesters need to realize the risks they are taking when they close down a freeway, risks they themselves especially face." He said law-enforcement officers handled the Wednesday incident as peacefully as anyone could under these circumstances.

"The state patrol supports the right to exercise one's First Amendment rights, but the freeway is not the place to do so," said Col. Matt Langer, Minnesota State Patrol Chief.

"The closure of an interstate freeway for the purposes of a demonstration is unacceptable. They are used by everyone and are an artery for emergency vehicles. It is illegal to walk on the freeway and blocking traffic is dangerous for both pedestrians and motorists."

Some of the rallies throughout the following months caused widespread disruptions around the Twin Cities metro area.

The first major protest happened when protesters spilled onto Interstate 94, July 11, 2016, closing the westbound lanes between Plymouth and Broadway Avenues in Minneapolis.

One of the current job descriptions of a Sergeant with the Minneapolis Police Department is monitoring and handling protests, demonstrations and other civil disturbances that occur in downtown Minneapolis.

He told me that Minneapolis experienced 130 demonstrations last year alone, for causes that included $15.00 minimum wage, Immigration rights, Anti-North Dakota Pipeline, and Black Lives Matter. He continued that fortunately most of the demonstrations are small, law-abiding, and peaceful. Some, however, grew to 1,500 people marching throughout the streets and onto highways purposely congesting traffic for miles and creating as much disruption as possible. He laments that many Minneapolis City Council members and the twin cities' Mayors rose to public office from various civil rights and activist positions. He believes that the politics are leaning very liberal. He has seen precedents set that have allowed protests and other demonstrations to be disruptive to the general public.

He talked of the rules of engagement for the Minneapolis Police to allow "reasonable disruption" to traffic and pedestrians, and not interfering with any protest actions shy of personal violence or major damage to property, which he sees translates into letting the protesters walk where they want, and disrupt other peoples' lives as much as they want.

The officer talked about his belief in the first amendment, which allows for peaceful and lawful protesting. He believes that's what makes our country so great. He also believes that as a law enforcement officer, he has a duty to ensure that the demonstrators, even if he disagrees with them, have the ability to protest lawfully without fear of retaliation.

However, he, as a policeman, also has the duty to make sure that the uninvolved public has the right to move freely and safely about the city without unreasonable delay from unlawful protest that intentionally congest and disrupt traffic.

He realized that a reasonable amount of disruption to sidewalks and streets, without personal assault or damage to property should be allowed. However, at some point, after an unreasonable amount of disruption and reading dispersal orders, offenders should be arrested and charged.

Protests were usually spur-of-the-moment events, but with social media, that is no longer the case. Police departments throughout the country have been under scrutiny since an unarmed black teenager, Michael Brown, was shot and killed the summer of 2014 in Ferguson, Missouri, by white police officer Darren Wilson. The sights and sounds of the protest that quickly became a riot horrified this television viewer. Every news channel was filled with the destruction of innocent store owners' property, and, I thought, we taxpayers had better be ready to open our wallets—we're going to be paying for this.

Newspapers and television broadcasts were filled with the results of the investigation from the Justice Department. It laid out a strong case in Wilson's favor. The physical evidence suggested Brown reached into Wilson's car during their physical altercation and attempted to grab the officer's gun. The most credible witnesses agreed that Brown moved toward Wilson before the officer fired his final shots. There simply wasn't enough evidence, especially given the struggle at the car, that Wilson wasn't justified in fearing for his life when he fired the shots that killed Brown. Although some witnesses suggested Brown raised his hands up before he died, witnesses who disputed major parts of Wilson's side of the story were discredited by the physical evidence and when they changed their accounts.

"The late evening of Aug. 9, 2014, I couldn't sleep," wrote Jonathan Capehart in an article for *The Washington Post* March 16, 2015.

"In those early hours and early days, there was more unknown than known. But this month, the Justice Department released two must-read investigations connected to the killing of Brown. They have also forced me to deal with two uncomfortable truths: Brown never surrendered with his hands up, and Wilson was justified in shooting Brown."

However, Jonathan also wrote that the Department of Justice went on to say it found an abuse of the constitutional rights of people, mostly African Americans, in Ferguson.

In a pool of about 75 people from the ages of 28 to 80, who are not in law enforcement, I ask, "Should protesters be arrested?"

Many, reiterated the right we all have to protest peacefully. That was the key word—peacefully. The majority went on to say arrests should be made only after they have been asked to leave the area and refuse or if it escalates to property damage.

Most went on to say that critical services should not be stopped. Protesters have a right to voice their views as long as it does not infringe on others' rights.

A related question: "What if it turns to violence and damage to property and physical injury? Should they be arrested?"

Overwhelmingly they wanted the police to do whatever it took to subdue the crowd. The answers on how it should be done? Arrest the whole bunch, bring in the mounted patrol, use tear gas, rubber bullets, firehoses, tasers, make the arrested clean up the mess the protesters make. Call in the National Guard. Police are not equipped to handle crowds with hundreds, perhaps even a thousand people, hurling objects, setting cars on fire, smashing windows in stores, and looting.

Another often heard response was the question: At what point or period of time did we develop a society, with no thought of responsibility or respect for anything?

One officer from a relatively small town said they had only experienced protests a couple of times. When they felt the situation was getting out of hand, fire hoses quickly took care of the situation.

Protesters arrive to participate in the chaos for many reasons. Comments came from the group of civilians.

Many thought they come for the excitement, that it is no different than the movie, Animal House, and someone yelling, "Food Fight!"

I am reminded of the many discussions I heard about bar fights. Monkey see, Monkey do. Someone throws a chair. Another, a drink in someone's face. The fight is on.

I realize people have differences and get angry about situations and perhaps are mad at life in general. However, when they disrupt people's lives, when they take away their ability to get to a doctor, hospital, an airport, to get to work, or, prevent them from getting home to their family after a day's work, they aren't getting my sympathy. They may be getting their attention but certainly not the public's understanding. I dare say if anyone of us were on the crew that cleans up after a protest, we would have little compassion for their gripes.

Mike was not often called to a bar brawl, but occasionally he was in the area or an officer was there alone. Just his presence seemed to calm things down. The officer he was assisting was glad when Mike walked in the door!

Solutions, answers we can agree on, may never come in ways we would like, but open minds and civil behavior to those who disagree with us will temper our angst. I watch the news as much as I can. I record and listen to people I may not agree with. When I hear others say I only watch a particular channel, I am sorry they are not willing to hear the other side. I believe the majority of us have friends that we may not agree with on every subject but we like them and enjoy their company just the same.

"I object to violence because when it appears to do good, the good is only temporary; the evil it does is permanent."

—Mahatma Gandhi

CHAPTER 11

LIFE IS A HIGHWAY

We spent Mike's nights off with friends, drinking coffee and sometimes playing cards. That was our entertainment. Many of the local policemen and deputies were about our age, with young children and no money also. We spent time with them, and life was good.

A call-out for a blood run was especially common when we lived in West Central Minnesota. There wasn't a large supply of blood at our local hospital. When more was needed, it often came via a trooper from a larger hospital. In nicer weather, sometimes the patrol airplane brought it. But the majority of time, it was relayed by troopers. While Mike was roaring down the road often in the middle of the night, there was another person with him in spirit in the squad—the dispatcher.

I remember the man I'm interviewing as young, maybe a 16-year-old. He's about 64 years older but looks very much the same. He had thick head of hair—a duck tail back then. Today it's gray and still thick but not a duck tail.

He went into the military after high school and went to security school. He flashes a smile that still looks the same. After the military he worked for an armored car company. He saw an ad in the paper that the state patrol was looking for dispatcher.

The dispatcher felt like he was riding with the troopers. Sometimes they were roaring down the road in a chase, other times on their way to an accident, but often they were after a speeder. He had sat in the passenger side of their car, knew what it looked like, the dashboard, the shotgun strapped into the front of the car. He had been there. When they called in, he was with them in his mind—right there with them.

He remembered the first day of training when he listened to the last minutes of a state trooper's life. They were called Minnesota Highway Patrol back then. The patrolman had been shot in his neck and could no longer speak, but, as a dispatcher asked questions, yes or no questions, the fatally injured man could key the mic. Once for yes twice for no.

Listening to the tape of that dying man made a lasting impression on this dispatcher. He was their lifeline. When troopers were called out in the middle of the night the only contact they had was their dispatcher and he was on guard for them. If he didn't hear from them for a while, he was calling their number wondering where they were. He felt responsible for the trooper out on the call...maybe too much. Could he leave his job when he walked out the door? Sometimes not. He worked holidays, nights and weekends and missed a lot of family life.

Summer driving was easier for Mike. When blood was needed, the patrol cars could travel fast with lights flashing and sirens blaring. Winter was a different. The voice on the radio would be asking, "When can you meet the officer bringing the blood?" "Roads are icey! I'm driving as fast as I dare!" would be his reply. Mike was young and driving fast was fun, so he secretly enjoyed these otherwise dire challenges. He didn't mind being called out often for much-needed blood.

Before there was air conditioning in their squad cars, it was difficult to keep blood cold during the summer months even though they started off neatly packed in ice. I remember when Mike told me about holding the container out the window, trying to keep the contents cold. Time was critical so airplanes or helicopters were also used but were not always available or, in inclement weather, not feasible.

I loved the town we lived in. The involvement with the community fit me. I taught Sunday School, belonged to the Ladies Aid, and worked many hours at the church, serving for weddings and funerals. "Is the cake for church?" Mike would ask if I was baking. I was on the Title One Board for school and an election judge. I intended to grow old in that quiet, friendly community. We had developed close friendships and a sense of belonging; so had our children. We would live in that house only nine months though before our lives would change again.

Mike was always an explorer and adventurer. He would often say he was born too late and would have liked the 1800s when the men were out finding new territories. As a woman, I would have been left behind to fend off the Indians and Mother Nature. Having been in our town for nine years, he knew every road in that area and had driven them many times. He wanted new roads and scenery to explore.

I heard Mike on the phone. He rarely answered it if I was home, but I was putting fresh sheets on the bed when it rang, and asked him to please answer. I could, of course, only hear Mike's side of the conversation. He thanked the person on the other end for being considered, but went on to explain that we had just bought a new home and had lived in it only eight months.

"My wife would not be happy about a move," I heard him say.

Mike had had a transfer request in for Northern Minnesota for many years. We often camped in that area, and he loved the woods and lakes. That phone conversation was with the captain of the district. There was an opening, and they needed an answer right away. My stomach ached as he told me about it. Five hours from our parents?! I hated the thought of it.

"I turned it down," he said.

He liked where we now lived but knew stations up north didn't become available often so wanted to have a request for the northern part of the state on record. My stomach ache became more intense as I asked for more information about the pending assignment. Mike was reluctant to talk about it, saying he knew I wouldn't go and to forget about it.

When I think back on it, what a good tactic he had used. Guilt works on some people, and I was one of them. We finally talked about it, and he told me exactly what was said. The captain wanted him to come up and look over the station and give him an answer within a few days. I encouraged him to drive up at least to take a look at the station and talk to the other patrolmen who worked there.

He spent two days there, staying overnight with a patrolman and his family. Mike came home acting as if he was not impressed. He would be leaving an area where we felt so welcome and five hours from our family.

On the other hand, Mike was the head of our household—the "bread winner." The children would be out of school by the time we needed to move, and we might be ready for a change. I told him I didn't want to be sitting in a nursing home someday, listening to him complain about never being able to move up north.

We had already planned a camping trip to that area in August, a plan made long before the transfer was offered. We would camp with our long-time friends. Their three girls, and our John and Julie would be there.

We had vacationed often with them in the past. Traveling on motorcycles, we had seen most of the northern and western United States together. Often taking two-week vacations, we usually left our children with their grandparents. My parents and Mike's would take turns, each having one child for a week, then switching children for the next week. It worked well.

This camping trip was different. Mike and I would look for a house to buy. A new life was coming our way.

We were in the middle-income bracket, and there weren't many homes for sale in that price range. Frustrated, we went back to the realty office and had a cup of coffee. We sat quietly, disappointed by what was available. But the phone rang while we were there. A contractor had a spec house ready for sale. The realtor smiled as he hung up and told us that this may be the home for us.

It was a great location—a dead-end road just a block from the river. It was a beautiful area, woodsy but still within the city limits. It was a pretty house. Its split entry gave a spacious look to the living room and dining room. John, age thirteen, and Julie, age nine, would have bedrooms on the main floor. There was also a roomy master bedroom for us. The lower level offered a family room, workshop, second bathroom and a tuck-under garage. We bought the house contingent on selling our home, which sold in four days.

Trucker Bob helped us move. Before meeting him for the first time, Mike told me he was "down to earth." That always meant that his language would be crass and his all-around behavior would be something I would not like. I didn't like some of his behavior; however, he would become a dear and cherished friend. He cleaned up his language when he was around me, and I enjoyed his company.

Bob would be in charge of bringing our belongings to our new home. The moving bill would not be paid by the State of Minnesota; it would be ours. Mike would pay for the gas, and our friend would provide the truck.

Moving day went well. I drove the car, leaving Mike's truck and squad car in Redwood. We arrived in northern Minnesota on a hot Saturday night. Mike and Bob would unload and go back to our previous town on Sunday afternoon. The high temperature was scorching, and son John worked hard, helping with unloading. The temperature was high and I cautioned him about working too hard and made sure he had plenty of water. By the end of the day he felt clammy and sick to his stomach. Fortunately, he was fine the next day.

The station was shorthanded, with a patrolman on vacation, one at National Guard Camp, and one on days off. Mike would go back and work alone for a week, taking calls and working the day shift. He stayed with one of the deputies.

I had only been that lonesome for Mike two other times: when he was in Thailand and when he was in Vietnam. I felt totally alone and sad that first day. The next day was better: my parents arrived to help me put our house in order. They were lifesavers and I thanked them over and over for coming. My mom loved to clean and scrub everything in sight. We laughed and talked as we arranged things in our new home. My dad loved meeting people and was soon a regular at the local coffee shop.

Soon the week was over and Mike was in his new station to start patrolling the roads of the county. Our neighbors, who had scarcely glanced at us during the week, were suddenly gawking and walking slowly by the house, intrigued by the squad car in the driveway.

The smell of pine in the air and the wooded area made us feel like we were on vacation. Walking a few blocks from our home took us to a quiet bay on the river. We had warned our children about the dangers of the wild. Unfortunately, the year we moved was a particularly bad year for bears coming into town. The weather had been dry, and berries were not as plentiful as in years past. John loved to go to the bay and roam around the woods. We had told John and Julie that if they encountered a bear, they should climb a tree.

When that situation came up, John did what he had been told. He climbed into the crotch of a tree. The yearling bear also climbed that same tree but up into the other crotch. There they sat, looking at each other. John waited the bear out, coming home to tell us of the experience, and also that climbing a tree was not always the best course of action.

Leaving the quiet community we had lived in was a huge adjustment. We gave up the farming area for The Range. John loved the area the minute we arrived. He was going into the eighth grade and was quite social.

Julie was going in the fourth grade, and like her mother, did not like moving. I am sure her feelings came from me, and for that, I am sorry. I was preoccupied with my own sense of upheaval and did not give her the attention she needed or the consideration a young girl needed for her own sense of loss.

My extended family lived two hundred and fifty miles away. I never wanted this northern community to feel like home and did not, at first, give it much of a chance. I have no complaint in the way we were treated. The people we met were welcoming and friendly. We were immediately included in parties and social gatherings. I was just plain homesick. I have always been close to my family. Mike would say we were the only family who went to third cousins' confirmations. I grieved for the comfort of having family close by. Through the years Mike apologized many times for taking me away from my family.

Mike was trying to adjust, too. The laid-back farming community was gone. Here we were in the shadow of the range. Hard working, hard playing, and hard drinking was at our back door. It also didn't help that he had a half-mad, half-sad wife to contend with.

Mike would say, "If I stopped ten people in our southern community, one wants to fight. If I stop ten people up north, nine want to fight, and the tenth one is from southern Minnesota." Mike was big, tall, and incredibly strong. He would often ask the question (though not really expecting an answer from me), "Why would anyone want to fight with me?"

Mike's job was patrolling highways. He enforced traffic laws, investigated accidents, checked out abandoned vehicles, and assisted the motoring public. Although he sometimes worked a day shift, at times a midafternoon or night shift, he was often on call. The phone ringing in the middle of the night was not odd. Though it startled me and set my heart beating faster the first few times I heard it, I became used to it. The phone was on my side of the bed, so it also woke me. I always stayed awake until he was out the door. I would guess his adrenaline was pumping if the call was about a crash. He didn't usually say what the call was about and I fell quickly back to sleep.

We would develop cherished friendships in the community. Mike worked for the Minnesota State Patrol for twenty-six years. He would attend an Advanced Accident Investigation Course, be promoted to Station Sergeant, and receive many thank-you letters from the motoring public.

Department of Public Safety – Patrol
To: Officer Michael T Jurgens # 280
From: Captain Norris Sletten
Subject: Advanced Accident Investigation Course

Congratulations on your very successful completion of the Advanced Accident Investigation Course held at the Training Center April 2-6, 1973.

The excellent final grade of 98.5 which you achieved is commendable.

We urge that you use these skills in your accident investigations, and further, that you assist your partners with their investigations at every opportunity.

Norris Sletten
Captain

To: Trp. Michael Jurgens #280
From: Captain Charles D. Geiger
Subject: Station Sergeant

I would like to congratulate you on your appointment to Station Sergeant in the 3130 Station. I am confident you will do an excellent job in this position.

If we can be of any assistance to you, feel free to call Lt. Fort, Lt. Anthony or myself any time.

Captain Charles D. Geiger
Commander – District 3100

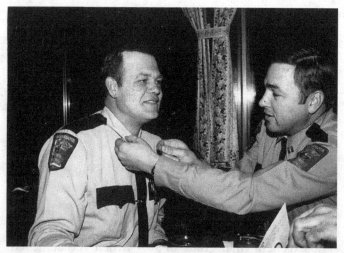

Mike promoted to Station Sergeant by Captain Charles Geiger.

Department of Public Safety – Patrol

To: Sgt. Michael Jurgens #280
Subject: Commendation

A man called our office on September 3, 1987 and expressed deep appreciation for your helpfulness and the professional way in which you handled an accident in which he was involved.

He went on to say he wanted Sgt. Jurgens' supervisor to be notified of this.

You are commended for this and for the many other times you were helpful to people in need.

Captain Charles Geiger
District 3100

Department of Public Safety – Patrol

To: Sgt. Michael Jurgens #280
From: Captain Norris Sletten
Subject: Commendation

A man called our office to say thank you very much to the trooper answering their need on Highway 14 the day of the accident. He was in a daze and could not remember your name. He also wants to thank you for insisting they go to the doctor. Their injuries were worse than they thought. They would also like your name and address and a photo of you and would be glad to pay the cost. They said we need more men like yourself.

Mike—Good Work. Maybe you should send them a couple of pictures. That's how fan cubs get started! Thanks again for leaving a good impression with them.

Norris Sletten
Captain

A thank you note came to Mike after receiving his name and address:

"The harder you work for something, the greater you'll feel when you achieve it."

—Anonymous

CHAPTER 12

COME FLY WITH ME

Formed in 1957, the Minnesota State Patrol Flight Section, spotting unreported crashes, traffic obstructions, stalls, and hazards for the motoring public were part of the airplane pilot's job. The planes were also used in traffic speed enforcement, and pilots were often "the Bear in the air."

The State Patrol Flight Section is responsible for the support of state, county and local aerial law enforcement support. The flight Section is based in St. Paul and Brainerd.

There are nine state trooper pilots in the Flight Section who fly two Bell helicopters, three Cessna 182 airplanes and a Cirrus SR22 airplane.

All helicopters are equipped with thermal imagers, Night Sun spotlights and microwave down link equipment capable of transmitting a live video picture from the helicopter to a receiver — this live video can then be streamed online. Most helicopter flying is done during nighttime hours and all the pilots are equipped and trained to fly using Night Vision Goggles. The pilots are also trained to fly firefighting and rescue missions in conjunction with the State Patrol Special Response Team.

"It's a Living"

—Story by Jim Hansen, Used here with his permission
First Published in *The Minnesota Flyer*. December 2011

Technically it is Minnesota State Patrol– aviation – but to most people accustomed to the old CB lingo, it is the "Bear in the Air." Most people continue to think of the Flight Section as "the guys that do speed traps." Being in the aviation business, I often see the State Patrol aircraft doing a multitude of other duties, and it's time that they get some recognition.

When I was doing the "It's a Living" series on unusual aviation occupations, I tried to get a pilot to do one on the state patrol – but he was reluctant to write the story. Law enforcement officers are often reluctant to attract attention, or talk about what they do. Three years of badgering him and offering to write the story myself produced an interview at the Aviation Division offices at Signature Flight Support at St. Paul Downtown Airport. As expected, there is a lot to tell about the operation.

THE PILOTS

I've known this pilot for a number of years, ever since he was a deputy. He worked for and received his Commercial and Instrument ratings in 1999. He applied for and was accepted to the flight section of the State Patrol in 2000, and was made Chief Pilot of the flight section in 2010.

I asked the man about the policy of most Law Enforcement aviation units of only hiring people with law enforcement experience. He replied "It's a lot easier to take a sworn officer and teach them to fly than it is to teach a pilot how to be a police officer. We require that the officer has a Fixed Wing Private Pilot Certificate and Instrument rating (with 100 hours of time) before applying. Upon being accepted into the flight section, a new pilot will obtain a Commercial fixed wing reading. A pilot can get the ratings in a relatively short period of time, but it takes a longer time for an officer to receive the training in law, procedures, criminal investigation, and experience than it takes to learn to fly. We're also looking for the qualities and background required of a state patrol trooper – Respect, Integrity, Courage, and Honor."

All state patrol pilots are troopers; their job assignment is to the flight section. The pilots will still go and work the road during inclement weather and during special assignments.

Once hired into the State Patrol Flight Section, if not already rated, the trooper will be trained to fly helicopters. An FAA Commercial Helicopter rating will be earned. After a total of about 150 flight hours in the helicopters, the new pilot will be sent to the Bell Factory School in Texas.

All Patrol pilots are "dual rated" in helicopters and fixed wing aircraft. In addition to the Chief Pilot, who still flies, there are currently eight pilots on staff. The pilots maintain proficiency in the airplanes and helicopters, as well as instrument proficiency, through a formal in-house training program. In addition, the unit brings in Bell helicopter recurrent training specialists for the difficult helicopter maneuvers – touchdown auto rotations, auto rotations from hovering out of ground effect, and operation with night vision goggles.

THE AIRCRAFT

The unit has three helicopters—two Bell Long Rangers and a Bell 407. Though the 407 looks like the Long Rangers, it can be identified by the 4-blade roto system. Each of the helicopters is configured for one pilot and six passengers. There are no hoist systems installed, but there is an external cargo hook that is used for the rescue work and firefighting. The other distinctly "cop equipment" is a 30 MILLION candlepower "Night Sun" surveillance light, a thermal imager/camera and a microwave transmitter.

Two Bell Long Rangers.

The microwave transmitter gives the troopers the ability to upload a picture from the helicopter camera/thermal imager to the Internet. They can do this by transmitting to either, three fixed sites that are based around the state, or to a mobile truck that transmits the picture via satellite to the Internet. The truck allows a picture to be transmitted from anywhere in the state.

The helicopters all look new—but these are not "hangar queens"—the highest time helicopter has 11,000 hours on it—and the newest has 1600 hours.

As for the fixed-wing airplanes, the Patrol (like so many other states) uses the Cessna 182 Skylane. They have three of them—two 1981s and a 1984. I asked what the trooper liked about the Skylane, and it was the same thing that has sold Skylanes for years—good short field capability, reasonable speed, good endurance, and a stable instrument platform. I asked what he wished for, and like all pilots, he asked for more speed, and an ability to fly in Minnesota's icy conditions.

"We maintain a 24-hour readiness," he replied. "That means that we fly night and instrument weather. If it *can* be flown, we fly. I guess I would like the weather capability, too, in that case!"

The unit also has a Beach Queen Air, with the Excalibur engine conversion to 400 horsepower, 8-cylinder, direct drive engines replacing the old geared engines. The aircraft was a former NASA aircraft. It can haul cargo, but the primary mission is transport of people. This includes prisoner transports under contract with local law enforcement agencies or the Minnesota Department of Corrections.

Because it is doing contract work, the pilots and aircraft maintain FAR Part 135 standards. Transporting prisoners by air can be far more cost-effective than surface transportation, when you consider meals and overnights. Of course, it is also far more secure than surface transportation. The aircraft is also used to transport State Patrol personnel, Department of Public Safety personnel, hazardous materials, HazMat Teams, structural collapse teams – like military missions, the State Patrol is often asked to do things that are out of the ordinary. The Queen Air supports FEMA missions, and has even been used to transport bomb disposal squads to outstate Minnesota. Though unpressurized, the Queen Air offers a good payload capacity, a range of over 1000 miles, and cruise speeds to 180 knots.

I asked about maintenance on the aircraft. The pilot said, "All a-frame, engine, and avionics maintenance is bid and contracted out." The contractors are specialists on the type of aircraft and engines used. I asked about other staffing – secretaries, dispatchers, etc., and was told that the unit has an office manager and the trooper pilots. "We self-dispatch" through the state patrol dispatch center or "MetroComm," said the pilot. "We maintain a schedule of 8 a.m. to 3 a.m.—and are on call after that." That's a lean operation!

THE MISSIONS

The missions by the unit are varied. I asked if they maintained a regular patrol, like the air units of many large cities. The trooper said "We do. We try to keep the helicopter up over the Metro during varied hours of the night. Not only is it a deterrent, but the fact that we already have an aircraft in the air means that we can be on the scene to render assistance within minutes. We may aid in a car or foot chase, or participate in any other police activity."

Some missions are unique. "We do short-haul lifts," explained the pilot. "There is no other short-notice lift capability for paramedics anywhere in the state. With helicopters based here, plus one in Brainerd, we can have paramedics on the scene quickly."

The State Patrol Flight Section also works with the St. Paul Fire Department to support rescue efforts. The fire department supplies the paramedics that will rappel into a scene if necessary. They do short-haul to get injured persons to a ground ambulance or in aero medical helicopter.

Taylors Falls rescue.

Snowy landing.

The unit specializes in searches – visual searches – or using the Nightsun light, night vision goggles or their thermal imager. The missions are varied – they may search for lost hunters, boaters, children, or someone that has wandered away from a nursing home. They also look for suspects of criminal activity.

Cirrus Airplane

107

The pilot brings up a good point "If it is an outdoorsman," he said, "we can usually find them in minutes. An outdoorsman will stop and build a fire—and we'll find them fast with the night vision goggles."

"We work with other agencies," he continues. "Our helicopters are equipped to use a "Bambi bucket" - a collapsible, 144-gallon water bucket used to fight fires. We're not in the business of putting out big forest fires—that's a job for the firemen and the DNR-contracted air tankers and helicopters—but those dedicated air tankers aren't available all the time. We will assist when the DNR needs us, but that is rare. We can assist the local fire departments in getting water on a fire before it GETS big." (Note: external loads on a helicopter, like the "Bambi bucket" require a different set of skills by the pilot – you essentially have to fly the load to the point where you want it, as well as fly the helicopter. It's a demanding task.)

He describes other missions. "We provide disaster response – floods, fires, structure collapse. We fly medical supplies – emergency equipment – damage assessment. We provided aerial platform to aid decision makers in making their assessment. We're transport specialists." I asked if the Patrol unit had participated in the recent fires in the Boundary Waters. "Yes. We provided the rescue response for the fire crews – having paramedics available in a situation like that can be a life saver."

As sworn law enforcement officers, the Patrol provides security for the Governor and high-level heads of State agencies. "If the mission calls for a fixed-wing aircraft, the Governor will usually fly with the Department of Transportation, but if they need a helicopter, we fly them," the trooper explained.

One of the most important missions for the aircraft is blood transport. The State Patrol is asked to transport blood from the blood bank to outstate hospitals. It may be a rare type of blood needed, or the need may be for a quantity of blood for an operation or multiple injuries.

Getting back to police work, he explained how the Patrol cooperates with other law enforcement agencies. "We may provide support for a SWAT team," he explained, "or we may do surveillance for them – or photograph the building they will be entering. We do photography, accident investigation photos, and crime scene photos." I asked about drug work. The answer was "We don't usually go looking for infractions, but we will deal with it if we find it. Our work in that area is mainly in support of other law enforcement agencies. As an example, we may follow a seller or a buyer."

Dual controls in the helicopter.

Finally, I asked about the "Bear in the Air" missions – traffic surveillance – the mission MOST people think about when they hear about the Patrol Aviation Unit. "We work with ground units," explained the pilot. "We'll have people on the ground in cars—we'll get to altitude, deploy 10 degrees of flaps, set up an 80 knot cruise, and lean the mixture to 7 – 8 gallons per hour. We'll time a vehicle crossing the painted markers, keep our eyes on them, and direct the ground units." I asked if anyone ever beat the system by claiming parallax. The pilot said, "No. We give them the benefit of the doubt. They start the watch as the front of the car gets to the mark, and stop the watch after the rear of the car leaves the next mark. Essentially, they get two "free" car lengths."

I asked about the problem of monitoring the radios – especially in the Metro area, and was told, "The helicopters have two com radios to monitor, plus three police radios, plus the normal VOR, GPS, and transponder."

It is obvious that this trooper/pilot is happy with his career in law enforcement AND flying. "I used to spend 7-8 hours on the road – then got the opportunity to fly. I never considered being in the administrative end of the unit, but I'm glad it worked out." Almost as an afterthought, I asked him, "You used to see State Patrol ground units changing tires for motorists on the side of the road. Does the Patrol still do that?" He replied "Our troopers are spread pretty thin – they often are dispatched from accident to accident – in the metro area, we have a roadside assistance unit for changing tires or bringing fuel – but yes, I'll stop and help change a tire for a motorist. I guess it's just the old farm boy in me!"

Nice to know that there are still people like that out there!

* * * * *

> *"Any landing you can walk away from is a good landing.*
> *Any landing that lets you fly the plane again is an even*
> *better landing."*

> —Chuck Yeager

CHAPTER 13

FLYING HIGH

Ken didn't know anything about the Minnesota Highway Patrol when he was young. Raised on a farm in northern Minnesota, money was tight and after graduating high school he decided to go into the army. There was a draft, and he knew his name would soon come up. Ken spent some of his army life in Alaska where 17,000 troops were stationed. They went on a maneuver called "Operation Little Bear." He likes to say he toured Alaska on a D-8 Cat in January, February, and March at night. It was cold. It would sometimes be as cold as -40 degrees. He was used to working on machinery in the cold, as Northern Minnesota could be almost that cold or colder at times. Once discharged and back home, in a café over coffee, he heard the patrol was hiring. He took the test, passed it, and in 1962 was invited to join the Patrol School. He was contacted via Telegram from Western Union:

> *Fax St. Paul, Minn. 9:35 A M CST Mar. 13, 1962*
> *KA Kammen*
> *You Have Been Selected for Patrol School. Advise at Once If*
> *Still Interested.*
> *Letter Follows.*

Twenty-six years old when he started on the patrol, he wonders whether the younger troopers have had enough life experience. Having had other jobs before coming to the patrol would perhaps be beneficial.

Good training made him ready for the difficulties and rewards that would come with the job. He talks of working closely with other agencies. He saw them as a family when talking about other law enforcement officers in the area he worked. They were a small group. They helped each other and counted on each other. Ken still keeps in touch with them.

He worked the road for 15 years. He liked the freedom of going where he wanted, heading in any direction. He talks of car chases as being the most exciting and the most dangerous. Decisions have to be made in a split second to chase, to continue chasing, or back off. It depends on the severity of the offense. Ken likes the idea of cameras. He thinks it makes for a better officer and answers questions that are raised that only a camera can sometimes answer.

1988 Plymouth. Trooper Ken Kammen by his squad car.

Yes, he missed a lot of family life. There were times he went several days without seeing his children. He doesn't feel like he was too hard on his children and yes, they were proud of him. Ken has not become hardened. He didn't nor wouldn't let it happen.

In 1969 he heard from a flight instructor that veterans in the service between the Korean War and Vietnam were now eligible for the GI Bill. He got his private pilot's license on his own and then could use the GI Bill for the Commercial, Instrument Rating, and Flight Instructor Rating plus hours upon hours of training needed to be qualified for a position with the patrol flight section.

After his years on the road, he was ready for a different job on the patrol—a new adventure. Exciting and satisfying are the words he uses for his flying experience. He started flying with the Air Division out of Bemidji. It was a fairly quiet area. Soon, however, he was flying out of St. Paul, and that was busy. The patrol pilots spend many hours helping other agencies. Acquiring a helicopter made search and rescue efforts easier. Calls for help came from around the state, and the flight crew responded. They stepped up to fulfill many requests. It was rewarding to help so many different agencies. They flew governors and state officials and also often transported expert witnesses to court. Ken talks of the enjoyment of getting to know many people from different agencies and working with troopers throughout the entire state.

There is a moment that stands out in his memory of all the thousands during his time as a pilot in the Minnesota State Patrol. It was Sunday morning of the Memorial Day weekend, a day that usually started out quiet, meaning almost everybody was at his or her destination and wouldn't be hitting the road until the next day. Ken's shift began at 6 a.m., flying out of St. Paul-Downtown Airport. Over the air, a trooper working the East Metro area asked if he would monitor the speed timing zone on I-35E north of downtown St. Paul and the junction of I-694. This is a method of determining speed by timing vehicles over a measured quarter mile (1320 feet). There are usually five white hash marks painted on the right lane, clearly visible to the pilot to time vehicles by use of a stop watch to determine the speed of the vehicle in the zone. There is such a zone on I-35E.

After preflighting the Cessna Skylane, he departed St. Paul Downtown Airport. It's only a short distance to the zone on I-35E where the trooper was waiting on the southbound side of the freeway. As Ken entered the area, he could see a vehicle traveling at a high rate of speed heading south toward the timing zone. He alerted the trooper and started timing the vehicle at the first mark. As the vehicle crossed the second hash mark the speed was determined to be 104 m.p.h. Ken again checked the vehicle over the next two marks and determined the speed at 106 m.p.h. He advised the trooper of the speed, described the vehicle to him and its position, which was in the left lane. The trooper stepped from his squad car and waved the vehicle over to a spot behind his squad car.

After a conversation with the driver, the trooper called for the time and speed of the violation. He then advised Ken of the ticket number he would be issuing. Moments later he advised that the driver was being arrested for DWI and they would be heading downtown.

Later that day Ken had an opportunity to speak with the trooper and asked why the driver was traveling at such a high rate of speed. The driver stated that he had overslept at his girlfriend's place and was in a hurry to get home in hopes that he might make it there before his wife woke up.

The flight section flies in all kinds of weather, although they do have a policy not to fly when the temperature is below -20 degrees. Yes, it's cold inside the airplane when one first takes off. It can be cold in the winter and hot in the summer. Flying the 182-single engine, the Citabria, and the Bell 47 helicopter (like the one in the TV show "M.A.S.H.") was Ken's first relationship with the skies and made him realize, *This a long way from the farm*. The Bell 47 was slow but one could see 360 degrees. He would soon learn to fly the Long Ranger. It could carry seven passengers but usually carried only five because of weight restrictions.

MSP Bell 47 helicopter acquired from surplus military equipment.

MSP Bell 47 landing on the transport cart.

MSP Bell 206B helicopter and the larger model Bell 206L.

Ken became a supervisor (Chief Pilot) in1985. "Did it distance you from the troops?" I asked.

He believes it did and always does. Once you get into management, it seems you have stepped over to the other side. He tried not to let that happen, but it does. You become more distant. It's just part of the job.

He doesn't know if he would recommend a career in law enforcement today. Attitudes toward those enforcing our laws have changed. It's more dangerous out there.

Do you think law enforcement officers are afraid today?

He doesn't think they're afraid. It's not the job to be in if you are. You have to be confident and careful.

Do you think people understand what the job of an officer of the law entails?

There's so much that goes on out there that he doesn't think they can appreciate or understand what an officer does. Things happen so fast, situations change rapidly. No, they don't get it. Officers are taught to run toward danger to protect the people.

Do you think the young ones are up to the task? Will they stand up, protect us from danger?

Yes, he has faith in our young people and believes they will step up and be our protectors.

Was he ready to retire? No. He loved his job but with the early out offer, it just didn't pay to work past the age of 55. He had done his best, hadn't bent anything, hadn't hurt anyone, hadn't had any forced landings or crashes. He loved flying, and when he walked away, he felt a sense of pride. There were times he missed the uniform, but that time is over. He has never regretted his career with the Minnesota State Patrol, but after 29 years with them, he embraced his retirement.

Ken feels blessed in his retirement years. He has traveled by motorcycle about 250 thousand miles. He has enjoyed life in Arizona during the winter where he volunteers at the Commemorative Air Force Museum at Falcon Field in Mesa, and he also appreciates his summer home on a lake in Minnesota. A few years ago, he went for a ride in the new Minnesota State Patrol helicopter. He just gazed at all the new tech equipment and was in awe. He does wish he had that when he was up there.

"It's Retirement Time for Whirlybird"

By Captain Ken Kammen
November 1989

After 20 years and nearly 7,000 hours of dedicated service, the state patrol's 1969 Bell 47 helicopter was retired on August 15. While making a test flight after an annual inspection, A pilot took her up. Upon coming to a hover before landing, the transmission failed, but the pilot made a successful landing by using auto rotation.

Product support for the old helicopter makes it impractical to consider repair. We are planning to dispose of it through surplus property sales.

The helicopter was purchased in 1969 by the Minnesota State Patrol. Throughout the years, the helicopter was used for many purposes, but mainly for traffic control. It has led an interesting life and escaped major damage, though it has made a few unscheduled stops including one in a pig pen at Farm Fest and another on the banks of the Mississippi River in Minneapolis, when a U-joint on the tail rotor drive shaft broke. Since it was on floats, it was towed down river by the Washington County Water Patrol boat to the St. Paul Downtown Airport. It was the first time a helicopter had gone through the lock and dam.

Because of the Bell 47's vast window area, it made an excellent search craft. The doors of the helicopter have been taken off many times in order to photograph crime scenes for police and sheriff departments. DOT engineers have made use of our service by doing preconstruction and long-range planning photography. It was used for many years as the morning and afternoon traffic-watch helicopter, but that operation was discontinued when gas prices skyrocketed in the early 1980s. Now there are four news service aircraft doing it.

The helicopter has also been used for rescues. One memorable rescue was of four young fishermen who fell through thin ice near Forest Lake in November 1984. Using the helicopter on floats, another pilot and I rescued the boys after dark and deposited them on shore in good, but wet and cold condition. Another time, a pilot rescued a duck hunter who was mired to the waist in mud. As far as I know, the man's shotgun is still out in the swamp.

Many marijuana fields have fallen victim to the watchful eye of the Bell's pilots. Observations by the MSP pilots have led to several arrests and destruction of thousands of dollars' worth of marijuana.

Those who did their training and received their helicopter rating in the Bell are going to read this article with tender spots in their hearts. They loved her, but they cussed her at the same time because she was so hot in the summer and so cold in the winter. One of the pilot's used to get into the helicopter in the hangar and have the line crew tape the door shut while he sat there with his snowmobile suit on. Then they would pull the helicopter out, and he would depart on his morning traffic watch. By taping the doors, he was able to conserve a little of the heat and fly with a mitten only on his left hand.

The past 20 years have seen drastic design changes in helicopters, but other than the advent of jet engines, they are still basically the same – just a lot more comfortable.

Mikhail and Raisa Gorbachev made a 7 hour stop in the Twin Cities June 3, 1990 after receiving and invitation from then Governor Rudy Perpich. The Gorbachev's were greeted by crowds chanting Gorby, Gorby, and waving Soviet flags.

Captain Ken Kammen was Chief Pilot for the Minnesota State Patrol at the time. An event of such national importance, with such short notice, required the help of a large number of people. Ken received commendations for doing an excellent job and going that extra mile from Governor Rudy Perpich. The governor praised Ken for making the visit of President Mikhail and Raisa Gorbachev a success. He complimented Ken for the excellent job he did of thoroughly covering every area with professionalism and efficiency.

> To: WCCO
> From: Bruce Kammen
> Re: WCCO Good Neighbor
> Date: February 28, 1991
>
> I am writing to you to request having my father be recognized as "Today's CCO good neighbor." His name is Captain Ken Kammen, and he is the Chief Pilot for the Minnesota State Patrol.
>
> On March 26, 1991, he will be retiring after 29 years of service to the State of Minnesota. His first 17 years on the job were spent in Northern Minnesota. After

about seven years on the flight section, he became the captain and has been ever since. "Captain Ken" has been involved in countless searches, chases, and a wide variety of incidents assisting law enforcement in Minnesota.

During retirement, he plans to do custom picture framework and spend a lot of time on Deer Lake.

Captain Ken's family all appreciate what he has done for them and for the State of Minnesota.

I would really appreciate if this could be aired on either March 18, his birthday, or March 22, his retirement party day. If I could be contacted to confirm whether this will be a broadcast or not, that would be great.

Thank you,
Bruce Kammen

Ken Kammen, Chief Pilot.

Denny's story:

The offer of the pilot job was something the trooper really needed to discuss with his family. They had it made, living in a small community in northern Minnesota with a little hobby farm and also had a herd of black angus cattle.

His daughter was a senior in high school. It would be a big change in their lives for her father to go into flying. He visited with his daughter about it, telling her he would understand if she didn't want to move.

She thought it over and knew it was a great opportunity for him. She would be going to college in a year anyway and was willing to make the sacrifice.

Being a pilot certainly expanded his horizons. He had a chance to meet many of the troopers and work with the other agencies. He believes it was a good move. He started taking Ground School after moving up north. Some of the pilots were war veterans, and they had a lot more experience flying. He was smoking at that time, didn't realize the health hazards, and it was kind of the thing to do. He decided he couldn't afford to learn to fly, but if he quit smoking, stashed the money he would spend on cigarettes, he might have enough to go to Ground School. He saved for two or three years and started his flying career. He kept saving, and soon the account was built up again. Seeing an advertisement in a magazine that a commercial pilot was starting a flight school. He took vacation and went for the accelerated course.

It took him about a month flying every day, getting as many hours in as quickly as he could. He received his commercial rating, then received a call from the Captain of the Aviation section of the patrol. Ken asked if he'd be interested in flying for the patrol. At that time, he worked at getting his instrument rating at Holman Field in St Paul.

Going into the flight section was an opportunity for him to broaden his horizons. He has really been happy with his decision and his career as a pilot.

He was flying when he received a call that a lady had just had a baby. The woman had a rare blood type and needed blood within the hour to survive. The hospital in Fargo had the blood. He took off and advised Fargo Airport that this was a dire emergency.

A Northwest plane coming in was held so he could land. A bunch of cones around another plane took up a lot of room. Instead of going around, he busted through some of them. Suddenly he was surrounded by FBI agents. He told them who he was and that he had an emergency.

He found out later that it was Air Force One, with President Ronald Reagan on board. A man came running up to his plane with the blood. Denny requested high-speed taxi to the runway for immediate take off. Air Control gave him permission. He landed and a trooper took the blood to the hospital.

The trooper/pilot received a call on a cold winter night. Law enforcement had been monitoring a person they thought was hauling a large amount of drugs. They had watched him enter his apartment but a search did not find drugs. The only chance they had is if Denny would fly to Duluth and pick up the drug dog, his handler, and bring them here. It was dark and cold. He really didn't want to make that flight, but the need was there. He crawled into the plane about midnight and headed for Duluth. He picked up the drug dog and handler; the police brought them to the apartment. The dog made a circle around the coffee table, they took it apart, and in the round center they found a large quantity of cocaine. The dog then ran to one of the bedrooms and started scratching on the wall. They broke out a part of that wall and found a large volume of cash stuffed in between the studs.

Denny received a call about a drowning. A man had disappeared out of his boat. They often helped other departments with searches. It was going to be a hot day, so Denny just put on his light street clothes, jumped in the squad car, and headed for the airport. On the way, he met a car that was westbound on the highway. The driver was all over the road. He pulled the car over and got the driver back to his car. When he started to process him, his passenger jumped out of his car, ran over to him, and said this guy had just raped her. The guy jumped out of the car and started running. Denny called for assistance from the city police. The guy ran in the direction of the airport.

Denny thought the best thing to do was to take the plane and see if he could spot him. He saw the guy lying in a little ditch on the edge of the airport. Denny chased after him with the airplane. They went back and forth for a while, but he was starting to get really tired. Denny was able to get along side of him, got the wing right next to him, then right on top of him, and the deputy with him jumped out with his headset still on. He had a fight on his hands. Denny got out of the airplane and helped the deputy. There were police cars on the runway. Denny got on the radio and told the control tower that this is the State Patrol and the airport is officially closed. Shortly, he called back to say that the airport was open again.

Denny received a call from the sheriff concerning a lost child. The little girl was about 10 and deaf. The sheriff got in the airplane with him, and they went looking. It was a hot muggy day. They got a glimpse of her in the heavy canopy of the forest. Denny called in and said he was going to turn his wing down and do tight circles around this child, otherwise they wouldn't find her.

The sheriff flying with him wasn't feeling too good. His stomach was really upset. Denny told him he had plenty of plastic bags for him to use. He also told the searchers to keep an eye on the airplane and they'll find her. Denny was keeping her in sight.

It took them a long time to go through the dense forest to get to her. The sheriff kept filling up bags. When the deputies finally came and took custody of the child, Denny was able to straighten out and finally land. The sheriff got out of the plane and laid on the ground. Denny asked if he could help, but the sheriff wanted him to go, just Go! Denny took off, heading back to Bemidji. A little bit later, he thought, he can't just let him lay there, so he went back. The sheriff was still lying there. Denny got out of the airplane, and told the deputy he couldn't just leave him there. Again, the sheriff just wanted him to Go! He never wanted to fly with Denny again. He and Denny have talked and laughed about that a lot over the years.

"For once you have tasted flight you will walk the earth with your eyes turned skyward, for there you have been and there you will long to return."

—Leonardo da Vinci."

CHAPTER 14

KEEP YOUR MIND ON YOUR DRIVING, YOUR HAND ON THE WHEEL.

"People, People, People," Mike would often say as he came walking in the door at the end of his shift. He would be irritated by what had gone on in the world of the "motoring public." "What are they thinking," he would ask, not expecting an answer. We called it not paying attention, today it's called distracted driving. I don't know if one phase sounds better than the other. Sometimes it was merely a fender bender or losing control and going in the ditch. However, there were too many times when it was an accident. They called it accidents back then, now it's called a crash. Whatever it was called, it was not only a smashed vehicle but smashed bodies as well.

Research by the University of Utah and reported by *USA Today* October 5, 2017 concludes that technology in cars is causing more—not reducing—distracted driving. The study tested 30 vehicle systems and found that all are distracting to motorist.

As a young driver, I took my eyes off the road to tune to a radio station. In that case, I could just as easily have taken out a pedestrian or hit another car or tree.

Cell phones and other technology in our vehicles are not the only thing that has led to distractions while roaring down the road. It is not a new danger. Cars full of teenagers years ago were as filled with commotion as they are today. We had our distractions: girls laughing, everyone talking, boys showing off and driving fast. I don't remember driving down the road eating though. We parked our car in the drive-in lot and waited for a carhop to come to the car, ordered our food, and ate it there.

Today however our vehicles are equipped to distract us from the minute we sit down. Bluetooth tells us the phone is hooked up. Other additions to the now high-tech cars give the feeling that we are almost able to fly into space. Instant phone access is what our love affair with instant communication demands. Humans cannot multitask. Our brains need to concentrate on the business at hand.

My sister Carolyn was a traveling nurse for many years. One of us siblings would often travel with her to her 13-week assignment and fly home. Another would fly out and drive home with her when the assignment was over. I planned to fly to Seattle and accompany her home. "I don't want you to go," Mike had said. "Why?" I asked. "I am so excited about the trip." "I don't want you to die. I know what you two are like together. You'll be laughing and talking and not paying attention to what you're doing. Your brains turn to jelly."

I let that discussion go for a while, knowing full well that, yes, he was somewhat right about our behavior but that I was certainly going.

Carolyn met me at the airport. As we drove to her apartment, I told her that I had promised Mike I would not die. We paid particular attention to our traveling to Minnesota and only made one incorrect turn during the entire trip.

I know I can't talk on the phone and drive at the same time, so I place my phone in the back seat when I drive. I put it on mute so as not to be distracted by the whistle that tells me I have a text or an email, or the voice singing "I Feel Good" when my phone rings. Even if I wore a headset, it would interfere with my focus.

How many of us will admit that we have driven down the road, thinking about an array of things not remotely connected to driving. I have, and then suddenly realize that I have driven many miles with no memory of the road I just managed to navigate. Some call it a brownout. My mind is somewhere else. I have to stop myself from writing in my head and not letting a scenario of something in a book I am writing overtake my concentration.

Drivers think about a number of things as they negotiate a highway filled with other vehicles. Piloting our vehicles is so commonplace that we forget the tremendous task we have taken on.

"I'm astounded," Representative Mark Uglem, R- Champlin, said, according to the *Star Tribune*. 2017, speaking of the attempt to pass a state ban on the use of handheld cell phones and other electronic devices while driving. It had the DFL's and Republican bipartisan support. But then, the measure died – for a fourth straight session.

Finally:

St. Paul, Minn. (AP) — "Motorists will be required to use hands-free devices to talk on the phone while driving on Minnesota roads starting Aug. 1, 2019 under a bill that Gov. Tim Walz signed Friday to crack down on the growing problem of distracted driving."

"The law bans motorists from holding and using cellphones or other wireless devices while driving. Built-in Bluetooth systems meet the legal requirements that systems be voice-activated, but so do cheap hands-free mounts sold by many stores and online retailers. There's an exception for emergency calls. Drivers can still use GPS navigation apps, stream music and listen to podcasts if they're voice activated or if they start them up while they're still parked."

"The penalty for a first offense will be a $50 fine, rising to $275 for additional violations. Minnesota already bans texting and emailing while driving."

August 1, 2019. Minnesota State Patrol reports they stopped 162 drivers for using their cell phone. By the end of the week the patrol gave over 500 tickets and warnings to people driving with their cell phones in their hand.

A Minnesota Trooper tells me that sometimes when he's at scenes of accidents, he's had people that pass by trying to film the incident.

Cell phones are not the only actions that take our thoughts away from tasks at hand. Distracted driving takes on many forms. Drivers have dogs on their laps. Mothers are trying to care for their children who are sitting in the back seat. Our vehicle is jam-packed with disruptions.

Distracted walking is putting yourself at risk also. Crosswalks provide a false sense of security for pedestrians. People of all ages cross the street, looking at their cell phones. They have a fight with a pole or bump into another walker also tuned in to their cell phone. They don't hesitate or even sneak a glance towards oncoming traffic before crossing.

People seem to think that they are invincible. We can all get sidetracked. Someone walking by may divert us from the task of driving. What's for dinner? Or, what time do I have to be at that meeting? Unfortunately, interruptions behind the wheel are more than just an annoyance. Put down the phone, the food, make-up, or the book. I have sat beside a car at a stop light while the driver reads the paper, eats, and talks on the phone. In the blink of an eye, not paying full attention to our driving can lead to a crash and we could be seriously injured or dead. The Minnesota Safety Council urges all drivers to keep their eyes on the road, hands on the wheel, and minds on driving.

"We simply can't do two things at once," says Paul Aasen, President of the Minnesota Safety Council. "Driving needs our full attention, and we're not being responsible if we're sidetracked. *We* are the solution to distracted driving crashes." According to the Minnesota Safety Council, inattentive or distracted driving is identified in one of every four reported crashes in Minnesota.

The State Patrol believes it is likely much higher, given the challenges law enforcement officers face in determining distraction as a factor. The Minnesota Department of Public Safety states distracted driving accounts for one out of every four motor vehicle deaths. Nationally, every day, 11 teenagers die from texting and driving; 21% of teen drivers in fatal accidents were on their cell phones.

A good friend of mine was a Driver's License Examiner. He talked of youth being good drivers because they had just learned the rules and of course wanted to pass their tests. They were rule smart but inexperienced. They hadn't driven down slippery ice-packed roads or learned the real art of defensive driving.

He would also comment about the bad habits' drivers fall into as driving becomes old hat and mundane. Driving instructors estimate that a driver makes an average of 200 decisions during every mile he or she drives. This leaves no room for multitasking while behind the wheel. If you are trying to solve business or family problems while driving, you are creating mental overload.

Sgt. Jesse Grabow's column:

Question: I am wondering what your thoughts are in the legal reprimands with people getting out of their cars to do with the Drakes "In My Feelings/Kiki challenge?"

Sgt. Grabow's Answer: This is a very good topic to have a conversation with your children and friends. I have seen the "nae nae" and the "floss" but this is the first dance craze I've seen involving a moving vehicle. The #KiKiChallenge is a dance trend featuring a willing volunteer who opens up the passenger door of a moving vehicle and hops out and proceeds to dance alongside this moving vehicle to Drake's hit single "In My Feelings." Meanwhile the driver is video recording the person doing this.

As one would expect, there are going to be multiple risks involved with jumping out of a moving vehicle and dancing alongside it in the middle of the road or even near the road in general. This is a safety issue for the driver, the dancing pedestrian and the rest of the motoring public. The risk of injury to a person getting out of the vehicle is significant and the driver can be distracted by the person exiting the vehicle. In addition, it is illegal to take a video while driving.

People involved with this receive a citation for distracted driving no seatbelt use or more. If a crash was to occur, a driver could be charged with reckless driving or even criminal vehicle injury or homicide depending on the severity of the crash.

The moral of the article? Don't Kiki and drive.

Minnesota State Troopers deal with what goes on when a driver gets behind the wheel. Deputies and local police also write tickets or give warnings for speed, stop sign violations, drunk driving etc. However, the traffic on the Minnesota highways mainly belongs to the troopers. Speed is a big problem with the driving public. You have less time to react when you are going fast. Things go wrong quickly. A trooper talks about the distance it takes to stop, losing control of the vehicle, less time to avoid a crash. The Department of Public Safety studies the behavior of drivers regularly. They have found that drivers using cell phones while driving took their eyes off the road for five seconds at a time, literally driving the length of a football field at 55 mph without looking. So why do so many people multitask while they drive? Because they drive so often it's become automatic, so they figure they can safely do more than one thing. Just one accident could instantly change your mind. This is what happens to your body during a car crash:

- First, when your car suddenly stops, your body – including your head - continues to move at the speed you were driving until it hits something – like the steering wheel, windshield or dashboard. On impact, your brain crashes against the inside of your skull, and then rebounds and smacks into the other side of your skull. At minimum, you have a headache or a concussion. At worst: brain swelling and death.
- Then there's your neck: The weight of your head whipping back and forth can cause whiplash, but if it's a high-speed crash, the motion could break your neck.
- Another thing that happens during a car crash: If your heart swings too violently into the back of your breastbone, it can tear off the aorta – the largest artery in the body, and you'll bleed to death.
- Then there are your lungs. A lot of people gasp just before impact. Filling their lungs, and making lung ruptures more likely.
- Finally, if there's enough force to drive the front end of your car into your knees, your thighbones will snap.

Other factors such as fatigue, weather, and traffic conditions can increase the adverse impact of distractions on driving ability.

Before you think about work, referee an argument, engage in intense conversation or use your cell phone, remember that you are driving.

For many of my younger years, almost every child I knew rode a bike. We traveled many miles around our area. Packing a lunch often consisting of baloney with mayonnaise on homemade white bread before we headed down the road to a bait shop about a four-mile drive away that also sold candy bars and pop. Sometimes we had enough money for a bottle of Coke, but often we just had a jar of water.

Our sandwich baked in the hot sun as we soaked our feet by the edge of the dam. We didn't get into the water, as the current could be quite swift. Our mothers didn't worry even if we were gone for hours. Riding bicycles or walking were our modes of transportation, our freedom, and our independence.

I don't remember ever seeing an adult riding a bike. In today's world, biking has become a form of exercise and a regimen of getting and staying fit. It is also used by many to get to and from their job. My brother and his wife bike around the Minneapolis area and also in Phoenix where they spend time in the winter.

Cyclists are struggling for space and safety on our highways. According to a report August 24, 2017 by the Governor's Highway Safety Association, with funding from State Farm Insurance the average age of cyclists killed in collisions in 2015 was 45.

"When we bike, we have as much right to the road as when we drive," says Vicki Harper, spokesman for State Farm. "Unfortunately, when bikes and cars collide, cyclists are much more susceptible to serious injury or death."

That is, of course, true. Bicyclists have as many rights on our highways as cars do. However, the small amount of space between the shoulder and the white line of the highway where many bicyclists ride is often extremely narrow.

Sgt. Jesse Grabow's Column:

Question: Can you drive in a bike lane? For instance, use it as a right turn lane?

Answer: No, motorists are not allowed to drive in the bike lanes. The solid white lines on any road mean do not cross. There are designated areas were the solid white line is converted to dashed lines and this is where motor vehicles our allowed to enter a bike lane to make a turn. Before crossing a bike lane, make sure it is safe to do so. Yield the right-of-way to approaching bicyclists when the bicycle lane is clear, signal your intention to turn and then move into the bicycle lane before making the turn.

Bicycles are legal vehicles on Minnesota roads and they share the same rights and responsibilities as other vehicles.

Bicycle lanes are designed to separate bicycle traffic from normal vehicle traffic. It is illegal to drive in these lanes except to park when permitted, to enter or leave the road, or to prepare for a turn. Each year in Minnesota approximately 35 pedestrians and seven bicyclists are killed as a result of collisions with motor vehicles.

As a group, pedestrians and bicyclists comprise nearly 11 percent of all traffic fatalities each year—72 percent of these fatal accidents occur in urban areas. 35 percent of pedestrians and 27 percent of bicyclists killed had consumed alcohol. 16 percent of bicyclists and pedestrians killed were not crossing properly.

The above information is using the five – year average from 2011 – 2015.

Bicyclists and motorists are equally responsible for bicycle safety. The number one factor contributing to bicycle – vehicle collisions is failure to yield the right of way.

About one half of all bicycle - vehicle collisions are due to a variety of bicyclist behaviors, such as disregarding a traffic sign or signal. The other half are caused by vehicle driver behaviors, such as inattention and detraction.

Rules and tips:

Bicyclists may ride on all Minnesota roads, except where restricted.

Bicyclists should ride on the road and must ride in the same direction as traffic.

Motorists must at all times maintain a three-foot clearance when passing a bicyclist.

Bicyclists must obey all traffic control signs and signals, just as motorists.

Bicyclists must signal their turns and should ride in a predictable manner.

Bicyclists must use a headlight and rear reflectors when it's dark. To increase visibility, add a rear flashing light.

Drivers must drive at safe speeds and be attentive – look for bicyclists, check blind spots.

Drivers should use caution and look twice for riders when turning.

Drivers should use caution when opening door upon parking on side of road.

When I'm driving along the highway with a bicyclist alongside, I am as careful as possible. I give them as much room as I can. However, sometimes sharing the road with a vehicle can be fatal. Bicyclists are in places where not getting hit is a miracle.

Pedestrians are also walking at their own peril and often times are inattentive. They are oblivious to what is going on around them and we cast some of the blame on their cell phone use.

"Life is really simple, but we insist on making it complicated."

—Confucius

CHAPTER 15

EVERY MILE A MEMORY

"Cross Roads" by Minnesota State Trooper Eric Hopkins.

How am I ever going to drive by this spot again?" I'll never forget those words, the words Matthew's mom told me when learning the "spot" where her son died. I think of her and her son when I drive by this cross, the cross marking the spot where Matthew left the road just outside a small, close-knit town. I remember the deadly combination of alcohol, speed, and lack of a belt that took his life. He had been speeding over 100 mph, hit an approach, and launched through the air more than half a football field. His body wasn't anywhere near his truck. What I remember mostly, however, is not this spot, but a porch light a few miles away.

It's 3 a.m., We knock on the door and moments later the porch light flickers on. I'll never forget her wail, the wail of a mother who has just learned she has outlived her son. On the steps of the entryway, her knees buckle and we moved to catch her fall.

Now, when I drive by Matthew's cross, I can see his camouflage baseball cap hanging from it, and I wonder if he liked to hunt. Come ride along with me in my mind's eye, as we travel in and out of the lives of victims and their families on the cross-littered Memorial Highway where I work. Let's head east.

Traveling east on Memorial Highway, I see the abandoned church perched in a corner at the intersection. There is Mr. Lund. He's the one laying over there in the middle of the road, motionless. The stop sign he didn't stop for is still upright. I wonder why he didn't wear his seatbelt. I'm astonished by how he, as the driver, flew out of the passenger side window. There's a man standing nearby. That's Mr. Lund's son. After today, I'll be bumping into him from time to time at the grocery store and I'll ask him how he's doing.

Next, let's travel a short distance from the church. I won't soon forget this spot in the road and Calvin who had his whole life in front of him. That's Calvin's truck we just passed back there. Calvin had too much to drink and drove his truck off the road. He lived through it though, but not long enough to tell anyone. You see, after Calvin got out of his truck, he walked here to the middle of the northbound lane. We'll never know what caused him to lie down. It's horrible what came next. Another drunk driver came along, driving north from the bar, towards Calvin. The other driver didn't stop though. He didn't even swerve. He said he thought Calvin was a deer. That blood and fluid trail leading from Calvin's body will bring us north to that residence below the hill where the driver will be arrested.

Driving south from the residence, we come to another scene in the road. It's a beautiful drive next to the lake that is only disturbed by all the debris on the road. In the midst of all that debris and broken glass and aroma of airbags, can you see that person over there? That's me. I'm holding Mrs. William's head and she's telling me that the other vehicle came into her lane, colliding with her head on. Neither of us knows that she has torn her aorta. Neither of us knows that she has only moments left to live. She seems to be so kind and calm. I can tell that she loves her family. Later, I'm going to learn how much her family loved her.

Now, were driving south and east and coming to another crossroads on Memorial Highway. Farmers have favored corn this year, and its brown stocks can be seen as far as the eye can see. The highway has turned yellow from all the corn that has been spilled. Those two scraps of metal in the distance are the remnants of a truck that has been severed in two. The overturned green truck in the ditch is what did the cutting. Hector's pale, lifeless arm is hanging out the driver's side window of his truck. The distraught and in despair man in the back of the ambulance is the grain truck driver.

After we're done knocking on another family member's door, let's travel north. I always notice the cross over there, sticking up from the ground. The storm that has just passed through has left a light show in its wake. The sky is a brilliant hue of pink and orange. Maybe that's why the storm chaser didn't stop at that stop sign. The new, but totaled minivan in the plowed field belongs to Mr. and Mrs. Larson. They were coming home from a fish fry at the Lutheran Church. There I am again. This time I'm holding Mr. Larson's cold hand, searching for a pulse. I can't find one. The responders are frantically working to free Mrs. Larson; she's barely clinging to life. I think I'll cover Mr. Larson's body with a blanket until they can free him from this wreckage. Soon we'll be standing on another porch. Then, another porch light and at the other end of the switch will be Mr. and Mrs. Larson's son.

Leaving the Larson's family's porch, we continue to drive north on Memorial Highway. We come to an intersection I've been at many times. However, none have taken a life yet. That is until today. I see this semi on the curb and the Saturn in the median. I see another pale and lifeless left arm. This time the arm belongs to Clara and is hanging out from underneath the blanket they are using to respectfully cover her. After today, I'll write countless emails and make numerous phone calls to Clara's stunned daughter. Her daughter will try and make sense of the suddenness and finality of losing her mom in such a manner.

Leaving the median, we continue on. If you look to the right, that's old Memorial Highway. It's much colder now, Christmas decorations are up and it's almost the start of a new year. A man on his phone is waving us down. He directs us to an overturned truck in a field off the old highway. A couple hundred feet away from the truck a body lays up right in the frozen black dirt. It's Noah. He has been driving and drinking and not wearing his seatbelt. He's too young, and he's going to die in the ambulance on the way to the hospital. Inside the overturned truck and wedged underneath the dash is Emma. On my hands and knees, I reach into the truck for Emma. She's already cold. It will take a couple of hours to untangle her body from the carnage. In a little while, it will be yet another porch light, but this time for the parents of Emma. At this ungodly hour, they'll see us on their stoop and know immediately what we're about to tell them.

Stepping off the stoop and into our car, we'll continue our journey. This time, we nearly make it to our lunch break. However, before getting there, we see another cross and an American flag in the ditch. Not far from the cross and flag is Raymond. Raymond is already covered up by a blanket. His motorcycle is resting on its side nearby. His helmet is of no use. The grown man sitting in my front seat, weeping uncontrollably, just told me he made a left turn directly in front of Raymond. The weeping man had been on his cell phone. I'll squeeze his shoulder to console him, but it's useless.

Still on Memorial Highway and nearing an ordinary Minnesota town, we come to the intersection at the crest of a hill. If I live to be 100 years old, I will never forget this day. The demolished car over there drove into the back of that fully loaded dump truck. How you ask? Well, if you look inside the car, you'll see Jacob. Not Jacob's face. That's covered by his air bag. What you will see though is that Jacob is still holding his cell phone. His thumb is still pressing down on the cracked display screen. He's dead. That's why we're zipping him up in this blue bag. I'm not sure about you, but I'm tired of Memorial Highway. I think we'll get off at the next exit. The exit says Valley of Tears Turnpike.

We're not too far outside another town for which we don't have to slow down. The memory of Jacob holding the phone is still hunting my mind. We're approaching another sign in the ditch, but I already know what it says. "Fly high boys." That's referring to the two boys (that's what they are really), Mason and Logan; Mason, barely old enough to drive, and Logan just able to vote. Senselessly, their lives were cut short when that guy over there decided to drink and get into that truck and drive. He veered into the boys' path, and they died right here by this sign. I don't like this road anymore either. I think we'll turn here.

On Lost Innocence Avenue, the reconstruction paint is still showing on the pavement, but fading fast. I expect it will be gone by summer's end. That cross will remain though, and so will the charred tree for a little while. The fire has already been put out, but the charred body of Gabriella remains. She didn't have the benefit of time to escape the flames. Thankfully, her family did. I'll be forever tormented by the recounting of the first person to arrive at this scene who described Gabriella's seven-year-old son trying in vain to get back to his trapped mother in the fully engulfed car. I can't imagine what it's going to be like for him to drive by this spot. If only the other driver in the other car hadn't used cocaine prior to getting behind the wheel, maybe Gabriella and her family would have made it home from the movies. I should leave. The memory is still too fresh, and I can still smell the smoke.

Driving west, we finally come to Cemetery Road. When I drive by this little unremarkable cemetery, I always feel an ache in my heart. I am overcome at the memories of holding her. I remember how she smelled and how she would look up at me and her angelic smile. I remember leaving the hospital with her and wondering where the instruction manual is that should have come with her. I recall the pride of placing her in her car seat and driving home. Then, I remember her small white casket at the front of the chapel and the fog drizzled March day. We led the long line of cars, as we pulled into this cemetery. This is the place of our daughter Gracie's final rest.

Even though Gracie wasn't taken from us tragically by way of a brutal car crash, she was taken from us tragically nonetheless. I remember wondering at this cemetery as Matthew's mom did, "how am I ever going to be able to drive by this spot again?" Then, it dawns on me. The feeling I have every time I drive by this cemetery must be a lot like the families feel when they drive by their crosses along the road.

The sun is setting now, so we leave this cemetery and drive west. I'm home now, with my family. I give my children a hug. Tomorrow, I'll take another drive. Tomorrow I'll try again to prevent any more crosses from cropping up on the side of the road.

Epilogue:

We named our daughter Gracie Darlene Pearl. She died in our arms on March 23, 2006, from complications of heart surgery. She was four months old. This Memorial Day we put fresh flowers on her grave for the 13th time.

CHAPTER 16

DON'T GET HOOKED ON ME

Speed continues to be a dangerous killer on the road. Add alcohol or any other drug that impairs us endangers us every time we slide onto the driver seat of our car or truck.

Webster's definition of addiction: *Compulsive need for and use of a habit-forming substance (such as heroin, nicotine, or alcohol).*

The word addiction has sadly become common place in our society. It can bring with it crazy, criminal, senseless, brutal behavior that at times seems accepted by the masses.

The drunk who staggers in the bar, spills a drink, swears, and acts foolish sometimes encourages a grin on the face of other patrons. His weapon could be a car, maybe a truck. All seems well out on the highway if the well-oiled driver just happens to arrive home without killing anyone or running the vehicle into an immoveable object. The laughter and good times end when or if he walks in the door. Even if he doesn't kill himself or anyone else on the highway, an argument and perhaps violence is often the end result of the so-called *amusing* evening.

Mike saw all forms of substance abuse during his working days, but what he saw the most was alcohol abuse. Chronic drunk driving was not a rarity. Law enforcement officers are not the only ones who have no time or sympathy for the drunk driver involved in an accident. Treatment from medical staff is not always gentle either. Stitching up cuts hurts, especially without anything to deaden the pain.

The occasional drinker would also find himself in the glaring light of the Minnesota State Trooper. Perhaps people reading this are relating to the time in their lives when they drove impaired. A night out with friends, a picnic on a hot summer day, or maybe a cool fall night sitting next to a fire. I have heard people say, "I've done it. I never set out to. I stayed too long. I drank too much. I didn't eat enough."

Some of those paid the price and were stopped by the patrol, a deputy, or a policeman who probably saved their life or the life of someone else. Many however told of getting home safely. They didn't hurt anyone or didn't smash anything up. They were grateful. The people I have just written about hopefully never drove impaired again. I would guess many have said, "There but for the grace of God go I."

The normal blood alcohol concentration where you would be given a ticket for DWI is .08. The penalties for driving sloppy drunk in Minnesota have gotten substantially tougher.

People generally age out of criminal activity. They are simply too old. However, that doesn't always happen on the addiction side of it.

The Minnesota Department of Public Safety announced in January 2018 that preliminary figures show that 380 people died on state roads during 2018. State figures go back to 1910 when there were 23 fatalities. The most deaths occurred in 1968, when there were 1,060—one of four years historically with more than 1,000 roadway deaths.

The Minnesota State Patrol, local police departments, and sheriff departments deal with addictions every day among the residents they are trying to protect and serve. It may be a fight with someone in their home. Maybe it's a traffic problem, an accident, or careless driving, a robbery of drugs, or a theft of something to sell for drug money. Additions can trigger fights in bars or the addict's own death where he or she passes out, sometimes lying on a highway, perhaps passing out in a ditch, their body found the next day. Addiction is epidemic in our society.

There are many forms of addiction. It may surprise the American public that drug overdoses have more than doubled since the end of the millennium according to The Centers for Disease Control and Prevention.

Even the small town where I went to high school has a drug problem. Drugs and the troubles they cause are often news in the small-town local paper.

Heroine leads the list of preferred drugs, accounting for a quarter of the overdose deaths, more than triple the rate at which it killed in 2010. "Overdose deaths are up for every age group," says The Center for Disease Control.

What is it we are trying to forget, trying to deal with?

New Year's is always a good time to make resolutions if you are addicted, or think you may be, to alcohol, drugs, food, sex, gambling, or even the Internet. Any time is a good time to break an addiction; it is the most important resolution of one's life.

"Addictions are not necessarily about feeling good or high or pleasure seeking, but more about simply feeling and escaping emotional isolation," according to an article in Consultant Magazine (September 2016).

Alcohol dependency is common; however, most alcoholics have difficulty admitting that they do in fact have a problem. People often minimize or do not admit how many drinks they have in a day; they often kid themselves.

"How much have you had to drink?" That question comes often from the law enforcement officer. "I had a few beers," is the usual answer.

Interestingly enough, group therapy for addictions is generally considered better than individual therapy. People are often more challenged and supported by others who are going through the same thing.

According to the 2015 report by the National Institute on Drug Abuse, addiction is costly to our nation, exacting more than $700 billion annually in costs related to crime, lost work productivity, and health costs.

In post-Civil War America, opium was the drug of choice. Cocaine became popular in the 1880s. Heroin was originally used to treat asthma, and morphine—discovered in 1906—became a popular pain reliver. The popularization of drugs during the 1960s made its way to college campuses.

The U.S. Department of Justice's Smart on Crime Initiative acknowledges that the arrest and jailing of drug users and dealers alone has not eliminated the drug problem, which continues to plague the United States.

"Fentanyl has appeared as a powerful synthetic pain killer and it's killing its users. Jan Malcolm, Minnesota Health Commissioner called the spike in fentanyl related deaths a public health crisis as stated in the *St. Paul Pioneer Press* Tuesday, May 15, 2018." Counterfeit pills containing fentanyl caused the death of Minnesota rock star Prince in 2016.

Minneapolis (WCCO – June 7, 2019.) Officials say 175 drug overdoses, including 17 overdose deaths, have been reported in the past two weeks across Minneapolis, St. Paul, South St. Paul and Washington County.

Narcan, a medication that blocks opiate receptors, can be carried in squad cars and is also available in pharmacies without a prescription. A law known as Steve's Law was passed in 2014 granting immunity to anyone who reports an overdose, and it also allows law enforcement and individuals to carry and administer Narcan.

"The use of Narcan has sparked debate. *The Arizona Republic* article dated Dec. 20, 2017, told the story of two sheriffs in Ohio. The sheriff of Clermont County firmly believes it's a call of duty for his deputies to carry the nasal spray that can save people from death by drug overdose. However, less than fifty miles away, his counterpart in Butler County is dead set against it."

"The sheriff from Butler County feels medical workers are more suited to this new duty. It sidetracks his deputies from fighting crime and can put them in danger. The sheriff also gets support from the citizens in his county. They have grown weary of people who overdose repeatedly."

The *Star Tribune* headline states in its July 26, 2017, issue, "Opiates Ravaging Red Lake." The Red Lake Indian Reservation in Minnesota has such a heroin and opiate epidemic that it has prompted tribal leaders to declare a public health emergency and consider the extraordinary step of banishing tribal members involved in drug dealing. The problem was so bad that the local hospital ran out of Narcan.

People I have talked to do not all agree on the use of Narcan. Many say the addicts have brought this on themselves. Brought back from the grip of death encourages the users to name a sober person much like naming a sober driver. They will be responsible to have Narcan ready in case of overdose. Many say it gives them an excuse not to seek treatment. Libraries are afraid of becoming hangouts for addicts who believe they have found a place to use drugs and also be saved in cases of an overdose. Drug use in bathrooms of fast food restaurants is also a concern.

I loved to smoke. I enjoyed every puff I took for almost 25 years. I never wanted to quit. I coughed in the mornings and even though my family did not have good lungs—I loved cigarettes. Cigarettes were on my mind. Did I have enough for the day—that evening? I know what it is like to be addicted to cigarettes.

I bought them by the carton and didn't usually run out but there was occasional panic. I loved to smoke. When I caught a cold, I ended up at the doctor's office diagnosed with bronchitis. I was addicted.

My doctor would remind me that I was going to get bronchitis every time I caught a cold if I didn't stop smoking. Then he'd give me that look. I ignored his warnings and continued. Sometimes seeing him at a social gathering he would walk by quietly and grumble about smoking.

I had the beginning of what was a bad cold one winter. I decided to quit smoking just until my cold was gone. Then I wouldn't have to listen to the doctor's scolding. After about two weeks my cold was gone. I wasn't coughing every morning. I decided to see if I could go a little longer. I carried a pack in my purse and a half a carton of cigarettes in my kitchen for years. I have no will power. It was simply the right time to give up my addiction.

Food addiction can be just as serious since food can trigger the same areas of the brain which give pleasure as addictive drugs. Foods that are rich in sugar, fat and salt can become potentially addictive. People over-eat for many reasons. It gives the body a feel good high.

Food addiction is particularly difficult to manage. Daily sustenance is needed to stay alive. We celebrate many occasions and situations in life by eating. Birthday parties almost always have cake and hopefully ice cream. Today's parties are often bigger than when I was growing up. I have attended some with more than 100 people enjoying the festivities.

If we buy something, we will probably go out to eat to celebrate our recent purchase. It could be a new car, a new house, or something much less expensive. We may celebrate a raise in salary or a promotion at work by eating. I personally don't need much of an excuse to celebrate something by eating out. There's food at happy times such as a wedding, and also food served at sad times. The funeral lunch is expected to be food of substance. Many have traveled a distance to attend. We celebrate with food for our emotions: loneliness, happiness, regret, and sadness.

"Recovery didn't open the gates of heaven and let me in. Recovery opened the gates of hell and let me out."

—Unknown

CHAPTER 17

A PICTURE OF LIFE'S OTHER SIDE

"Gambling: According to the Mayo Clinic Health Letter, America's gambling habit has grown from $80 billion a year in 1986 to over $600 billion. Illegal gambling is flourishing alongside the legal version.

People addicted to gambling aren't thought of as addicts—at least not in the way we look at alcohol and drug use. They aren't a danger behind the wheel, don't slur their words, lose control of their bladder or bowels. They don't pass out at the restaurant table after ordering their food or want to start a fight. However, they may hurt their health. Paramedics talk of being called because people get so caught up in gambling, they forget to take their medications and also just to eat, which is especially threatening to diabetic gamblers.

"According to a study conducted in 2010 by neuroscientist Reza Habib, they discovered that in the brain chemistry of a pathological gambler, "near misses" actually caused the same brain activity as if they had won."

We went to a dinner at a shooting range. We had raffle tickets in our hands, hoping to win a prize. The winning numbers came up on a huge screen, four at a time. Voices reverberated around our table: "Oh, I was just one number off," or "I had two of the numbers." I smiled and thought, *it doesn't matter how close you were. You didn't win.*

Scratch-off tickets seem to have the same effect. I have sat next to people with a basket full of scratch off tickets or pull tabs. According to a state lottery consultant, "Adding a near miss to a lottery is like pouring jet fuel on a fire…that's why sales have exploded? Every other scratch-off ticket is designed to make you feel like you *almost* won."

"Project Turnabout is a facility that offers hope for those who have lost hope," states the *Montevideo American News* in its publication of February 23, 2017. The paper interviewed Sherry Parker, Director of Residential Services, who said, "The people who come here deserve a chance, so being able to help those people is very important to us." "We are in the business of helping people rediscover their value as human beings," says Mike Schiks, Executive Director and CEO of Project Turnabout.

This treatment center has been in existence since 1970. A group of men turned an abandoned sanitarium into a facility that offered inpatient and outpatient services to addicts. A new facility has been built.

My sister Carolyn and I went to that sanitarium several times. It was a tuberculosis sanitarium back in the 1950s. My sister and I each had a reaction to the Mantoux test that was given at school to test for tuberculosis. If the injection site turned red, students went to the sanitarium for a chest X-ray.

I was young, perhaps eight years old, the first time. It was a spooky place. Led into the basement, we were told to take off our blouses and were then given a small white cover that looked like a sheet. I remember standing in line, Carolyn holding my hand, then taking the sheet off, and standing in front of a huge X-ray machine when it was my turn. It was cold when I placed my chest up against it and held my breath. A man in a white coat told us what to do. I was scared. However, Carolyn being with me and assuring me that it would be all right made it easier. The sanitarium housed patients for many months or sometimes years. I was afraid that when I went there and walked down those steps, I might never get out, might never go home again. I do not remember my parents ever talking to me about the results of the X-ray.

I drove by the old building in the late 1980s. It stood empty. Vandals had broken windows and partied in the building. Glass and weeds covered the ground. I was fascinated by the old building and decided I should go in. Although I walked in a small side door, I was soon at the main entrance. It was a huge area and years before had a beautiful fireplace. I had actually used that setting in my mind when I wrote my first book, *A Small Pile of Bones*. I did not venture down the basement stairs. The main floor housed many offices with a few file cabinets still intact. There was also a large kitchen and patients' rooms, some with bed frames. The stairway to the second floor was a challenge. I walked gingerly around the second floor; a bit concerned that I might fall through. I even carefully ventured into the huge sunroom solarium that had three sides of broken out windows and overlooked the river below. I took some video of it and, yes, as I look back, it was scary, precarious. Luckily, I did not fall through. The old brick sanitarium was removed in the late 1990s after sitting empty for over twenty years.

The campus for Turnabout is now located on the northwest edge of town. Support for patients continues after they complete their treatment program. Project Turnabout works with each patient to develop a continuous care plan.

Gambling has cost people their jobs, their marriage, their material possessions; homes; cars; and at times their lives.

One man related that while he was in treatment, he was told he had three choices: end up in prison, commit suicide, or seek treatment. He had treatment and it worked. It has been many years since a casino drew him in. However, he has said that he cannot even hear the sounds in a casino.

I am not a gambler but occasionally we have gone to a casino, sometimes for lunch or to stay overnight in the adjoining hotel while traveling. I have asked myself what it is that excites people. What is it that draws them to keep putting their money into a machine?

Of course, I can certainly imagine that the first thing they would tell me is that they want to win. They want to put money in, pull the handle or press a button and see the images flashing across that machine telling them they have won. Many things in a casino get your attention: lights flashing, noise, and commotion. I find it unsettling—too much going on. I have spent $20 the few times I have been in a casino; but when the money is gone, I'm done.

Mike and I traveled to Arizona in February 1996. While eating at a restaurant, we visited with a couple as we were leaving.

I had picked up a real estate pamphlet as I like to do whenever we traveled, and immediately the couple told us they had a house for sale on the edge of town. I told them we were not interested in buying a place, that we just liked to look at real estate brochures in the areas we visit.

Later that afternoon we took a drive and decided to drive to that new development. As we drove around the new homes, the owner we had met earlier was standing outside, pulling a few weeds in front of the house. We stopped. I rolled the window down, and we talked a little bit about our chance meeting.

He said we should take a look if we'd like. He opened the door, called to his wife, and I walked in. He and Mike stayed outside.

His wife smiled and told me that at our meeting earlier, she had thought I looked like her favorite author, a Minnesotan. She told me that she herself was a writer. As we walked into her library, she showed me her four latest books and then autographed copies for me.

The woman thought anyone can write a book. She told me to just write about something you know. Embellish the story and characters. She went on to say that it doesn't matter how much trouble or heartache your characters go through; it has to have a happy ending. If people have misbehaved in one way or another there have to be consequences for them.

Then she took out one of the Minnesota writer's books, turned it around for me to see the back cover, and showed me a picture of the author. I can't say that I thought I really looked like the woman. However, she was blonde-haired, blue-eyed, and I did fit that description. She then invited us to stay for coffee.

The woman opened the door, called her husband to say she was making coffee and to come in shortly. When she said that, her husband, Mike would tell me later, told him he couldn't believe she had spent so much time with me and asked us to stay for coffee. Apparently, she didn't like women. I didn't know that her husband had made that comment until we left. We stayed there for several hours. I'm quite sure she liked me because of the resemblance to her favorite author.

As we sat drinking coffee and eating cookies, she told me she was a gambler. She went on to tell us how good the casinos treated her, and as she got up to get more coffee, she said that they even serve them drinks and dinner for no charge. Under his breath, softly so just Mike could hear, her husband told Mike it always cost them a lot of money.

"By three methods we may learn wisdom: first by reflection, which is noblest; second by imitation, which is the easiest; and third by experience, which is the bitterest."

—Confucius

CHAPTER 18

BEHIND CLOSED DOORS

A woman knocked on our door shortly after she and her husband moved into our neighborhood. The frightened look on her face gave me pause. Mike was getting ready for work. She was attractive and probably about my age at the time—late forties. A social worker and newly married, her husband had beat her that morning and left the house. She started crying as she talked and said he would be coming back soon. Mike asked if she wanted to call the police? No. Did she have a friend to stay with? Yes. Mike told her to pack a bag and leave. She knew all the phone numbers to call for help; she had given them to her clients many times.

Even before becoming involved, this smart and well-educated woman had heard about her husband's history of violence from others. Thinking, believing he truly loved her and that he had changed, they had married. It wasn't long before their house went up for sale and they were gone. I don't know if they stayed together.

The headlines in the *West Central Tribune*, June 12, 2019 said "Grove City man goes to prison for domestic assault." Below, a separate headline said, "Man sentenced to prison for assault by strangulation." Different women, different men—same result.

Has dealing with domestic abuse changed you?

A new report from the National Law Enforcement Officers Memorial Fund documents what police officers have known for decades: Domestic violence calls are the greatest danger for responding officers. Calls to private residences for family disputes, calls for assistance in the sanctity of one's home— these are the most treacherous calls for police. Yet they come. They are the people standing at your door to help.

The pattern of repeated abuse makes domestic violence calls particularly dangerous for officers. A 2008 study by the National Institute of Justice determined that victims of domestic violence are more likely to call police after repeated assaults thus putting police officers in an even more volatile situation when they respond.

"If someone breaks into your home, you're going to call the police. You're not going to let someone break in 10 times. But with domestic violence, it's unique in that way, that the call could represent something that's been percolating over time," said David Chipman in an interview in the *Arizona Republic* April 9, 2018. David is senior policy advisor at the Gifford Law Center to prevent gun violence and a former agent at the Bureau of Alcohol, Tobacco, Firearms and Explosives for 25 years.

Police policies towards domestic violence have changed from considering abuse a family dispute to a serious criminal offense that requires a response, including specialized domestic violence units inside departments and comprehensive service centers for victims.

"As officers started getting injured and, in many cases, killed—and victims being killed, we started analyzing and assessing and identifying better methods for responding to domestic violence," says Frank Fernandez Director of Public Safety in Coral Gables, Florida, and chairman of the International Association of Chiefs of Police Firearms Committee.

A policeman had a sad look on his face as he talked about domestic abuse. He related that first the man wants to kill her, then to kill the policeman, then many times it switches, and they both want to kill him.

A BCA officer has a lot of compassion for innocent victims. He has seen way too many of them.

In the heat of the moment, when violence erupts in the home, a call goes to 911 and police are dispatched. The end result may not be what either the victim or the abuser expects. One of them, the person deemed most aggressive, is going to jail.

Sometimes the police take both to jail. At times, they've gone to try to protect the wife, then she's the one who eventually jumps on their back.

A retired sheriff many times has asked the question—What brings them to the assault side of it? He has looked for a long-term solution in a domestic abuse situation. Domestic violence still bothers him today.

When the radio goes off, if the call is for a shoplifter, it's pretty straightforward. You get a description of the person, what was stolen, if a car was involved, if anyone knows the make, if anyone got a license number.

When the call is for domestic abuse, police know they are going into something that has so many different parts. The officer needs to know: Are there weapons? Are there guns? Have there been previous calls? Is the incident in progress? Or, if it's past, are the parties still there? Is the abuser still there? The situation can go from calm to chaos in the blink of an eye. The nature of the crime adds another dimension. Domestic violence is about one person's desire to be in control. The officer arriving at the scene is attempting to take away some of that control.

Law enforcement think it's one of the toughest calls to go on. A policeman shook his head and talked about the small town he works in.

He's disappointed that he knows these people. They may be someone he sees at his children's sporting events. The people that fight brutally with each other on Saturday night after too much to drink may be the same couple he has seen at the football game or basketball game the night before.

You can't assume that the victim is a female, although that is the usual situation. It becomes a he-said, she-said state of affairs. An officer sighed as he stated that he has seen too much of the problem between husband, wives, or significant others. He shook his head in disgust. He was just so sick of it. He felt compassion for the innocents, the children, witnesses to that struggle between his/her parents.

Harvey Dahline wrote this in his book - "Dedication to Duty."

"The Robe"

There was a little man around 40 years old who lived in the southeast part of town. I was surprised to see him very late one warm summer night standing on the sidewalk. He appeared to be crying and looked to be a little beaten up. What really stood out was that he was barefoot and apparently only wearing a terry-cloth robe.

After I quieted him down, because he was quite distraught, he proceeded to tell me that his live-in of some years had come in after a social night on the town in somewhat of a bad mood. Not thinking, he had asked her where she had been since it was so late. That was his mistake. She went over to the coffee table, breaking off a leg, and went after him with it, striking him several times before he was able to get in the bathroom, grab a robe and make it out the door. Not knowing what to do or where to go he had wandered downtown.

The man was well known to me. He was a gentle person and this was not the first altercation between the two. The lady, somewhat larger in stature, was also well known to me as she would be again in the future.

After asking what he would like to see done or if he would like to make a complaint, he said all he wanted to do was get home, get some clothes, and leave. The night finally ended by my taking him home and her being removed to her father's house for the night.

These events continued for some years with him always going home.

Seems we have heard this story before but with a different twist.

Officers I interviewed talked of the anger as they walk into a home.

Law enforcement officers are walking into their home, their so-called castle. It should be their private space and here they are walking into their home. Picture this scenario: A police officer often tells the husband he has to leave. The goal is to protect the victim and hold the right person accountable.

The National Law Enforcement Officers Memorial Fund study states that 22% of the 911 calls are about domestic abuse. This is why training is so important to help understand the undercurrents of domestic violence and also safety. If you don't get through it safely, you're not going to help anyone.

A New York policeman talked about a week of excellent training at one point in his career. It consisted of what was called "Family Crisis Intervention" training. It involved roll playing and learning a whole new way of dealing with domestic abuse. It brought a team of non-police to his department who would get a brief memo from them about the original call. They would then follow-up that day or the next and get people referred to social programs to try to solve their issues. The members were very good and their domestic calls went down considerably.

One of the biggest questions is why people stay? Why don't the victims get out? And stay out? Victims may go back to the abuser. They're doing what they think is best for themselves at that moment. In my interviews, officers called to domestic abuse calls still have difficulty wrapping their minds around the person's decision to stay trapped in the abuse. One officer said he had many times arrested the abuser and the abused is the person coming to bail him out.

Many officers had this to say: If someone hits you, they don't love you. Get out!

According to the National Coalition Against Domestic Violence, an estimated 1.3 million American women experience domestic violence each year. Despite this, most cases are never reported to the police.

The impact violence has on a family unit is horrific. According to *AZcentral.com* "A man walked into a salon February 2, 2018 and stabbed a woman to death. She was later identified as his former girlfriend."

The man lived in a mobile-home community close to the salon and was shot and killed when he attacked officers with a knife. Any one of us could face this situation. We could be getting our hair done, buying groceries, or sitting in a restaurant, and get shot because an estranged angry person comes in to kill his girlfriend or wife. She is the person styling your hair, the cashier checking out your groceries, or perhaps the waitress who has just brought food to your table. Families in crisis affect us all. They are our neighbors, our friends, people we work with—people we come in contact with every day.

★ ★ ★ ★ ★

She met him on a blind date. She usually didn't go on blind dates, but a friend talked her into it. They talked for hours and he seemed like a really nice guy.

I look at her sitting across from me. The woman is "pretty in pink" and classically beautiful.

They dated for about a year and a half and then married. The abuse started about six months into their marriage. She left him after the first time and spent a few days with her parents. Flowers, apologies, and promises never to hurt her again brought her back. He was a con man, and she wanted to believe him.

He beat her again. This time she went to an attorney and filed for divorce. Her husband was once again repentant—so sorry—and talked her into seeing the minister who had married them. The minister told her to stay, to work it out.

She is angry and doesn't think a pastor would say that today. The woman believed she should at least try to do what the pastor said.

She stiffened a little as she said that she knew people say that women marry men like their fathers, but that's not true in her case. Her dad was a kind, gentle man and would never have hit a woman.

On the other hand, her husband's father had died in World War II; and he took notice of his domineering mother only when he needed money. Alcohol and women—and he wanted—both.

Life would go on, and things would be good for a while—maybe six months—and then something would set him off. It would normally involve alcohol. She didn't call the police, although she tried. There were no cell phones then, and he would take the cordless phone away. When the crisis passed, she kept the secret, telling no one. Although her clothes often covered contusions, her face at times bore bruises from the night before; but she always had an excuse for her marks.

He would threaten that if she left him, she would have nothing. He would get the children because she couldn't support them. No one would want her. She heard the threats and belittling regularly.

The years went by. She was on a merry-go-round and couldn't get off. The physical and verbal abuse took its toll. Her self-esteem was gone.

Caught up in the cycle of abuse, she stayed in their home while he moved in and out of her life on a regular basis. He sometimes lived with another woman and then showed up at home. Wanting sex was normally a part of the process. If she refused, violent behavior would erupt. She fooled herself into thinking the kids didn't know. Trapped in the cycle, she began to think of her circumstances as normal. It was her life.

The woman was an accountant. When her son, now grown, started his own business, she was going to do his books in the evening. However, her husband had other ideas and had let the air out of all her tires. She called her son to come over, telling him that his father had deflated her tires. Her son aired up the tires and told her that if she wasn't going to do something about it, he didn't want to hear about it again, *ever*.

She had every intention of leaving him at this point. Her abuser suggested marriage counseling, and she agreed. He went only twice. She continued to go. The counselor was a wonderful woman, just who she needed at that time. After joining a women's support group, she grew stronger and stronger with every session.

When asked if she had been tested or was fearful of having a venereal disease, she told her counselor that she had never thought about it, never realized she could be at risk. She once again went to see an attorney. He told her that the best advice he could give her was to leave the house, that leaving it could keep her safe. Although her home had been a place of abuse and trauma, it was home and the thought of leaving it was extremely difficult.

The woman enlisted the help of friends to find an apartment. She escaped. Her friends were sworn to secrecy. He stopped paying the mortgage. He did not find her, and for some odd reason, he never came to her workplace. Her attorney had told her that she would not be able to collect anything from his pension as she already had a job. This was in the 1980s. Later, of course, she would realize that that was bad advice. He had a retirement that she could have legally tapped into. That realization came too late. She walked away with no financial help...but she had her life.

What should you do if trapped in that situation? Tell someone, get out and get professional help.

"You can't control the past, but you can control where you are going next."

—Mark Twain

CHAPTER 19

HOME IS WHERE THE HURT IS

Years ago, we called it wife beating, although it wasn't exclusively women who were beaten. Most likely the female, then and now, is normally considered to be smaller in stature and in weight and not capable of the strength needed to inflict bodily harm. The National Coalition Against Domestic Violence tells a somewhat different story and has found that women and men can each be violent. However, its statistics also state that the majority of abusers are men.

There are many reasons for cruelty toward a person you profess to love. Power and control seem to be at the heart of conflict; but jealousy, alcohol, drug abuse, and a feeling of losing control of a situation also fuel the brutal behavior.

Back in the old days, rumors would occasionally surface about a particular man whose drinking would lead him to hurting his wife. Those episodes were shameful for the woman; and, if she chose to tell, it was only to a close friend. At times the bruises were difficult to disguise, and tongues would wag. Thinking back, I'm sure there were children abused as well, although as a child, I was not aware of it.

Police were rarely called. Perhaps a trusted neighbor or close friend would be summoned if the husband came home after having had too much to drink. Many times, furniture in the home was busted, and dishes broken. Today, local police or county deputies are called on a regular basis and expected to be referees, therapists, marriage counselors, doctors, lawyers, all the while watching their backs as the caller— often the one being beaten—turns on them. Chaos and out-of-control behavior quickly replace rational thinking.

A seamstress sewed clothes for me. A stay-at-home mom, as were many in the 1950s, she had her young children playing near her while she measured and pinned the material for my new wardrobe. Over the span of many years, there were new babies born to this seemingly normal family. They moved to another state. We heard of her murder several years later. A beating by her husband had taken her life. There had been a long pattern of abuse. He was convicted of manslaughter but served only a few years in prison. I think back on that kind, quiet woman who fitted me with many skirts and blouses; but I remember with particular fondness a baby-blue ensemble she sewed: I wore it for prom. She wanted to hear all about the dance the next time I saw her.

Newspapers and television provide graphic information about abuse. The constant question is, "Why stay?" Numerous reasons are given by the abused—from their feelings of love for the abuser, fears of being alone, money, religious beliefs, breaking up a family, their children's need for a father, and always the promise by the abuser never to do it again. Many who hurt the person they live with, or are married to, are apologetic for their seeming loss of control. Promises to change and loving behavior after the beating are compelling. Also, the belief that violent behavior will change is something the victim wants desperately to believe.

I belonged to a morning church circle with young women of my own age after moving to West Central Minnesota and I intended to do the same in our next move. A morning part-time job made that impossible, so I joined one that met in the afternoon. That circle did not meet at the church but rather at members' homes. It was a wonderful way to get to know the town and surrounding area. The women in this circle were considerably older, and although at first I was disappointed that I wasn't with younger women, I soon began to relish my time with them and appreciate the wisdom of the older group. One of their conversations was of particular interest. They had all grown up in that area and talked of how they met their husbands. None had actually gone on a date alone before marriage. They had, however, been with their prospective husbands many times at church and school social gatherings.

They really didn't know them or their families very well until after they were married. Another one quickly added that the women only hoped their husband would be a good provider and not beat them. If he did hit them, there was no reason to tell anyone. No one could help you, not even your own mother.

I was astonished when the women nodded in agreement. The looks on their faces, so matter-of-fact, with little emotion, were unbelievable to me. I didn't ask any questions at that time but would bring it up in one of our Bible discussions much later, when I felt less like an interloper and knew them better. They spoke of abuse, whether they had been the victim or had a friend who was abused, in a surprisingly calm manner. It was never talked about in a social setting, one woman lowered her eyes to the floor as they talked. However, apparently, sometimes one told a trusted friend. Often that friend was in the same boat.

It seemed as the years went by that many of the men calmed down and the abuse stopped. They didn't call it abuse. They called it hitting, slapping, hurting, or beating. *Abuse* sounded almost like a sophisticated, nice word, for something that was so vicious.

I was shocked at the thought of these women having to go through a relationship with such fear and brutality. They were young when they married, and I came to realize that somehow, they had come to terms with their lot in life and had found a way to forgive their husbands. Some were widows and spoke of missing their spouses.

They lovingly talked of the good qualities of their husbands and the often-kind behavior that followed beatings.

Family violence is a difficult thing to understand and extremely difficult for the police to deal with.

Officer Weldy had written this:

Late one evening, my partner, and I received a call for a family dispute. I knew this family. Now domestic disturbances are probably the most dangerous call an officer runs into.

Normally, by the time it's over, the man and wife have teamed up, and the officer is the fall guy. We rolled up to the residence and I climbed out. I looked in the window and saw the husband loading a rifle and I thought "Oh Shit!" His wife was sitting on the couch holding their baby. I told my partner to wait outside and I would talk to the man.

I opened the front door and yelled "Hey, it's Weldy," and he yelled, "Come In." He stepped out of the bedroom without the rifle and I asked him "What's going on?" And he told me that he and his wife were fighting. I walked over to the couch and sat down, and he came over and sat beside me, and things were going good. He was on one side, his wife on the other, when my partner came in. He was a good cop but could make people mad when he opened his mouth. He came in and the man of the house became unglued. Into the bedroom and out came the rifle barrel. I knew the rifle was loaded as I had seen him load it.

I told my partner to get out and told his wife to go out the back way. She seemed shocked so I pushed her down the hallway while I watched the rifle barrel sticking out of the bedroom.

I had drawn my gun and I was hoping I wouldn't have to shoot. I got the wife and baby out, and about that time, along comes the man's brother-in-law, and in the house, he goes. The next thing I see is the owner pulling on the stock and the in law pulling on the barrel. So I yelled to the brother-in- law that the gun was loaded. "Nah," he said, "It isn't loaded." The man of the house quieted down and I took the rifle and jacked out seven shells. The brother-in-law said "God, I could have been killed." I just looked at him and said "No shit, Kemosabe!" The man of the house was really a nice guy and we're still friends. He asked me one time, "Would you have shot me?" I said, "Just as fast as I could."

A deputy told another story about a fight between husband and wife that seemed to take place quite often. The call would come in usually on a weekend. There was always lots of drinking involved. The deputy would settle everyone down and the wife would often fix them breakfast.

The National Coalition Against Domestic Violence tells us that domestic abuse knows no color, age, or financial situations. Every facet of American culture is affected. Also, one in four girls will experience some form of sexual violence before the age of 18.

Girls are the fastest growing population in the juvenile justice system. It's not because they are becoming more violent. It is because they have been sexually abused. Sex trafficking is the blatant example of how poverty and sexual abuse trap girls in the cycle of abuse. These young girls are arrested for prostitution and thrown in jail. They are treated as perpetrators rather than supported as victims.

Apps such as Find My Phone can easily be operated for malicious use. GPS tracking, social media, text messages, and online purchases can be used by stalkers to track and discover where their victims are living or hiding. But technology is also used to combat domestic abuse.

Better work on the part of police, prosecutors, and victim advocates has fueled a progress. Significant changes in domestic violence laws have also been a big part of that change. Better training for law enforcement advocates and prosecutors is stepping up to the plate to convict offenders. The law enforcement community is struggling to do a better job of convincing the victims to be proactive for their own safety, to get out of the situation as soon as the abuse starts. Officers are now asking all victims a series of questions and revisiting high-risk victims to investigate further.

Partner abuse takes many forms. It can be verbal or physical. It may begin with a simple push or grabbing shoulders. It may be a condescending attitude: Where are you going? Who are you going to see? What time will you be home? Those are simple questions, not in and of themselves problematic, but in the context of a controlling partner, they may be the beginning of rough times.

Dating abuse has become an enormous problem. If it was around when I was young, I didn't hear of it, see it, or experience it. And to my best recollection, no one ever talked about it. If you are in a controlling relationship early in life, chances are that that relationship will either continue or you will find another similar type of relationship.

What is it that draws an individual to a person who wants you to be with them exclusively? *Don't be with your friends, just be with me.* Jealousy sometimes is a heady thing and may be an aphrodisiac for a young girl. It's flattering if a boyfriend wants your undivided attention. Giving up time with your friends doesn't seem like a huge price to pay for someone who just wants to be with you—hug you—kiss you, and make you his entire world. It is only looking back that one sees how scary that can be.

Law enforcement often deals with that kind of obsession. It may be called stalking. There are many words for it, but what it represents is the beginning of control and abuse. That is not to say that women and young girls cannot be controlling and jealous. Girls can also insist that their boyfriends see only them and that other friends be excluded from their relationship. All in all, those relationships usually flag trouble.

Twitter is working on new plans to prevent people who have been permanently suspended from twitter from creating new accounts. According to CEO Jack Dorsey and USA Today, "safe search" results are being turned on for users. These results remove tweets that contain sensitive content such as violent or pornographic images or language or traits that come from blocked or muted accounts.

Twitter, known for its 280 character messages, has struggled to broaden its appeal. For years, Twitter billed itself as "the free speech wing of the free speech party." But as it grew, that hands-off approach contributed to a dramatic rise in abuse, harassment, and hate speech.

People don't have to use their real names on Twitter. And with that anonymity has come racist, sexist and even anti-Semitic taunts and full-fledged campaigns from trolls.

According to the National Domestic Violence Hotline, there are ways to help someone you suspect is being abused; and you can protect yourself as well.

Call the police or 911. You may overhear a fight that you suspect is turning violent; and, if this occurs, you should call the police. These calls can be anonymous; but if you choose to get involved and offer your report to the police, they can help protect you.

Keep a record of what you see or hear and when it happened. Sometimes arguments can turn loud and scary but they may not be violent. Keep a record of what you have heard if you suspect an argument has escalated into violence: This record may ultimately help the victim if you come forward with this information.

Approach your landlord with concerns. If you suspect a neighbor is being abused, talk with the management team on site who may be able to approach the neighbor and offer support.

Talk with the victim. If you know your neighbor, you could be the person to ask if help and guidance to the right resources and to leave the abusive situation are needed.

Don't get involved in the argument. If you suspect someone is being abused, it may be dangerous to get personally involved. These difficult situations are best left to trained professionals. The National Domestic Violence Hotline offers advocates who can be reached at 1-800-799-SAFE (7233), or online at www.thehotline.org"

> *"Do the thing you fear the most and the death of fear is certain."*
>
> —Mark Twain

CHAPTER 20

THERE'S TROUBLE ON THE TURNPIKE

Webster's Dictionary states the word *rage* means a furious, uncontrolled anger or a great force of violence.

Why is everyone so angry? What are we all so mad about? Is someone cutting you off on a highway actually worth taking their life, or beating them senseless?

Road rage has become the popular term for uncontrollable behavior on the highway. The shocking death of an ex-NFL player—Will Smith April 9, 2016— followed an argument after his car was rear ended. A fight between motorists can erupt over a driver who changes lanes, and a brawl can occur over a parking space.

I think of the scene in the 1991 movie, "Fried Green Tomatoes." Laughter filled the theater as we watched the character Evelyn Couch, played by Kathy Bates, ram a car repeatedly and said, "Face it, girls. I'm older and I have more insurance," after they stole her parking space and had said to her, "Face it, lady. We're younger and faster." We laughed at the older woman taking on the younger, spoiled, rude women, smashing her car into theirs. However, serious consequences and even death can and has resulted from road rage.

A male movie star was arrested Friday Nov. 2, 2018 and charged with assault and harassment after allegedly striking a man in the face during a dispute over a parking spot outside his New York City home," His face and story were on many television news casts and newspaper.

The actor claimed a family member was holding a parking spot for him. As he attempted to park his black Cadillac Escalade around 1:30 p.m. A man driving a black Saab station wagon pulled up and took it.

Police said the men were arguing and pushed each other before the movie star, 60, got more aggressive. He was ordered to appear in court Nov. 26, 2018.

National Highway Traffic Safety Administration (NHTSA) data, based on police reports, shows road rage or aggressive driving were reported as factors in 375 fatal crashes that resulted in 418 deaths in 2014, the latest year statistics are available. The numbers do not include violence after a crash.

On Friday, June 2, 2017, the *West Central Tribune* reported:

"A truck driver is facing two criminal charges. The 34, year old man made a first appearance Wednesday in Kandiyohi County District Court. He is charged with first-degree criminal damage to property, which is a felony, and disorderly conduct, a misdemeanor."

Later, he was sentenced in Kandiyohi County District Court to three years' probation. In addition to probation, Judge Michael Thompson ordered him to pay restitution to the victim and write a letter of apology.

The incident started with an alleged road rage incident in May 2017 on Minnesota Highway 23. The complaint states:

"A woman driving beside a truck attempted to pass in the passing lane. The man driving the truck sped up to 70 mph and would not let her pass. When the next passing lane became available the women stated he moved into the center of the road to again block traffic before pulling back into the right lane. The woman and several other vehicles were finally able to pass."

Road construction further down the road stopped everyone. The man got out of his truck and pounded on the window of one of the women he had blocked from passing. The woman called 911.

The man told the officers that arrived on the scene he thought she had been following him too closely.

Law officers say there has always been road rage but not to this extent. There have always been some people who cannot control themselves in tense situations. They think people have become more selfish and it's all about them—that they are more important than anyone else. The officers want you to know: If you are one of the "special people" who believe your appointments, your work, your time is more valuable than others—get over it. Road rage could end your life.

Many motorists believe road rage is much worse than it ever used to be. People are so much more aggressive. They are angry. I think they're mad at everything. An officer thinks it still stems back to the bottom line, and that is that people are not taking responsibility for their actions, their behaviors. It's always somebody else's fault, and they're lost. He believes that's where it starts. They lack basic coping skills. He believes you have to start with the parents.

It's about conflict resolution. It starts in childhood. There was always work to be done around the house especially if there was arguing. I don't ever remember the word "conflict" used or "resolve" Bad behavior simply wasn't put up with. Most of us can remember our parents, particularly our mothers, teaching us to say please, thank you, excuse me, and I'm sorry. Rude behavior was not tolerated and there was swift punishment for that conduct.

Who is teaching children to find peaceful solutions to everyday problems? Where are the mothers and fathers showing their children patience and kindness towards others? School teachers have learned that they are the ones expected to bring civility to their students. Basic manners are no longer taught in many homes.

In the small school where I attended grades one through eighth grades, everyone in our class was invited to our birthday party and everyone got a Valentine on Valentine's Day. We left no one out, including our teachers. Kindness was the order of the day. No teachers stood watching us during recess, no bully tormented us on the playground. The "big kids" (8th graders) would have protected us.

We were not afraid of anyone or anything at school except maybe a surprise test, shot day, or the cook occasionally in the dining room. We cleaned our plates, and drank our milk, or we didn't leave the room.

A 2017 study by the AAA Foundation for traffic safety found that nearly 80 percent of drivers expressed significant anger, aggression, and rage behind the wheel at least once in the previous year.

Troopers respond to a number of calls daily based on driving conduct and many other issues and actions occurring on our highways. If confronted by an aggressive driver, the troopers give this advice: Get out of their way. Stay calm—reaching your destination safely is your goal. Do not challenge them. Ignore gestures and don't return them. Find a safe place to call 911 and report aggressive driving (including vehicle description, license number, location).

Road rage, fighting, vandalism, we can go on and on about what people do when they get angry. In today's society, it seems more and more people are lashing out. Let's face it, we all get frustrated from time to time. We all have seen every day people flying off the handle at little provocation. Is it the economy? Bad drivers? Is it the number of vehicles on the highways?

Drivers moving too slowly in the left lane could be ticketed under a new law in Minnesota that bars "slowpokes" from unsafely preventing faster drivers from passing beginning Aug.1, 2019. The *West Central Tribune reports* July 30, 2019. If you're passing, pass in the left lane. When done passing, get back in the right lane. "If drivers around you are speeding, leave it up to law enforcement to deal with. Don't take the law into your own hands," said Col. Matt Langer, chief of the State Patrol.

Why are we living in such an angry society?

We've all read or heard about the celebrity meltdowns. Sometimes anger is actually fear or frustration. A popular singer shaved her head at a salon in California. She stunned the public days later by attacking a paparazzo's car with an umbrella.

In December 2011, an actor was kicked off an American Airlines flight refusing to turn off his iPhone.

In March 2011, a singer became visibly agitated during an interview with Good Morning America's Robin Roberts when asked about the 2009 assault of his ex-girlfriend. After the interview, the singer stormed off stage, ripped his shirt off and threw a chair at a studio window.

Anger seems to also be the Internet's most powerful emotion. People are raging online using social network sites like Facebook, Twitter and YouTube to go on a tirade. People seem to be mad about almost any subject and like to vent.

Whether you think our country is angry or not, whether you are one that displays rage, one thing is for sure, at some point we all have to find ways to tame our tempers and let the little things that bother us go. We've all been angry at one time or another. When I get angry my heart races, my stomach churns, my breathing speeds up, and I'm sure my blood pressure goes up. There are times in our life we will need that response. However, most situations in our life are annoyances. They don't rise to the need of placing ourselves or others in danger. Overreacting to a situation will bring unnecessary stress to our bodies. Save yourself for the "real battle" whether it be physical or mental. We're going to need that strength someday.

Try to remember, the next time you're roaring down the highway late for work or an appointment—it's not all about you. There are other people perhaps on the same mission with the same problems. They're late too…in a hurry just like you. There are older drivers on the road. They might not signal, may not even be going the speed limit. Should they be on the road at all? Maybe not, but there are many reasons to keep your anger in check for some day, you will be just like them.

Exercise is one answer I hear when I ask others what calms them. Meditation, prayer and spending quality time with family and friends can also help ease irritation. If you find your day fraught with anger and frustration share it with a friend, talk it over with your family. We know our own triggers—take a deep breath and settle down.

Put a smile on your face, a smile given a stranger won't hurt and it might even help their disposition. Say excuse me, even if it's not you that bumped into the person in the grocery store. Everything you do causes a ripple effect so be the best person you can be.

"Anger is never without a reason, but seldom a good one."

—Benjamin Franklin

CHAPTER 21

GOING DOWN THAT LONG LONESOME HIGHWAY. GONNA LIVE LIFE MY WAY.

I'm interviewing a soft-spoken man. As he speaks, I wonder how he came to be in law enforcement. His father had migrated from Syria. He doesn't know how his father ended up in Northern Minnesota, intermingling with blond-haired, blue-eyed Scandinavians. His mother was Swedish; his dad was fairly dark skinned.

His dad did not encourage a job in law enforcement. He didn't believe that there should be struggle or conflict in people's lives. I myself find it difficult to imagine the now-retired trooper in a fight. A physical altercation seems almost impossible. Even a verbal argument seems too harsh for him. He is a gentle man.

As a youngster, he had seen a couple of highway patrolman (he about as tall as their gun belt) going into a restaurant. He decided then and there he wanted to be one of them.

He met his wife while both were in the military. He was an MP when he saw her in the lunchroom. She looked at him and smiled. He decided someday he was going to marry that girl. When he went back to the line she had disappeared. When he went to get some milk, she ran towards him, right up to his face and asked him his name. He knew she was the one for him.

He joined the patrol when he got out of the service. After going through training, he waited 5 weeks to start work until more money was appropriated for the patrol. He found the nicest people on the Iron Range. "The Range" was often a problem for outsiders but the officer found a home and wonderful community there and was told he fit like a glove.

He believes he worked in the golden era. The now retired trooper is pleased that they were allowed to be individuals. They weren't monitored. He believes human nature is to be left alone. The trooper feels that people like to be a little autonomous and make their own decisions. He made a choice, felt like he did a good job, and was comfortable with it.

"Were there some gray areas in your life?" I asked. Yes. There was very little black-and-white—lots of gray. He worked different shifts and weekends and was quick to point out that many others in different occupations did the same. He says he was strict with his children, although they don't seem to feel that way. Their Mom was the parent who played cards, games, and watched TV with them. When he had time, he liked to be alone—to read Max Ehrmann and study philosophy. Max Ehrmann, widely known for his prose poem "Desiderata" (Latin: "things desired") is buried at Highland Lawn Cemetery in Terre Haute, Indiana. He has visited the grave site several times.

Small town is different. He smiles and talks about his town. They know you and you know them. He was told by a townsman that he had heard the trooper was always fair and asked how he accomplished that. Although the man wasn't sure he always was fair but felt confident that he had certainly tried to be. He stopped a woman for speeding late one night. She was driving a beat-up old car, no back seat and had several young kids standing with their hands on the back of the front seat. To inflict a ticket on this woman would mean less money to buy cornflakes for the children's breakfast. He did not give her a citation.

He told of his wife's observation one day as he sat in his squad car filling out paperwork.

She told him of the hard look she saw on his face and that she would have been afraid if he had stopped her with that look on his face. She went on to say that he usually had a gentle look but not that day.

From then on, he paid more attention to his look.

This trooper weighed every traffic stop very carefully. He believed the key to a good and smooth interaction with the public was the expression you had on your face and the tone of your voice. He didn't have one complaint throughout his career.

Loving the job, he would have stayed working until 60, but the early out offered at 55 along with health insurance, were too good for him to turn down. He had never wanted a supervisory job; his love was the highway. When asked if he missed the job, the uniform, the squad in the driveway, his answer was no. But would he do it all over again? Yes.

Because of his admiration of Max Ehrmann, I will add his prose poem Desiderata to this story.

Desiderata (1927)
By Max Ehrmann

Go placidly amid the noise and the haste,
and remember what peace there may be in silence.

As far as possible, without surrender,
be on good terms with all persons.
Speak your truth quietly and clearly;
and listen to others,
even to the dull and the ignorant;
they too have their story.

Avoid loud and aggressive persons;
they are vexatious to the spirit.

If you compare yourself with others,
you may become vain or bitter,
for always there will be greater and lesser persons than yourself.
Enjoy your achievements as well as your plans.
Keep interested in your own career, however humble;
it is a real possession in the changing fortunes of time.

Exercise caution in your business affairs,
for the world is full of trickery.
But let this not blind you to what virtue there is;
many persons strive for high ideals,
and everywhere life is full of heroism.
Be yourself. Especially do not feign affection.
Neither be cynical about love,
for in the face of all aridity and disenchantment,
it is as perennial as the grass.

Take kindly the counsel of the years,
gracefully surrendering the things of youth.
Nurture strength of spirit to shield you in sudden misfortune.
But do not distress yourself with dark imaginings.
Many fears are born of fatigue and loneliness.

Beyond a wholesome discipline,
be gentle with yourself.
You are a child of the universe
no less than the trees and the stars;
you have a right to be here.
And whether or not it is clear to you,
no doubt the universe is unfolding as it should.

Therefore be at peace with God,
whatever you conceive Him to be.
And whatever your labors and aspirations,
in the noisy confusion of life,
keep peace in your soul.

With all its sham, drudgery, and broken dreams,
it is still a beautiful world.
Be cheerful. Strive to be happy.

> *"And though age and infirmity overtake me, and I come not within sight of the castle of my dreams, teach me still to be thankful for life, and for time's olden memories that are good and sweet; and may the evening's twilight find me gentle still"*

—Max Ehrmann

CHAPTER 22

BORN TO RUN

What are your thoughts about car chases?

Roaring down the rural roads late at night with no one around, there was an exhilaration when the chase was on. A retired trooper talked of loving it. He has second thoughts about it these days when the chase is going on in populated areas and putting the motoring public at risk.

Generally, this Minneapolis officer is not a fan of vehicle pursuits.

His experience with pursuits is that they seldom rise to the point where the need to apprehend a suspect outweighs the risk to the public or the officer involved in the pursuit. He has found that the most common reasons for people who flee in a vehicle are because they do not have a valid license; they have a revoked license; they have a warrant for a non-violent crime; they possess a small amount of marijuana; or they are driving a stolen vehicle, for which the punishment is negligible.

On the other hand, there is the argument that someone may be fleeing for a good reason; such as, a gun in the car, or having just committed a serious crime. He believes there is a time for a pursuit as long as the justification outweighs the risk to the public. As a supervisor who takes on the responsibility of allowing a pursuit in his precinct, considerations such as crime committed, time of day, road conditions, and traffic conditions on the roadway need to be heavily considered and evaluated. Due to public and officer safety, he generally is more inclined to terminate a vehicle pursuit without the absolute need to apprehend the offender.

Car chases – he loved them when he was a young officer on the midnight shift. He was young and it really spiced up a quiet night for this New York City Captain. He doesn't agree with the Do Not Chase policy but does understand the liability issues and danger to citizens.

The trooper knows an officer has to weigh the risk of a chase, being aware of their surroundings, getting into a residential areas or heavy traffic. She continues to say that if it's risky, they have to call it off. The adrenalin kicks in and then relief comes when it ends. There's anger with the person fleeing, anger that they would put themselves and others in such jeopardy. However, she doesn't want a policy that says never chase.

Sometimes it's necessary. Shortly before the police officer retired, he was checking out a suspicious car and the car ended up being stolen. They took off, so the chase was on. They had actually pulled off some robberies as well. He's worried about covering himself. As he's chasing, he's thinking at what point does he need to back off. The officer doesn't want anybody getting hurt, including the people they are chasing, and especially, of course, the public.

Officer Weldy writes:

One night I and a fellow officer were patrolling around town when we spotted a suspicious looking vehicle aimlessly driving around. We ran a 10-28 (license check) and sure enough, back came a hit. Vehicle was stolen in Minneapolis.

I hit the reds and the chase was on. It really wasn't much of a chase.

Out jumped two men and ran into a small woods alongside the river.

It's dark and we don't know if these guys are armed or not, and we're sure to go stumbling around in the dark to find out.

My partner is a real outdoorsman, and in fact an avid raccoon hunter. It just so happens he keeps his dogs a short distance away, so I asked him if his dogs would track these guys. He said he didn't know, but we would give it a try. He's got a dog, a big black and tan named Ranger.

Ranger had a voice that would scare you to death, but was a lovable dog who would climb in your lap and lick and slobber all over you. We turned on the PA system and I informed the men to come out with their hands up or we would turn loose the dog. Then my partner spoke to the dog, saying "Coon Ranger, Coon." Ranger started to howl. What a racket inside the squad, but it was also going out over the PA system.

Within a minute came the cry from the woods, "Don't let the dogs loose, I give up!" Out of the woods comes this young fellow with his hands over his head. We placed him under arrest, put on the cuffs, and then he saw the dog. The look on his face was incredulous as he said, "you are going to track me with that dog?" We picked up the other fellow just west of town about four days later, cold and hungry.

One of the retired troopers is well known for his delightful incident reports. When his shift actually ended and he retired, his interesting reports were put into a booklet called *Poor Richard's Almanac*. He has given me permission to share them.

Nature of Incident—fleeing—fleeing—Squad—ker—banging.

It was already over an hour passed quitting time, due to a coffee break. I had one day to go before my 2-week vacation started and I was kinda looking forward to it, even if it was going to be spent wading in the mud in the rice patties. But don't count your eggs before the chicken lays them! About five minutes short of my quitting location I saw a vehicle parked on the side of the road with four people in it. They were passing a brown paper sack between them, I ascertained that from past experiences that in all probability is that inside the brown paper sack would be a bottle of an intoxicating liquid of some kind. As I drove by, I pretended that I hadn't seen them, so they would not notice me. I then very quietly turned around and was going to sneak up behind them and yell Ah ha! Gotcha!! But alack & alas they were hot footing it west on # 100.

Not to be concerned, because my Red Chevy had proved herself in the past and I was sure she could do it again. In a very short flight into the ditch on right side of the roadway, side-by-side, motors roaring, metal grinding – driver screaming, passengers passing gas, I came up out of the ditch and made a power turn and met them head on as they were coming out of the ditch – bet that put a stain in their underwear – he must've thought I was bluffing because he kept coming. I met him – nose to nose – once more Red Chevy roared – tires screaming, bumpers bumping, backwards into the ditch I push them – more stains in underwear – doors flew open on culprits car and everyone headed for the woods – I jumped out, kept my eyes fixed on the drivers and with one mighty leap I was going to nab the driver by the nap of his neck – but that was not to be – at the beginning of my mighty leap I stepped in a hole or on a no deposit – no return item and turned my right ankle. Pain – yes – but did that deter the dauntless dummy – no – following on pain I caught up with them, where before I had tried to ignore them, they now choose to ignore me. When they ran a stop sign, I turned on my siren, they still ignored me. It could be that my siren wasn't up to snuff as some weeks earlier the cone had fallen off and I drove over it so that it was no longer cone shaped. I didn't put it back on, I felt it would give off a flat sound.

Back to the present – the culprits wouldn't stop – drove right down the middle of the road causing much dust to rise from the roadbed. I called radio to advise them on my predicament at about the same time they switched drivers, speed increase considerably. Dust – my goodness for dust. All of a sudden – the pot lickers slammed on their brakes – put near ran into them. Twice more they tried same maneuver. I was now getting the feeling that they were serious about trying to get away. I tightened my jaws and bit down – oww – had tongue between teeth – when they came to the junction of Highway #1, I was truly amazed, they never stopped for the stop sign! Away to the West we went. I eased up alongside of them and was about to motion them over when the son of a gun tried to run into me – I shot ahead of them and thought – now it's my turn. I slammed on my brakes – hard. They made a U turn and went back to where they had just been. I did same – once more I eased up alongside them, intending to give the driver a stern and steely look - calculated to freeze him on the spot. Instead he ran into the side of the squad car -that upset me. I put Red Chevy into roar and rammed those pot lickers, faint order of stained underwear. I took off through the woods, twice I got a fleeting glance of the driver but after about a quarter mile I came to the sad conclusion that I had been bested. A bitter pill to swallow but a 20-year-old brain in an over 50 body just couldn't hack it. I limped back to the highway – licking my wounds and pride.

One bright spot was that I could still hear my siren and it wasn't getting fainter as it would have been had it been going west down the highway. A dinged-up squad was bad – but a disappeared one would be worse.

When I got back to the highway, I got me one fellow who was hampered by lugging a 12 pack with him. I took him in custody – he said he was the owner of the vehicle and proved it by showing papers – good enough – 1 arrest for permitting. Radio said help was coming, Red Lake squad showed up SB 24, air force 928, Belt 809 all arrived. I put the owner of culprit car in right front seat of my squad. I wasn't too concerned because up to that point he had been *calling me brother and shaking my hand all the time, but just as SB 24 arrived he put my squad into gear and head first into Culprits car. I had been ready to do a one-legged strut because Red Lake Squad had the driver – Belt 809 had a passenger and air force 928 was keeping everything covered, but the sound of tinkling glass, sure takes the strut out of you.*

Retired game warden showed up, and by the glint in his eyes you know he wanted to get into the thick of it again, but after we compared the elements we decided to stick to golf – though come to think of it, the last time I played golf I hit myself on the back of the head with a golf club, fell down and rolled around on the ground. They said I had swung too hard. The wrecker showed up, got my squad out of the ditch and hooked up culprit's car.

Red Lake squad took passenger back to Red Lake – Belt 809 took driver and owner of culprit's car to Bemidji. That left us in need of a driver for my squad. A friend of mine lives close by so I had radio call him to see if he could help us out. He was one of the older fellows, who, when we were growing up tried to lead me astray at times – but when in need – you know – I don't think there was that much brush hanging on the squad before he took it.

SP 24 took me in custody and took me to see Dr. Radio had made an appointment for me. Dr. put my foot in a cast and told me to take it easy for a month – not broken – just bent.

"A Man's got to know his limitations."

—Dirty Harry

CHAPTER 23

SUNSHINE ON MY SHOULDER

Game wardens, often referred to as wildlife officers, conservation officers, or fish and game wardens, are recognized members of wildlife conservation teams, whether at the state or federal level.

Fish and game wardens are law enforcement officers who patrol lakes, rivers, beaches, wetlands, back country, deserts, and even metropolitan areas of a specific region. They may partake in undercover operations, and their work may include using jet boats, airplanes, canoes, all-terrain vehicles, and horses, just to name a few.

Conservation enforcement officers' (CEO's) work is often done alone. They are tasked with checking the licenses and bag limits of hunters and anglers and to investigate areas where illegal hunting has been reported.

*A comprehensive knowledge of the environmental sciences is often achieved through a bachelor's or graduate degree; therefore, a formal degree program has become a minimum requirement for federal game warden jobs and for many game warden jobs at the state level as well.*www.gamewardenedu.org

The smell in the air after a spring rain or leaves falling from the trees on a sunny fall day bring delight to this Wisconsin conservation officer. He always had an interest in law enforcement. He has a quick smile and a twinkle in his eye. He was hired full-time at 22 years old. He doesn't feel like he worked a day in his life. He really never had a job. He never had a profession. He was just privileged to live his lifestyle. This game warden was as excited on his last day of work as he was on his first day. These are the words of a dedicated conservation officer.

He had worked as a fisheries research assistant for the Iowa Conservation Commission for two summers before the name changed to DNR. He transferred to law enforcement at age 31. He was single when he was first hired but, after marrying, did discuss transferring to law enforcement with his wife. She was not excited, but it's what he really wanted and she relented. His marriage did not last, and, when asked if his job played a part in that. Yes, he supposes it did to some degree since he was gone a lot and didn't or couldn't spend as much time at home as he should have.

He thinks there is too much paperwork in the job today, and less time doing actual field work. He has also found more illegal drug labs on fish and game management areas.

He was excited on his first day of work—not nervous, just excited. He had been deputized as a temporary peace officer by the department for six months each year and would enforce fish and game laws when he encountered them but also worked as a fisheries biologist.

Yes, he has feared for his life a few times. One memory comes quickly to mind. He was unhooking a 12-point buck from a 10-point buck, tangled up while fighting. His supervisor, witnessing the event, told him that if he ever did that again he would give him two weeks unpaid vacation. He admitted it was not his smartest decision but both deer made it, unharmed.

He almost lost his life saving the lives of two firemen in a river rescue training exercise. He was the swift water rescue trainer and their boat went over the boil below the low head dam. Using another boat, he was able to pull them and their boat back over the boil, and they were safely rescued.

High-speed pursuits also enter his mind as he talked of close calls—called Jacklighting arrests. "Jacklighting" is a game warden term that is used instead of saying "hunting with an artificial light." Although states have different laws concerning shining an artificial light in search of game at night, Iowa prohibits that activity while possessing a weapon in a vehicle or on a person.

Encountering someone in the woods or hunting area, he thinks of safety first, analyzes the surroundings, and observes as much as he can before he approaches. How many are there? What are they doing? Do they have firearms? Is anything illegal going on?

Did he miss family life? Lots. He worked weekends, and of course his kids were *home* on weekends. Game wardens work holidays and all season openers. He regrets that he never took his boys out for opening day of pheasant season, waterfowl season, turkey season, or trapping. He did, however, have a good friend who took them out. Missing time with his boys was hard on all of them. Whether it was in the woods or at school functions, he tried hard to rectify that later in his career, and thinks he has done a pretty good job of it. His sons were always interested in his stories and adventures; however, he was selective in what he told them.

He enjoyed his days off—fishing, garden work around his acreage, and spending time with his boys during the evening. When I asked what he liked about his job, he liked everything except paperwork and reports. Yet, yes, he was ready to leave.

Vehicle computers were coming in, budgets were tightening. He had a couple of cancer events, and there were a lot of things he still wanted to do, and now he's doing them.

My question: Do you think law enforcement people are scared in today's world? He thinks if they aren't, they should be. Attitudes about law enforcement are horrible—lawsuits and the total lack of respect for authority and human life. It was different in the old days. He talked about the difference back then when he first started. Of course, he always stayed alert and ready, but people were different years ago. It really wasn't the hunters that concerned him as much as the nonhunters. He believes hunters seem to be dedicated to the sport and, in most cases, realized that the future of their sport depends on their actions and attitudes.

He and his partners were good friends. He said they had a very tight district. He was one of two sergeants, and they were all close at work and at play. He thinks about how easily you are forgotten when you retire. You become one of the old guys who are dinosaurs now.

"Do you think the public understands the job – the dangers that come with it," I ask? He thinks they understand the CEO's job to a large extent, but doesn't think they are aware of the dangers that are inherent with the job. "Is there something particular you would like people to know about your job," I asked. He wants people to know that CEOs are real police officers. They are extremely well trained in many areas and extremely dedicated.

A former Department of Natural Resources employee thinks every Minnesotan has an idea of how the DNR should run. If you don't catch fish, it's the DNR's fault. If the trail isn't groomed, it's the DNR's fault. If you didn't get the campsite you wanted, it's the DNR's fault. It seems like wherever you go, the DNR is getting bashed over something.

"The falling walleye population has many blaming the DNR. Resorts are having a tough time because of the fishing limits. Conservationists are claiming that row crops destroy habitat and pollute waterways, while farmers say it's their livelihood. Business groups and organized labor have cast a spotlight on the DNR as well," says the *West Central Tribune* October 26, 2015.

The Lac qui Parle Lake Association has stocked nearly 24,000 walleye fingerlings into Lac qui Parle Lake this fall. The stocking is part of an ongoing effort by the Lac qui Parle Lake Association and Minnesota Department of Natural Resources Fisheries to help build up the walleye population in the state says a report at www.dnr.state.mn.us.

I have fond memories of Lac qui Parle Lake—A resort, the sandy beach, and the roller-skating rink. When we had decided we were too old to go swimming at the swimming pool, we went to the beach on Lac qui Parle Lake. Sun bathing and cooling-off with a swim to the big rock and enjoying a cold Coke went along with a good day of summer fun. Another resort has been around for a long time. I have over the years had lunch there many times and as a child roamed that area often. It is a well-known lake in the area for fishing picnics and swimming. It has been a gathering place with a restaurant noted for tasty food and good visiting for years.

Deer hunting is another sport loved by Minnesotans. Hunting deer was a staple in Mike's life whether along the river below the small town where I grew up, in the cedar swamps of northern Minnesota, or hunting in Colorado. We ate venison on a regular basis when we were first married. I can't say I developed much of a taste for it, but it provided food. Also, I don't think I knew the proper way to prepare it. I added onions and spices to the meat when using it for chili, meatballs, or meatloaf; however, it always had a wild taste to me.

My daughter and son-in-law love to feed the deer in the winter. Their ideal setting on the Crow River is a drawing card for them. Starry nights with a blanket of snow highlight the beautiful wild animals as they jockey and skirmish for the perfect spot along the wooden box filled with corn. Feeding the deer in winter was not permitted in 2017 and is continued through the year 2019.

Deer enjoying the corn in the feeder.

"The *West Central Tribune* Friday, August 25, 2017, stated that a deer feeding ban goes into effect Monday, Aug. 28, 2017, for all or portions of 11 Minnesota counties. The Minnesota Department of Natural Resources announced the ban in Central Minnesota. The ban includes Stearns, Kandiyohi, Wright, Meeker, McLeod, and the portion of Renville County north of US Highway 212."

The ban was put in place because chronic wasting disease was known to exist in wild deer. While deer in the Central and North Central Minnesota areas were not known to have chronic wasting disease, the feeding ban as well as mandatory testing were precautionary steps the DNR took after captive deer infected with the disease were found on farms in Crow Wing and Meeker Counties.

Hunters in the Willmar area were required to bring deer that were harvested during the first two weeks of the 2017 firearms season to testing stations. The testing was a precautionary measure to prevent chronic wasting disease from spreading, according to the area Wildlife Manager with the DNR in New London.

Conservation officers (game wardens in every day parlance) play a variety of roles. As mentioned at the beginning of this chapter, game wardens are often referred to as Wildlife Officers, and this anecdote gives new meaning to "wildlife officer." An officer received a dispatch on August 12, 2018. Dudes on water scooters were the gist of it. He was soon launching his boat from a resort on a lake. He would later arrest a pair of naked troublemakers operating vintage standup personal watercraft. They were allegedly drunk, belligerent men in their birthday suits.

"Nature gives to every time and season some beauties of its own."

–Charles Dickens

CHAPTER 24

I AM WOMAN

Angie Dickenson, starring on NBC in 1974 as "Pepper" Anderson in "Police Woman," and Sharon Gless, along with Tyne Daley, starring in television's "Cagney and Lacey," are who my mind conjures up as I write about women in police work—Angie, looking beautiful, and Cagney and Lacey, tough but also gentle. I did not like the portrayal of Tyne Daley as inspector Kate Moore in "The Enforcer" with Clint Eastwood. With an oversized purse slung across her shoulder, running in high heels, and a deer-in-the-headlights look in her eyes, the portrayal was, in my opinion, completely unrealistic.

The real women in police work today look vastly different. They are weighted down with the uniform, encumbered with the trappings of a bulletproof vest, and many pounds of extra weight on their gun belts. Their hips always hurt. They talk of having had difficulties finding uniforms that fit. Some started earlier in their careers having to wear skirts, a gun belt, pumps, and pantyhose, but they really couldn't do anything about it. It is often said that clothes make the man. It's also true that clothes make the woman, the female police officer. But ill-fitting uniforms, designed to fit a man's body rather than a woman's, do more than just create a clumsy appearance. They also hamper a female officer's ability to do her job.

Female officers say that women's police uniforms have improved, but it varies from department to department. Larger departments have been able to change faster than smaller ones. Often, women were still issued men's uniforms, just in a smaller size, and they did not fit the female body well.

Other contrasts? It still takes some getting used to when a woman speaks with a loud, stern voice. "Stop where you are. Get your hands out of your pockets. Show me your hands. Put your hands on the hood. Stay on the ground."

One female trooper talked about when she first started. The motoring public seemed surprised to see a woman walk up to their car. Sometimes they called her sir, and in a surprised voice would say "oh, you're a woman."

Women often wear their hair pulled back in a braid, bun, or really short. It makes it harder for someone to yank on it. On guard, watching what's going on around her, and also watching the person she has just stopped to question, she is doing what every other police officer, male or female, would do. Attention to detail is what their training teaches them.

Although female officers still comprise a small percentage of the law enforcement workforce, early forerunners paved the way for women in the previously male domain.

Nicole Norfleet and Paul Walsh write in the April 30, 2018, *Star Tribune,* "While working as a Honeywell assembler and desk clerk, Dee Dunn saw a newspaper ad that would jumpstart her law enforcement career. It was the mid-70s and the Minneapolis Police Department was about to diversify its ranks.

"Dunn was in her early 30s at the time. In 1975 she went on to become the first black female police officer in Minneapolis and one of a small group of women in the department.

Dunn's obituary, published in the *Star Tribune,* said, "... She was truly a trail blazer."

Helen was an even earlier pioneer. She was my sister's mother-in-law, and I saw her often. After the birth of my nephew, my sister developed a staph infection. I stayed with her several months and took care of her new baby while she struggled to fight the infection. Helen visited regularly and loved to tell about her adventures while working on the Minneapolis Police Force and, even more, about being one of the first Minneapolis female police officers.

Helen did have a way about her. She was a tough, plain-speaking woman. She joined the Minneapolis Police Department in 1951. As a female officer, she was not allowed to work on the street. Her working garb consisted of a dress, pillbox hat, nylon hose, and shoes with high heels. She also carried a purse to hold her makeup, gun, and handcuffs.

Helen had earned a nursing degree at the University of Minnesota and was a nurse at the former Swedish and General Hospital in Minneapolis. Her working days had also consisted of being a supervisor at the Sister Kenny Institute during the polio epidemic.

Her husband, also a police officer, died of a heart attack in 1949, leaving her with two young boys to feed. Needing more money to be the sole supporter of the family, she knew she could make more money as a police officer. So she joined the Minneapolis Police Department in 1951.

Helen worked in juvenile crimes for many years. She was proud to tell the story of how she and another officer, passed the written and marksmanship test in 1961 to become detectives but that the police promotions board had refused to promote them. They sued the city and won to become the department's first female detectives. They were assigned to the homicide and sex crimes unit.

During interrogations, Helen had a way of asking questions as though it were a normal conversation. The person she was talking to wouldn't realize that an interrogation was taking place. Perhaps that is why her granddaughter Theresa became an attorney. Helen had a wonderful sense of humor and would often talk about the difficulties of working in the sex crimes unit. Tongue in cheek, she would tell me that men believed there can't be anything like rape for the simple reason that a woman can run faster with her skirt up than a man can with his pants down.

"In 1972, Congress passed an amendment to the Civil Rights Act of 1964, prohibiting state and local agencies from job discrimination based on gender. Police departments were required to hire women for jobs on an equal basis with men. www.eeoc/gov/eeochistory/35/thelaw.

The Metropolitan Police Department of the District of Columbia conducted a study, assigning a number of newly hired women officers to patrol work traditionally reserved for male officers. www.bjs.gov/content

"The study observed the women for a year. It stated that women patrol officers tended to be more effective than their male counterparts in avoiding violence and diffusing potentially violent situations. It also found that women were less likely than men to engage in serious unbecoming conduct. It went on to prove that citizens involved in incidents with police officers have the same level of respect for and favorable attitudes towards patrol officers of both sexes."

It took a lot of persistence, but today women play as major a role and are as much a respected part of the police force as men. At the police academy, however, women were not necessarily treated as equals. They had lower targets for physical ability and were not, back then, allowed to drive pursuit cars or shoot shotguns.

According to the National Center for Women and Policing, "In the 1960s a few women police officers were allowed to work undercover in a vice squad to bust drug dealers and prostitution rings that led to some changing times.... Police departments across the U.S. worked to desegregate and allow women into all levels of law enforcement."

"The Navajo Nation also wants more female police," says Navajo Nation Police Chief Philip Francisco. He wants to encourage more women to join the police department. "Women comprise only a small percentage of the local law enforcement in agencies around the nation," reports the *Community Policing Dispatch,* a publication of Community Oriented Policing Services, which operates under the US Department of Justice."

"The Community Oriented Policing Services goes on to say that "Navajo Nation Police Sargent Shirley Sanisya said Navajo women face gender taboos associated with the culture. Women in traditional Navajo culture do not hunt and are not supposed to handle weapons." Sanisya started her career in law enforcement as a dispatcher and was able to overcome those taboos with the support of her family. She is also married to a law enforcement officer.

What, you might ask, do women actually bring to law enforcement jobs? They believe they have a different, seemingly better way of dealing with conflict. They likely do not have the physical strength of some men, but their bravery, creativity, and verbal skills may make them ideal for the job. They also believe that good self-defense skills and knowing the right moves enable them to protect themselves, not just brute strength. Women in policing talk about being less likely to use excessive and deadly force and are less likely than their male coworkers to be involved in fights or acts of aggression on the job.

The women I interviewed say verbal skills and interaction with civilians are some of the vital skills they bring to the profession. Generally, women seem to have the ability for interaction beyond just skills in dealing with dangerous situations. Perhaps it stems from the way mothers interact with their children. Sibling fights can be calmed when mothers intervene. Sometimes telling children to go to their rooms is the same as telling people who are fighting to separate, to get away from each other.

Policewomen tend to be mediators and seem to find common ground, particularly when dealing with a mental health crisis. A calmer, less aggressive tone tends to diffuse the situation.

Some women in police work also consider themselves somewhat of a social worker. One of the women I interviewed said she had thought that's the field she would go into. Police work is about stopping conflict, not adding to already chaotic situations. As women in police forces have found out, many see a law enforcement position as the SWAT team going into combat, hopping over fences, busting doors down, armed to the hilt with guns.

Much of what they do is act the part of the parent. Police officers are often involved in doing mundane things, like taking care of a dog complaint or a problem with the neighbor. It's not all blood and guts.

Peer acceptance seems to be one of the greatest pressures operating within a police organization. The desire to be known as a good officer and partner is a strong motivating factor, and failure to achieve that status can be demoralizing and devastating. Women must also overcome the social prejudice of being known as the weaker sex. Female officers report feeling that they have to work twice as hard to prove themselves and to be accepted. I would think that would be the reaction of any female entering any male dominated profession; the problems would be much the same. Women going into law enforcement is likely no different than women going into other fields that are typically considered to be a male domain.

A female trooper believes she was treated well by the other officers. She goes on to say she was stressed but not by her partners. It was stress she put on herself. Because she was a woman in a man's world, she was hard on herself, wanting to prove herself and do a good job. She found great support in the training, but was surprised how hard patrol school was. She had never been in the military but some of the guys had and they helped her a lot. They let her know that some of the training was just playing head games.

She talks about the camaraderie she felt with her partners and that she worked well with all the departments. Working in a rural area they relied on each other. Talking of the dangers of her occupation she said the biggest concern was a vehicle running into her while she is taking care of a crash on a narrow rural road.

Women were not in construction work when I was young. When I graduated high school, few young women went to college. If they did, the professions of social worker, nurse, or teacher were what they usually chose. Many entered the work force as bank tellers, secretaries, waitresses, or married and were housewives and mothers. Of course, there were exceptions. There were women who became doctors, lawyers, even politicians. However, the prospects for women were slim. They were not going to be electricians, mechanics, or plumbers, and certainly not many were policewomen back in the 60s.

The women officers that I have interviewed talked about their goal of wanting to help people. That's why they went into the profession in the first place, and the majority of them said that Yes, they believe they have helped people. They've been there—they've been there for them.

The fact that the profession continues to be overwhelmingly dominated by men is something that will continue for a long time. It took some time for men to get used to women in police work. Some spoke of being shunned by their male counterparts; the men were leery and suspicious early on. Perhaps that is diminishing today.

Women also have a different problem than many of their male counterparts: they have to juggle childcare, have mouths to feed, clothes to wash, and houses to try to keep clean. They, like all who work weekends, holidays, and rotating shifts, have to find a way to have family time yet still be a force in their workplace. Just as men have long lamented their lack of family time, women have those same guilt feelings.

"It seems to boil down to this: A woman is like a tea bag— you can't tell how strong she is until she gets in hot water."

– Eleanor Roosevelt

CHAPTER 25

HELLO DARKNESS, MY OLD FRIEND

Shortly after we moved up, Mike received a call about a naked man standing on a highway not far from town. Before long he saw the man wearing only a baseball cap. Mike stopped at the pile of clothes lying along the side of the road, searched them, then brought them to the man, and said in the sternest voice he could muster, "Get your clothes on." The young man complied. They were soon traveling back to a mental health center.

"Mental illness is a prominent issue in police shootings. A joint report by the Treatment Advocacy Center and National Sheriff's Association examined cases between 1980 and 2008. Its findings estimated that roughly half of all police shootings involve people with mental illness.

The report goes on to say that outsourcing the severely mentally ill to law enforcement is a tragic symptom of our already troubled medical system. Police are expected to be front-line mental health workers. They are effectively armed social workers, and jails have become our psychiatric hospital system. Why do the families of the severely mentally ill need to rely on police for assistance? Because there's nowhere else to go."

Between 1955 and 1998 we emptied our mental institutions. 488,000 mentally ill people were discharged from state hospitals. www.

thebalance.com. Instead of finding solutions these castoffs are often left to suffer their delusions with overwhelmed, frightened family members or to rot in the streets or in jail.

The mental health industry essentially has given up when it comes to the severely mentally ill. The responsibility of the police is increasingly to serve, protect, and deal with desperately ill, irrational people. In 2013, *The Arizona Daily Star* reported that the police in Tucson, Arizona, received more calls about mental illness than about burglaries or stolen cars.

Television stations were filled with the story of the man accused of a bloodied shooting spree that left five people dead and six wounded at the international airport in Fort Lauderdale. His motive is not known still he was no stranger to Federal Law Enforcement. He had been in the FBI office in Anchorage eight times telling them that his mind had been taken over by the Islamic State and they were telling him to fight.

An article written by Rich Lowry, dated January 1, 2016, about a police shooting in Chicago was all too familiar—and not because it fits the story of police racism. Quintonio LeGrier's father called police after locking himself in a bedroom when his 19-year-old son threatened him with a baseball bat. When the police arrived, the young man with emotional problems allegedly charged them with the bat. An officer shot him dead.

Another police shooting in California involves a sheriff's deputy who was charged by a mentally ill woman with a kitchen knife. A 26-year-old Los Angeles area man suffering from bipolar disorder, lunged for an officer's gun in a hospital. For all the attention devoted to police involved shootings and race, mental illness is the more prominent issue.

In its analysis of 2015 police shootings, *The Washington Post* states dozens of cases in which the police were called as a means of getting treatment. Shirley Marshall Harrison called the Dallas police when her schizophrenic, bipolar son was out of control. He was shot down while allegedly charging police with a screwdriver.

She didn't call them to take him to the morgue, she called for medical help. It's a poignant cry. What's the answer?

Police need better training in how to de-escalate situations, but there always will be legitimate danger in these incidents. Mentally troubled people killed by police are often armed with guns and knives or other sharp objects. Mental health advocates do not second-guess officers facing potentially treacherous situations. Law enforcement officers deal constantly with people with mental health problems. The cries for help when there is no crime are dangerous. Often it is someone off his or her medication, hallucinating, busting up the furniture. Officers have no idea what to expect when they walk in that door.

"Mental health is the most pressing public health crisis facing Minnesota," states Michael Schramm and Lawrence J. Massa in a commentary article in the, *West Central Tribune* August 20, 2016. One in five adults will experience a mental illness this year, and half of all mental illnesses begin by age 4. Is this new or has the number of people with mental health issues grown along with the population?"

"*USA Today* reports March 30, 2018 that authorities have found 64% of the mass attack suspects had symptoms of mental illness. Mental illness plagued many suspects that are linked to violent attacks in schools and other public place."

Mental problems have always been in our society. We had individuals in our little community that were considered "different." I don't remember being afraid of them or police being called to handle them. I was a child and perhaps the adults, if I could ask them today, would tell a different story.

I remember a man walking down main street opening car doors and then slamming them shut with tremendous force. The car would rock as the door closed. "Shell shocked" was the term used by adults to explain his behavior. I don't remember anyone ever trying to stop him. As I think back, I wonder why people didn't just lock their car doors to stop him, although that would also have been strange: No one ever locked their car doors; often, we even left the keys in the car overnight.

Minnesotans experiencing a mental health crisis are too often sent to hospital emergency rooms hundreds of miles away from their families and communities. They have no choice as there are no local treatment facilities for them.

Once doctors say treatment is complete, there is often no place for those who have received help for their mental illness but are still in need of transitional housing to transfer back into society. Adult foster care, residential treatment programs, or group homes are often full. As a result, patients stay in state hospitals for weeks, months, or even years longer than they are supposed to.

We need more psychiatric hospitals, beds, and trained staff to care for the most abandoned part of humanity. We have been expecting police to pick up where society has dropped the ball.

People have taken to social media, telling others about their mental health issues. The new openness also coincides with increasingly calls to the police by concerned friends.

Following the suicide of renowned fashion designer Kate Spade and world traveler Anthony Bourdain, their admirers had great difficulty wrapping their mind around why this happened? Their suicide serves to accentuate the serious growing problem that demands action. Particularly upsetting evidenced no known mental health conditions in many that attempt or succeed at ending their life. They were instead influenced by factors such as relationship breakups, substance abuse, or health or financial setbacks. The CDC's finding that suicide is an issue that affects not only the mentally ill but also others struggling with stressful life problems.

Because it is often an impulsive act, efforts are needed to teach people about coping with lifestyle issues such as troubled relationships or unpaid bills. I believe the majority of us learned that from our parents. Aren't we teaching coping skills anymore?

Metro area counties will soon be testing a single telephone number that should make a request for help with mental illness as easy as calling 911. Using cell phone relocation, Minnesota will route the call to that county's crisis line rather than require a caller to figure out which of dozens of numbers to call.

Instead of calling the police or going to an emergency room, an increasing number of people are using crisis lines. Social workers can help de-escalate a crisis and assess the situation. They can also access hospital records and previous social worker contacts along with criminal records. A mobile crisis team will go to the person's home, manage and stabilize the situation, and help to arrange for therapy. If a person in trouble needs a crisis team to respond, they will reroute the call to a county mobile team. The *Star Tribune* says on October 15, 2016 that the state of Minnesota has funneled $13.6 million to individual counties to bolster existing mobile crisis teams. This will also reduce the likelihood that police need to be involved.

> *"You are a child of the universe, no less than the trees and the stars; you have the right to be here."*
>
> — Max Ehrmann

CHAPTER 26

LIFE THROUGH A LENS

What are your thoughts about using video cameras?

Many said they were in favor of video cameras as long as their use was monitored and policies and procedures were carefully written.

Per Natalie Tarangioli/Cronkite Jan. 24, 2017:

> *"Police wearing body cameras can promote a better relationship between the community and police, including members of the public, saying police officers treated them with respect, early results of an ongoing Arizona State University study show.*
>
> *Nearly 90 percent of the citizens strongly agreed the officers treated them with respect, treated them fairly, they were honest, they listened, they cared and they acted professionally," said Sgt. Josie Montenegro, a spokesman for the Tempe police department."*

Some of the officers I interviewed had concerns about using the cameras. They wondered how the public would feel when they realized they were being videoed. A small number of law enforcement were opposed to cameras and were discouraged about the lack of trust the public has in police officers.

What about the public taking videos of police?

An officer questions, with today's world of photo editing, and the public taking videos of the police usually after the incident has already started, do we know if we're really seeing the original or a modified version? He knows people can make it look any way they want. He absolutely thinks it benefits the police to have cameras, and that it's nice to have traffic stops filmed so you actually could see what was going on.

Many said they were just trying to get used to turning them on when they were en route to a call. "When the shit hits the fan," several believed that people would be less aggressive when they knew that the officers had cameras.

Besides training police to turn the cameras on more often, police chiefs and sheriffs are schooling departments on why cameras are helpful. The body cameras show what's really going on. It encourages greater accountability on both sides. Officers I spoke to also believed that with the advantage of cameras, there would be fewer false charges by the public.

A police officer wants the public to see how people act when they are in a drunken stupor. He wants us to see how our neighbor, friend, or the person we think is an upstanding member of the community behaves when they have had too much 'hair of the dog'.

As he spoke, I thought of Mike who would often ask me, how I knew someone when we were out somewhere and a fellow said hello to me. "They're my customer," I would say.

Some of the customers I waited on were not the same person Monday morning they had been on Friday or Saturday night when Mike dealt with them. I'm sure seeing them on camera, behaving like drunken slobs, would have colored my opinion of them. "Don't tell me what they do on the weekend," I said. However, at times, if they came in with a bandage or an obvious injury, I would ask what happened, already knowing the answer. The explanation they gave me was never the real story.

One of the deputies liked the idea of the cameras, but he was also in favor of a mechanism that automatically turns them on. He talked about in-dash cameras in squad cars that come on automatically. He says his biggest obstacle to camera use is when he jumps out of his squad car. There is so much going on, he forgets to turn it on. It's just not his first thought.

A trooper likes video cameras, but thinks they are limited in their scope. He's always worked with a camera. The video also refreshes his memory when it comes time for a report.

A Minneapolis police officer personally likes the cameras. More often than not, the camera will show that the officer acted correctly, and the suspect or the complainant was lying or misbehaving. In his experience, the camera has shown that an allegation made by a suspect or a complainant was false or very exaggerated. He has noticed that by activating his BWC (Body Worn Camera) suspects often change their behavior for the better because they realize that they are being recorded. On the flip side, he also believes that a BWC has a positive impact on officers' behavior, knowing that their actions are being recorded. Video camera/Body Worn Camera can also be helpful in court for charging.

Although this officer favors the use of cameras, he also sees a down side in their use. In this day and age of video cameras and BWCs, an officer's word is not what it used to be in the eyes of a jury or court system. He grumbles that more juries and prosecutors are relying on video to prove or charge a case. Often, if the event wasn't captured on an officer's BWC, it is getting more difficult to prove the event actually happened. Also, the camera often does not capture the entire event, which can be unfair to an officer who often makes a split-second decision while using all of his senses, which can't be captured on video.

The officer took great pains to explain the workings of the camera and what he expects it will do to help people understand its use in law enforcement. The video camera takes away a certain expectation of privacy for an officer, such as conversations between partners on a call, etc. Also, under high stress calls and situations, it can be difficult for an officer to remember to turn on the video camera or BWC. When this happens, there is an automatic assumption that an officer is intentionally attempting to cover something up or hide something. He has noticed that senior officers with many years of service, including himself, are not adjusting to the BWC as quickly as the new officers because they have been working years without the camera and lack the muscle memory in high-stress situations to turn the camera on.

The Minneapolis Sergeant also believed that when an officer is being recorded, there is the possibility of the officer's under-reacting to a situation, fearing how it will be perceived on video. He knew of situations where the officer should have used force sooner, resulting in the officer getting injured or killed. The officer hesitated to take the necessary action for fear of how it would look on video. Often Video/BWC Department Policy can be vague and confusing to an officer as to when to turn on the camera or when to turn off the camera.

On Saturday, June 23, 2018, Minneapolis police shot and killed a black man on the city's north side. This, another all too often shooting, sent protesters yet again into the streets over the weekend. Reports of the shooting filled the TV news and newspapers. The Minnesota Bureau of Criminal Apprehension investigated the case.

The released 911 call said:

> *"There's a guy walking around shooting his gun and he looks intoxicated and that's just not safe around here. He's firing off shots and that's why everybody started running away, like man this dude's drunk, man, you gotta, uh, move before he shoots somebody."*

"When the officers arrived," states the BCA, they found a man sitting on the curb with a woman holding a small child near the intersection of 48th and Camden Avenue.

The officers got out of their squad, and the man ran from them carrying a handgun. After pursuing the man on foot for several blocks, the officers shot him.

Witnesses gave conflicting accounts of the shooting, some saying they didn't believe Blevins had a gun. However, another man said he heard and saw much of what transpired directly behind his house. He heard yelling and, moving towards the alley, he heard voices shouting, "Drop the gun."

He said he heard two or three shots, and then, after a short delay, more shots. A few seconds later, he stepped out from around his garage and saw a man lying in a pool of blood. A foot away from the man's right hand lay a handgun. The officer ran around the body toward a handgun, kicking it away, and calling out, "Clear."

I recorded NBC, CBS, and ABC broadcasts of the 911 call and the uncle's statements. A man who identified himself as Blevin's uncle said to the protesters:

"We don't know what happened but we appreciate everything that you are doing here today because Black lives matter. We just want to know the truth. No one deserves to be shot down like a dog. We know he (Blevins) made some bad decisions, but we want everything to come to light. We're going to review the video, were going to review the body."

Release of the video cameras on television channels showed Blevins running as the police commanded, "Stop, drop the gun," many times. It also showed Blevins turning toward the police and pointing the gun at them.

County Attorney Freeman said, "There was no basis to issue criminal charges against either officer, because Blevins fled from the officers with a loaded handgun, refused to follow their commands for him to stop and show his hands, and then took the gun out of his pocket and turned toward the officers."

A trooper knows cameras are not the answer to everything. However, he hopes officers realize that this is a tool that benefits them more times than not. He also hopes that this will help build credibility with an increasingly skeptical public.

Cameras can also bring the focus back to an often-overlooked party in the officer-camera debate: crime victims. How does it feel to be a victim of a crime? How does it feel to be taped? A deputy hopes they don't feel it's too much, having a camera on during the worst time in their lives.

Many police departments are embracing the cameras because they create a complete audio and video record of incidents, rather than a cellphone video that generally captures only a portion of an incident.

A police chief thinks this technology represents an opportunity to demonstrate transparency. He told me they have nothing to hide. It's like an olive branch to the community.

Officers hope the camera generates a civilizing effect. They also hope that the use of force is not used unless necessary. It will protect the officers and the citizens.

A retired deputy said he's amazed to see what priority departments are putting into the new buzzwords, accountability and transparency. He finds it fascinating to listen to a brother-in-law talk about the new body cameras that officers are required to wear in Minneapolis. He had told the retired deputy about the policy and procedures associated with wearing the body camera. The deputy continues that he never had to wear a body camera but that he did have a dash cam in his squad. Generally, he found it to be more of an asset than a liability. He is hopeful that in time officers will get to the point where they would rather have a camera than not.

A retired trooper thinks the camera is good for police. He believes if they don't want a camera on themselves then they are probably doing something they don't want the boss to see. He has faith that if their actions are done right, this will prove to the world that they did their jobs in a correct manner.

We need the help of our communities, the many eyes and ears who see and hear what is going on in our neighborhoods. In the small town where I grew up, if a car drove through our main street or down one of the residential streets, they were noticed. If the car was driven slowly around the houses, someone may very well have walked over to the car and asked who or what they were looking for and could they help. The eyes of a small town watch your every move.

Since the attack on 911 and subsequently the many acts of terror, we are often reminded that if you see something, say something. Busy lives can sometimes be overwhelmed with the tasks of the day. Tunnel vision sets in, and we are in our own world, unaware of what is going on around us. The police need our help; our neighborhoods need our care and concern.

Cameras may very well be a game changer in police work and community involvement. Shining a brighter light on police and the people in communities, I believe, simply must be a good idea.

An article January 4, 2018 in the *Star Tribune* by Libor Janny speaks of community involvement in North Minneapolis.

The main man in the story runs a flower shop. He is a part of a small but growing number of Minnesotans who live in neighborhoods with high crime rates. He listens to emergency dispatches intended for police, firefighters and other rescue workers. When his portable scanner comes to life, he quickly logs into Facebook and taps out a hasty message to his 5,500 True North followers. Then he races to the scene. He represents a new generation of scanner junkies.

An officer says such online networks give people a place to have honest conversations about inner-city crime, poverty, and police community relations.

Our neighbors need help and also need to be the helpers. Police can't be expected to fix everything in our lives. We need to be our own support and peacekeepers in our communities. Where I grew up, the residents of our little town took care of each other. The government programs were few, and most did not want to have to take handouts from the county. We knew the word *pride*. The Dictionary says Pride means a feeling or deep pleasure or satisfaction derived from one's own achievements. Some people seem to have lost that feeling.

215

In an article in the *Arizona Republic* Nov. 24, 2017, Megan Cassidy, writing about police assistants, wrote:

> *"Beginning next week, the first responder to a minor Phoenix burglary or fender bender may not be a police officer. There's a good chance it could instead be a police assistant — a civilian employee hired to help shoulder non-emergency service calls for their sworn counterparts".*

This, I believe, is a step in the right direction. We need everyone engaged to protect and enhance safety in our world.

> *"Facts are stubborn things; and whatever may be our wishes, our inclinations, or the dictates of our passions, they cannot alter the state of facts and evidence."*

> —*John Adams*

CHAPTER 27

WHAT A DIFFERENCE A DAY MAKES

For fourteen years we lived on a dead-end road. Our neighbors of course knew Mike was a trooper but we did live in almost anonymity on quiet 8th Ave. Mike and I purchased 250 feet of lakeshore property in 1989. It was nestled in a forest hidden location with access to three more lakes, and the Mississippi River. We knew we had bought lake property but it was hard to tell: we couldn't see the water for the woods. We started clearing it on July 4th 1989. Heavy Buckbrush needed to go first. It was thick and took strength to cut it and haul it to a brush pile. We learned quickly it was an arduous task, but we were young. Mike 45 and I 43. We had cleared away enough trees and brush for a wide path to the place where our home would eventually be when Mike's parents came for a visit. We were excited to show them our lot and talk over our plans. As we sat on stumps, his dad said, "If someone gave this to me for nothing, I wouldn't take it." He shook his head and said, "too much work." Mike was irritated but later realized his dad knew more than he did. Our days off from work were spent clearing the lot, and it took two years to get it ready to have our new home built.

That time was good for us. Hard physical work took off pounds and shaped our bodies. We were mean and lean. Except for smoking (Mike still enjoyed cigarettes; I had quit a few years prior), we were in great form. Some days we could hardly walk to the end of the road where our pickup was parked and crawl in because we were so exhausted.

Occasionally visitors would stop by to see how the lot was progressing. I loved it when somebody came to visit. It gave me a chance to catch my breath and sit down for a few minutes. What a difference a *visitor* makes!

One of those days is burned into my memory. Two deputies had stopped the previous afternoon. The next day they were back. As I saw them drive up, I was again grateful. *Good*, I thought, *this is another chance for me to take a breath.*

They were standing a distance away from me. Mike was standing with his back against a tree that he was just going to cut. The look on his face had changed to an expression I couldn't quite read. I wasn't sure what it was: sadness? shock? I didn't know what I was seeing, but he looked different. I then remembered that a dear friend of ours was in a Minneapolis hospital close to death. A retired deputy had battled leukemia for a long time and was soon to lose that fight. I assumed his death was the news Mike was getting.

They stood there quite a while, and I wondered why they didn't come and sit down and visit like they had the day before.

Soon the deputies drove away. Mike still had that look of shock on his face as he walked over to where I was sitting. I asked, "Is it ...?" "No," he said. "It's dad. He died this morning."

After I had asked the questions of how, when, where, I asked why he didn't come and sit down. He said he had to lean against the tree so his legs would hold him up.

Although we had taken a week's vacation leave and had toyed with the idea of going out west, we decided to stay home to work on our lake lot. Our daughter had called the Sheriff's Department, told them what happened, and they sent the deputies to tell us. They later talked of how difficult it had been to bring that news to us.

We hurried home and packed our bags. We would stay the week. Mike called Julie to tell her we were on our way. She and her family had gone to visit her grandpa and grandma for the weekend. We thanked God that they had been there. Mike's dad, just sixty-seven, had suffered a heart attack and died during the night.

As I was preparing to go to the funeral service, Mike's mom walked into the bedroom. Standing just inside the doorway, she said, "What if you didn't love me?" I stopped what I was doing and said, "But, I do love you." "I know," she replied, but I was just thinking, *what if you didn't?*" I walked over and hugged her. She and I were dear friends then and have been through all these years.

Many troopers attended the funeral, including the Chief of the Minnesota State Patrol. I can still picture a trooper stopping traffic and saluting us as Mike drove his mother's car into the cemetery. The salute by that trooper stays embedded in my mind. Little did I know that ten years later I would see that same salute from a trooper as our son John drove my car into the churchyard for Mike's burial. We stayed a week with Mike's mom after the funeral. We wrote thank-you notes and comforted each other.

What a difference _____, 1989, had made!

For the next many years Mike and I would come back to help his mom and his grandma living right next door, every couple of weeks. He would have them make a list of household things they wanted done. I was a good *gofer*, getting the tools he needed to complete whatever he was working on.

If their lists were long, he would ask them what was number one on the list. That way he could take care of the most pressing issues. He was kind to his mother and grandma.

Mike always had a sweetness in him when he dealt with his grandma. He and his mother were close but not afraid to tell each other what they thought. He trusted her, and her opinion meant a lot. For example, after he retired, he decided he should have a mustache and beard. I never liked facial hair on him and expressed my dislike to him about not shaving but to no avail.

While visiting his mom one weekend, I woke up on a Saturday morning, walked out to have my coffee, and saw clean-shaven Mike sitting at the table. I commented that he had shaved. He said that his mom didn't like it. His mom had told him to shave that dumb stuff off. Obviously, she had the clout.

My mother-in-law often talks about the first time we met. I was fifteen at the time, and we liked each other immediately. Sometimes she says that she still thinks of me as fifteen. Oh, if that were only true.

I could not have asked for a better mother-in-law. She is a perfect example: always supportive, never critical. She often told Mike how lucky he was to have me as a wife. I, of course, smiled and agreed. He rolled his eyes.

Mike's mother loved to travel. Her father had worked for the railroad, and she loved trains, traveling on them often with her mother to visit relatives in a town, which was not far down the track from their home.

After Mike's death, she and I would go by plane, train, or car for the next ten years. We flew to Washington, DC, for a tour in the spring of 1996. We each loved history and savored our trip.

She, Mike, and I had taken a train trip to Sandpoint ID after Mike retired in 1995 to see Mike's cousin and his wife. We continued to visit Mike's cousin and his wife for the next ten years. After Mike's death, She and I also traveled to Bozeman MT. to spend time with friends. David was from my hometown. He had lived with Mike's parents his last year of high school while his father was ill. He and my mother-in-law loved each other then and still do now.

Another day that made such a difference was December 24, 1984, the day my father died. He had just turned sixty-nine in November. We had arrived at my parents' home December 23rd to hear that my dad had gone into the hospital that morning with a heart attack. He was in intensive care. The doctor told us that if he lived 24 hours, then 36, then 48, he had a good chance of living through the crisis. I was worried, of course, but didn't think he would die.

As I write this, I can still see my mother's face when the phone call came from the hospital. He had lived about 36 hours at that time. She had a white dishtowel over her shoulder, and her face turned just as white. She had seen him in the morning, and he had told her, "Go home. The family is all there for Christmas. Be with them. I am fine." That afternoon he died.

That evening we sat in the living room with heavy hearts. The funeral director came. He did not come to plan a funeral. We would not plan a funeral on Christmas Eve. He came to cry with us.

He had been a dear friend of my parents since grade school and would eventually become my stepfather. My brother's birthday was the 28th; my sister's, the 23rd; and my daughter's, the 26th. We would *not* have a funeral on one of their birthdays.

There were many staying at my mother's house, and we moved quickly, getting ready for church. Even with the death of our father, we were not going to miss the Christmas Day service.

I looked out an upstairs window that Christmas morning. People were driving by in their cars, and folks were out shoveling and walking. I wanted the world to stop for just a minute to let me catch my breath, to mourn, but it was Christmas Day. A sad long night had given way to a bright, cold, sunny day. Life moves along and will leave you behind if you don't move along with it.

My dad loved Christmas. He enjoyed the decorations, Christmas Carols, and the gathering of family. So it was fitting that a Christmas tree should adorn the church the day of his funeral and that we sang familiar songs from over the years.

Many people said how sad it was to lose him at Christmas time. I don't know that we were particularly sad because of the time itself. Perhaps it was fortuitous. There were Christmas decorations not only in the church but also all around town. It was also the first time in many years that we had all been together at the same time during Christmas. We were all married and had trips to the in-laws to make also. So, it took some planning to get all seven of our families together at one time. Even as the years have gone by, I have not noticed that *the time* is any less joyful than it was before Dad's death.

We are an emotional family. Tears come to our eyes for the strangest things—Perhaps a sentimental song, a sentimental memory, a sad movie, or someone crying in front of us. The day of dad's funeral, we surprised ourselves. We were tough. It was perhaps because we wanted to be strong for each other but particularly for our mother who was just 65 at the time.

Mother had grown up when women's and men's roles were highly defined. She took care of the inside of the house; he provided food, clothing, and shelter. Although as I write this, I am reminded that he was perhaps the first father at least that I knew who could have had the title "Mr. Mom." When he was 39 my brother was born on May 26. 1955. He was nine years younger than me. I had been the baby in the family of four children prior to his arrival. On May 15, 1956 twins, a boy and a girl arrived. Dad turned 40. My dad washed clothes in the morning—we hung them on the line before going to school and took them off the line when we came home for lunch. That did change when our little school house across the alley from our house started to serve hot lunch. My dad helped in many ways with the babies. Actually, we all did and thought it was fun. Our family of six had grown to nine in a very short time.

December 27, 1984, was bitterly cold. A raw wind blew across the snow-covered cemetery, tears froze on my cheeks, and profound sorrow filled my heart. I learned these three life lessons with the death of my father:

1. I can feel deep sadness and be okay.
2. I can and will be happy again.
3. Life goes on.

Those we love don't go away, they walk beside us every day. Unseen, unheard, but always near; still loved, still missed and very dear.

—Anonymous

CHAPTER 28

WALK A MILE IN MY SHOES

What has happened to our society? People assume that anything they can't handle should be handed over to someone else, often the police. Growing up in a little town in Minnesota, we would occasionally see a county deputy drive through town. My dad's cousin was a deputy and his mother lived a block from us. He sometimes stopped to check on her as she was getting on in years. I can't remember anyone ever talking about calling the police or know anyone that did call the police. Family conflicts happened, but whatever went on was handled at home. There was excess drinking by some with a liquor store and pool hall in town. After the Saturday night free movie, children sometimes fell asleep in the back seat of the parents' car until they left the liquor store or pool hall. During the summer, a peek through a screen door gave a glimpse into that dark and smelly pool hall, although our mothers had told us not to look inside.

A call in the middle of the night at our house was not usual, but it occasionally happened. Someone was out of fuel, and my father delivered fuel and gas. We had two phones in our home. When my sister and I moved into the bedroom that had been my parents, we now had a phone in our room. On one particular occasion, the phone rang late at night with someone asking for my dad. My sister woke him, he picked up the phone, and I remember his saying he'd be right there. It wasn't until years later that he told us who was on the other line. A man had come home drunk and began busting what little furnishings they had. My father's presence, just standing in the doorway, calmed the man down, and he went to bed.

What has happened in our families that we are unable to handle most or, at the very least, much of what happens in our day-to-day life? Police are expected not only to *always* make the right decision but to make a life or death choice in a split second.

Everybody should have *the talk*. Parents and all of us as citizens of this country had better have the talk with ourselves and with our children. Every person, young or old, should know how to behave in the presence of law enforcement. That's because almost everyone, law enforcement personnel as well, will someday find themselves in the gaze of a suspicious police officer. When that situation comes about, no one wants any misunderstandings. All will want to *COMPLY*.

What does that mean? Webster's Dictionary gives this definition: "to act in accordance with a request, order, etc." A person will want the officer to have absolutely no reason to think he or she is a threat to his or her safety. Officers are not only trained but *authorized* to use force to get compliance, and also to use deadly force when confronted by what the officer views as a deadly threat. Do you, the person reading this, understand what the word *view* means in this instance? It of course means *sees* as a threat, but it can also mean *thinks* is a threat, *understands* as a threat, or *takes* as a threat.

If the world were perfect, Philando Castile would have kept his hands on the steering wheel and stopped moving the precise moment he heard the policeman say the word "Don't."

Expert witness Emanuel Kapelsohn, in the trial of Jeronimo Yanez, said, "Perfection is not a reasonable goal to achieve." He stated, "The shooting was partly the result of Castile's mistakes, or the fault of circumstances. Instead of a young man on his way home from the grocery store and a young officer going back to his home, we have lived a nearly year-long tragedy. Jurors have had their work cut out for them."

The judge who presided over the case against the police officer who shot Philando Castile has written a letter of support to the jurors who acquitted Castile, saying there was "a failure to understand what you were asked to "do" by the public and media outlets."

The June 16 decision to acquit Saint Anthony, Minnesota, Police Officer Jeronimo Yanez was met with widespread criticism after dash cam footage showed him shooting at 32-year-old Castile seven times in quick succession during a routine traffic stop. Castile was hit five times, according to court records.

Castile had told 29-year-old Yanez that he had a legal firearm in his possession, and Yanez told him not to reach for the gun. Castile said he was not pulling the gun out, but seconds later, Yanez shot Castile while his girlfriend and her 4-year-old daughter watched in horror. Castile's girlfriend, Diamond Reynolds, broadcast the aftermath of the July 2016 shooting via Facebook Live.

In his letter to the jurors on Wednesday, July 5, 2017, published in many newspapers and read on television stations, Ramsey County District Judge William H. Leary III said, "The criticism of the jury's decision, of which I am aware, has focused primarily on a reaction to the squad-cam video and on consideration of issues you as jurors were never asked to address. You were simply asked to determine, beyond a reasonable doubt, whether a crime had been committed."

According to one of the jurors who found Yanez not guilty, even the Black members said Yanez was legally justified in his decision to use a lethal weapon against Castile.

Toxicology reports found THC in Castile's system at the time of his death. The defense maintains he was high during the traffic stop and therefore *culpably negligent* in his death. According to a story on KTSP-TV, the judge defined *culpable negligence* in his jury instructions as "intentional conduct that the defendant may not have intended to be harmful, but that an ordinary and reasonably prudent person would recognize as involving a strong probability of injury to others," adding the concept includes gross negligence coupled with an element of recklessness.

The Legal Defense Fund stepped up to pay for the defense of Geronimo Yanez. I have added this to my story with their permission.

Legal Defense Fund
By Bill Space, Legal Administrator

The MPPOA LDF Defense of St. Anthony Officer Jeronimo Yanez.
By Paul Engh, Esq.

On July 2, 2016, St. Anthony Officer Yanez was dispatched to investigate an armed robbery of a convenience store. In broad daylight, two African-American males walked up to the counter, one in front, the other from the rear, directed the clerk to the floor, pointed pistols at his head, and grabbed the available cash and a carton of cigarettes. One of the robbers was thin, had a beard, shoulder length dreads, and wore glasses. He leaned over the counter in full view of the in-store camera.

Officer Yanez studied the video of the robbery. Still photographs of the suspects were posted at the St. Anthony Police station.

Four days later and within a stone's throw of the convenience store, Officer Yanez observed an African-American male driving eastbound on Larpenteur Avenue, who fit the description of the robber, the dreads, the thin build, the glasses. The driver exchanged a furtive glance while passing, leaning back into a reclined driver's seat. Officer Yanez followed to find out who this individual was, and if he had a connection with the robbery. As he drew closer, Officer Yanez observed a taillight out. Mr. Philando Castile's car was thus stopped for legitimate reason.

What happened next has been widely reported. The dash cam video will be shown over and over again in your training for years to come.

What can't be seen, though, and what the trial was ultimately about, was the gun in Mr. Castile's hand. Officer Yanez ordered Mr. Castile "don't reach for it." Then he repeated, "don't take it out." And again," don't take it out." He wasn't shouting about a wallet or any other benign object.

Rather than obey the clear and shouted commands, Mr. Castile stared straight ahead, and continued to grip his gun. Officer Yanez Wood testified that without any doubt he saw Mr. Castile's right hand around the handle of the dark colored pistol. A pistol that was recovered from Mr. Castile's right front pocket, just where Officer Yanez said it was.

Had the case been submitted to a grand jury, our counsel was convinced a "no bill" would have been the result. The Ramsey County Attorney, as an elected official under immense public pressure, took a different course.

In anticipation of charges, two veteran assistant county attorneys from that office were assigned. An Assistant United States Attorney was called in to be the lead litigator in this purely state court action. This was now, in many ways, a case run by the US Department of Justice, venued locally.

When manslaughter and intentional discharge of a firearm charges were filed, the MPPOA Legal Defense Fund (LDF) assigned seasoned lawyers Tom Kelly and Earl Gray to defend Officer Yanez. I was also assigned to the defense team. The LDF directed the team to litigate with ferocity and gave them leeway to do everything that they thought appropriate. The LDF did not second-guess any decisions made nor the legal trial strategy employed. Every motion counsel thought necessary was filed.

For example, after the defense change of venue motion was denied, the LDF funded an interlocutory appeal to the Minnesota Court of Appeals and authorized that a petition for review be filed with the Supreme Court. No stone was left unturned.

A criminal investigator with over thirty-years of experience was retained. Dozens of witnesses were interviewed, including the officers at the scene, and Mr. Castile's firearms trainer, who testified that the permit holder's response to a police inquiry must feature hands visible, as opposed to what Mr. Castile chose to do.

Three expert witnesses were also secured. A former BCA toxicologist evaluated Mr. Castile's THC levels in his blood and testified that he was stoned on marijuana that evening.

Two more experts were hired to evaluate Officer Yanez's use of force within the meaning of Minnesota Stat. 609. 066 – Authorized Use of Deadly Force by a Peace Officer. Both experts concluded that Officer Yanez's actions were reasonable in light of the evident danger he faced and Mr. Castile's refusal to remove his hand from the pistol. The resulting shots, five of the seven which struck Mr. Castile's chest and left arm, were consistent with the officer's training.

At the defense's request, the jury was instructed as to the classic United States Supreme Court's Graham v. Connor language. The reasonableness of Officer Yanez's contact was to be judged from what he saw, and not with the 20/20 vision of hindsight. How Officer Yanez was forced to make split-second judgments in circumstances that are tense, uncertain, and rapidly evolving.

The trial – from jury selection to verdict – lasted three weeks

The well-publicized reaction condemning the acquittal is dismaying. Some, including those who did not attend the trial and even those who did, have suggested the jury system is flawed and racist. Yet two of the jurors were African-American. Those same critics never raised any objection to the fact that there were no jurors of Hispanic background seated. The case was fairly and carefully tried by a seasoned jurist. The LDF trial team anticipated the verdict.

Officer Yanez's case was historic, featuring the first police officer in Minnesota to be charged with manslaughter. If there is a sobering lesson to be learned from this litigation, it is that serious charges can be lodged against the innocent.

We hope no other police officer will face what Officer Yanez did. Still, Ramsey County's shift and prosecutorial method – favoring a complaint and discounting the importance of the grand jury – may be employed again with similar arbitrary results. But what will not change is this: When a member of the MPPOA LDF is charged with an alleged crime committed in and during the course of duty, the legal defense fund will be there for you, too.

Officer Yanez told the jury the cost of his defense was far beyond what he could have ever paid. It was worth every penny for the MPPOA and you, it's members.

The Legal Defense Fund is available 24 hours a day through its toll-free hotline number 1 – 855 – 533 – 6466. If you or one of your fellow officers is involved in a critical incident, criminal proceeding, civil proceeding, P.O.S.T Board matter, or are aware of a Case of General Importance, call 1 – 855 – 533 – 6466 to speak with the Legal Defense Fund about the incident. The Legal Defense Fund is here to serve you.

The shooting and the subsequent trial filled the newspapers and television stations. I asked a Minneapolis police Sergeant about the Castile shooting. This was his response:

As a police officer, he could easily put himself in the position of Officer Jeronimo Yanez. Having been in similar situations, he could understand the stress and heightened vigilance that Officer Yanez was feeling as he was conducting that traffic stop. He could also understand where a citizen who has never been in that situation could have a different perspective.

From what he knows about the Castile shooting, Officer Yanez believed that he was pulling over a possible robbery suspect where a gun had been involved. Prior to the start of his shift, Officer Yanez had been made aware of a robbery suspect and was given a photo of the suspect. The robbery suspect was a black male, facial hair, long braided hair and wearing glasses with gold rims. This description also closely matched the description of Castile. The Minneapolis officer had seen the photo of the robbery suspect and it looked extremely similar to a photo of Castile and he knew that he, too, would have certainly stopped Castile given the same information.

He could understand where Officer Yanez, driving past in his vehicle, may have observed Castile, who closely matched the description of the robbery suspect, would have wanted to investigate further. Shy of any more concrete suspicion or probable cause, not wanting to potentially violate Castile's civil rights by conducting a traffic stop at gunpoint and risking a potential lawsuit if Castile was not the robbery suspect, Officer Yanez conducted a traffic stop to investigate further. Yanez informed Castile that the reason for the traffic stop was actually an equipment violation so as not to alert Castile in the event that he was the actual robbery suspect.

He appreciated why Officer Yanez may have approached Castile's vehicle with a heightened alert, believing he may be pulling over a potential armed robbery suspect.

He also recognized why Officer Yanez became even more suspicious when he learned that Castile was in possession of a gun, furthering the thought that Castile may in fact be the armed robbery suspect.

He could realize why Officer Yanez became even more apprehensive when Castile began to reach into his shirt or jacket, even if it was to grab his ID, when ordered several times not to do so. Knowing that it only takes a second for someone to produce a handgun and shoot, he could understand where Officer Yanez felt that he was faced with a split-second, life-or-death decision. Police officers face these decisions as part of their job, where an average citizen might never be faced with one in a lifetime.

This event was incredibly unfortunate but he believes that Officer Yanez was placed in a very difficult position and was forced to make a very difficult split-second decision.

The Minneapolis Sargent feel strongly that Castile would be alive today if two things happened during that traffic stop.

1. Castile had not smoked marijuana and carried a handgun.
2. Castile had listened to Officer Yanez when he was ordered several times not to reach into his jacket. He believes Castile's judgment was clouded because he was high on marijuana.

Jon Tevlin writes in *The Star and Tribune* Sunday, June 11, 2017:

> *"Numbers that are mind boggling: 265,728—That's how many Minnesotans have a permit to carry a gun, a statistic that must be considered by officers, along with those who are carrying illegally, when they make a traffic stop."*

> *"Gray haired women on their way to the hair salon, older men on their way to the barber shop, and all most likely in a hurry better think about their own reactions to being pulled over or questioned in any way. Every stop, every answer to a call, has the possibility for a deadly encounter. A knock on a door can bring a shotgun blast."*

The thought of an older person pulling out a gun and killing someone isn't usually in our thinking; however, it happens. We expect better behavior from the old and riskier behavior from the young. The tattooed young man or woman is more likely to be looked at with suspicion than the mother with small children in the car, searching through her purse for her license. We may assume the usual; however, that can no longer be trusted. We have seen that in killings and in terrorist attacks.

Police train for the unusual. They encounter people at their worst. Motorists involved in a crash, even if normally pleasant and gentle, become different people when they are injured. Even if not injured, the sight of their beloved vehicle smashed to smithereens can enrage them. Whoever attacked their car, truck, or van is instantly their enemy.

A New York retired policeman recalled his first experience with *Shoot Don't Shoot* training. It was new and his department created hundreds of video scenarios of routine police situations. Standing alone on the indoor firing line, they started the video with a brief radio call that set the stage for what he was walking into. The instructions were to react as you would on the street. At first he thought it seemed phony, but about 10 seconds in, it became real because the situation became real, and they had to draw, issue verbal commands, and shoot or not shoot as they felt appropriate for the situation.

A traffic stop was one scenario that he went through. The driver came out shooting. He shot him and started to relax, not seeing anyone else in the car. All of a sudden four guys popped up, and the trunk of the car even popped up and the men poured out shooting. The lesson was, don't let your guard down!

A local TV reporter had come to go through training the same day. He started out cool and calm, but when he had gone through a few scenarios, he was wet with sweat from the waist up.

Police are trained to expect the unexpected...the ordinary person who will in a second become a murderer, the young woman searching for her license who pulls out a gun. They train for what would have been called far-fetched not too many years ago. It's training for the unexpected, the unthinkable in years past. This leaves law enforcement with these thoughts every second of their working hours...be cautious on every call...don't trust stereotypes. Someone who looks like a threat may be their assistant in an altercation, and a seemingly harmless person could be the one who kills them.

Keep these words of wisdom in mind when dealing with law enforcement. Do what you are told. Keep your hands where they can see them. Don't make sudden movements. Try to see yourself through their suspicious watchful eyes.

Are officers perfect? Of course, not. They are human beings. They make mistakes, like all of us, in our jobs, and our personal life. The police will never be perfect, but there are more good ones than bad. As in every occupation there are good and bad but mostly just average people, ordinary individuals.

Experience is the hardest kind of teacher. It gives you the test first and the lesson afterwards.

–Oscar Wilde

CHAPTER 29

SCHOOL DAYS, SCHOOL DAYS, DEAR OLD GOLDEN RULE DAYS

When we were young we looked forward to summer vacation…No more homework, no more books, no more teacher's dirty looks. If you got into trouble in school and your parents found out, you were in much bigger trouble.

Oh, how things have changed. If we weren't playing on the playground, we might be at the swimming pool. It was above ground and a beauty to behold. Also perched high above us in white chairs suspended on what resembled stilts pretty high school girls and handsome boys sat poised and ready to save us from drowning.

We walked through shallow disinfectant water that supposedly kept us from getting athlete's foot or any other fungus that tried to invade our toes. Entering the pool area, we either jumped right in or walked gingerly up the stairs where a magnificent high metal slide and or equally terrifying diving board stood ready for the next daredevil. Misbehavior was almost nonexistent. Running or even walking fast was met with a short whistle and a pointing finger. Dunking anyone was an automatic sit on the sidelines.

Our teachers as well as law enforcement have had to experience a change in the behavior of their students and of their parents. I met a man in our Arizona park last winter who had been a teacher for 30 years. Have his students changed over those years? No, his students have remained the same, but the parenting has changed.

There was no doubt that the teachers I had in school had the upper hand. Strict verbal discipline was usually adequate, but if physical discipline was needed, so be it.

In the hot lunch line, I remember a teacher grabbing a boy by the front of his shirt, lifting the student off the floor and placing him not so gently against the wall for disrupting the lunch line. Women teachers were less apt to have to be physical but that didn't mean they couldn't be. Of course, we were still kids. We giggled, whispered in class, and passed notes to our friends—minor infractions to be sure.

At one point, seeing somebody get hurt, I myself said, "Oh, God!" in front of my fourth grade teacher. That language kept me in the classroom for an entire week during recess. Neither the teacher nor my mother tolerated taking the name of the Lord in vain.

At a class reunion, I asked a former teacher if he had ever felt frightened by a student. He said that he himself had not, but he knew of other teachers who had. He also said that in the climate of the 80s, the other students looked up to children who threatened their teachers and were disruptive. When I was in high school, whether we liked our teachers or not, we would have never allowed a student to hurt them.

When I asked a principal of a high school if he was every afraid for his safety, no he has not been. However, he has been concerned for the safety of some of his teachers. He went on to say that the police have been called to the school several times and that he is grateful for their presence and their handling of the situation. The police have even been called to the elementary schools in our small towns.

We had eight grades in our school and three schoolrooms. First and second grades were together; third, fourth, and fifth grades were in another; and, when we had reached the sixth grade, we felt so grown up because we could walk up the stairs where sixth, seventh, and eighth grades were in the third schoolroom. The library and the hot-lunch room were also upstairs. When we were in eighth grade, we could even work at the library.

We weren't by any means perfect. Many carried knives to cut into stolen water melons. I think one woman planted them in her garden just for us to take in the dark of night and enjoy. We also swiped green apples from people who we knew would be angry about it.

My grandmother had an apple tree with the best apples in town. Although we could have as many as we wanted, we chose to take the apples from her neighbor because she made a fuss about it. It's not that we never misbehaved. The difference between then and, in too many instances, now is that we had discipline. Our parents didn't presume to be our *friends.* They were our *parents;* and if you liked them, that was fine; but if you didn't, that was okay, too. But we knew that *they* were in charge.

In Minnesota, flexible seating in classrooms is becoming a trend. It was implemented more than 10 years ago in the fifth-grade classroom in the Rochester school district. The Mayo Clinic study showed students who moved around more during the day had increased health and educational benefits.

Teachers have learned that students have different learning styles. Perhaps classrooms were more orderly, and teachers thought it was easier to control students who were sitting at desks.

Teachers feared disorder when they began to remove desks and tables and chairs from the classrooms, however many I talked to said they liked it. Students can now stand at a tall table; they can sit at a regular height table with a chair or even an exercise ball. Some students may sit on the floor on a yoga mat or a cushion and use a lap desk or clipboard. They have choices. There is less conflict because they are not all sitting around a table. Even noise levels are lower. Students can fidget if they like.

A teacher I spoke to said that what teachers talk about is that they are unable to prepare students for what lies on the other end of pomp and circumstance—the real world, that is.

He pointed to policies that are designed more to ensure that students pass than to prepare for life after high school—policies that allow students to retake tests over and over until they get a grade they like, that allows them to turn in work weeks late and get full credit.

Lest we leave the total blame on bureaucrats, he will tell me that parents are part of the problem. He complains that there are a lot of parents who are not engaged. If anything, he would be trying to find a way to force parents to be engaged in their children's school work.

Give him back his classroom, let teachers set the bar for students. He believes that when teachers were forced to take the element of failure out, that is not getting kids ready for college. He worries that teachers are producing students who are not ready to walk off into real life.

I sat across from a retired teacher during dinner one evening. I had met her briefly before, but that evening we spent time visiting. She said that in her last years of teaching, she had to do more mothering than teaching. She spoke of the changes she has seen—the lack of parental involvement in the small town where she had taught for years. She longed for the days when she first started where both the mother and the father parented their children.

Schools have also seen the rise in poor sportsmanship in high school athletics. February 9, 2018 the *Arizona Republic* reports that the Apache

Junction's gymnasium had to be evacuated during a girls' basketball game in January. After the winning team pulled out a close win the girls were escorted by Apache Junction security to their bus. He also reported in December after a Glendale - Deer Valley's boys basketball game that a bottle was thrown into the crowd and a verbal altercation occurred. Nobody was injured but police had to break up the crowd.

I was a cheerleader at a high school in Minnesota. We did not ever have to call the police to quiet spectators or athletes. Obviously, we are now seeing the good, the bad, and the ugly exhibited in sports. The newspaper article in the *Arizona Republic* goes on to say that since the 2017 – school year began there have been more than 800 athlete ejections in all of the fall and winter sports. Soccer has nearly half of those ejections and there have also been nearly 50 coach ejections for all sports. Referees no longer are part of the sport's traditional postgame handshake line because they need protection from the athletes, players, and sometimes the parents who have crossed the line of abuse.

Our schools are no longer a safe place to be. School shootings have become too commonplace within today's society. These killings are being perpetrated by students themselves.

Parents I spoke to say that we need to deal with and recognize that we have huge problems within a portion of our youth. Are they evil? Are they maniacs?

What has happened to our youth? Mental illness is a plague on some of our young people. Our main goal needs to be the protection of our students, security at the schools. We have tight security all over, in the courthouse, you can't board an aircraft without a TSA inspection and you can't even attend a baseball game without a security check. It's insane to continue to leave our students unprotected at school... any school.

Children need discipline. They need two parents. I realize that some students are depressed and that they feel bullied and that they feel overwhelmed. Why did we feel safe at school? Because our teachers were in charge. We respected them and they disciplined as they saw fit.

Teachers, along with police, are also being pressed into being the role model, parent, grandparent, counselor, mediator, as well as educator. Teachers I spoke to have advice for parents: Teach your children to be respectful in their behavior whether it is in school or to those in authority. You have done them a great disservice if you fail to do so. You have damaged their chance to be productive in life and a contributing member of society.

> *"Teach the children so it will not be necessary to teach the adults."*
>
> —Abraham Lincoln

CHAPTER 30

LOVE BY THE TELEPHONE

New technology may find those with addictive behavior tendencies fighting a new battle with the swell in popularity of social media.

People are becoming increasingly dependent on their cell phones. Last summer, studies by Informate Mobile Intelligence showed Americans check social media sites 17 times a day and spend 4.7 hour per day on their smart phones.

It's not just the young who get caught up on social media. Some older users actually get defensive if you mention how much time they spend on their phones. Life goes by quickly when you're looking at Facebook.

May 31, 2019 *The Washington Post* reports that four out of five teenagers with mobile devices keep them in their room overnight and nearly a third of them bring them into their bed while sleeping. Many reported using their phones moments before bedtime, almost immediately upon rising and at least occasionally during the night.

There's another problem that has arisen writes Isaac Stanley-Becker of *The Washington Post* June 25, 2019. The headlines say "Horns are growing on young people's skulls." It continues, "Mobile technology has transformed the way we live-how we read, work, communicate, shop and date. But we already know this."

"What we have not yet grasped is the way the tiny machines in front of us are remolding our skeletons, possibly altering not just the behaviors we exhibit but the bodies we inhabit. New research suggests that young people are developing horn-like spikes at the back of their skulls-bone spurs caused by the tilt of the head, which shifts the weight from the muscles at the back of the head, causing bone growth in the connecting tendons and ligaments."

Four people sitting in a restaurant, intending to eat dinner, hardly have time to look at the menu or order. They're all busy on their phones. Especially annoying is when sitting someplace and someone not far away is talking loudly on his or her phone. There are lots of articles written about cell phone use. There is even no shortage of apps to save us from addiction to apps.

The one I found the most intriguing, or might I say foolish, is an app called the Freedom app. You set a timer, put your phone face down and don't touch it until the time is up. If you can make it, you get to plant and grow a tree in a virtual world. However, if you blow it, your virtual tree dies.

An article written by Dr. Mehmet Oz and Dr. Michael Roizen goes on to say that it looks like an increase in the screen time spent on new media—Facebook, Twitter, Pinterest, Tumblr, and even Google, Yahoo and texting—is associated with an increase in teen self-harm and suicide attempts.

We often hear therapists on one television show or another talk of the increase in teen suicide. Teens are particularly vulnerable to criticism by their peers, and bullying is rampant on social media. There seems to be little to be done about it by the person being victimized. Facebook and Twitter have given voice to anyone who has any number of electronic sources to communicate. Total strangers "pile on" with an array of criticism and advice.

A study reported by npr.org March 6, 2017 says "users of Snapchat, Facebook, twitter and Instagram all lead to increased feelings of depression, anxiety, poor body image and loneliness. Teens continue to keep themselves occupied in the hours after school. When they're not doing their homework, they are online and, on their phones, texting, sharing, and scrolling."

Before the impact of the Internet, teens were more likely to be chatting on the phone one on one or in person and maybe hanging out at the mall. They were experimenting, trying out their skills, and personally interacting.

Young people enjoyed small real-time interactions. Children today are missing out. Teens are learning their communication today while looking at a screen, not another person. A recent survey conducted by health insurer Cigna says that many Americans are considered lonely.

"Young adults born between the mid-1990s and the early 2000s had among the highest loneliness scores. People are feeling disconnected, isolated and alienated," said Jennifer Ally Kern, a St. Louis Park-based executive coach and leadership consultant. She goes on to say, "I can't tell you how much I hear people say they are lonely."

Isolation is another result of all that screen time. We didn't know the current meaning of the word *isolation* when growing up. Granted, that was a long time ago for me, but I can't think of a youngster in town who felt *isolated*.

Country kids did not have the luxury of playing school games and being a part of after school or summer fun because there was no way to get into town. However, their parents visited their country neighbors regularly, and there were usually children around to play with, to interact with, although interact was not a word I ever heard to describe being together.

Growing up, no child that I knew wanted to stay indoors. We played in groups of at least two or three but most often with eight or ten so we would have a ball team or a group of several to play a certain game. We didn't come home until we had to.

Our dinner was at 12:00, supper at 6:00, and when the siren blew at 9:00, we were to start for home immediately. If we were at the skating rink or sliding on Champion Hill, it took a while. I can't think of one person who did not participate in outside activities when possible.

Is your teen struggling with thoughts of suicide? That was the question asked in an article in the *Arizona Central* weekend newspaper on April 7, 2018 written by Nikki Kontz. *"Parents, take heed of the warning signs your teen may be in trouble if they are talking about death, wanting to die, or feelings of falling apart."*

"Depression knows no age, social connection, or financial status. Among the factors were social isolation, lack of mental-health treatment, and drug and alcohol abuse. Most disturbing is the fact that over half of the people who died by suicide had no known evidence of mental illness but fell apart after things like a break-up, using drugs, or money worries."

According to the *New York Times,* it's hard to know whether to laugh or cry over the demand by some U.S. college students for *trigger warnings* to alert them that something they are about to see or read in one of their classes might traumatize them.

"All Cap letters frighten college students," writes Dave Basner Nov. 20, 2018, in the Express C UK.

The memo says: "Generally, avoid using capital letters for emphasis and 'the overuse of do, and, especially, DON'T."

According to the Center for Collegiate Mental Health at Penn State, "Anxiety and depression, in that order, are now the most common mental health diagnoses among college students."

So, what's going on? Is life really that bad for these students? Are these the people who are someday going to stand "on guard" for the rest of us? Are they going to protect us? Will they someday be our police force?

Teens live in the *fake world* of social media. They see posts of pictures of an unrealistic life and believe it to be real. It is much like the young woman or teens looking at magazines. They see touched-up photos of celebrities they envy and adore, believing they look like that every minute of every day. They don't realize the gorgeous people we see in a magazine, on TV, or in a movie are just like us when we crawl out of bed in the morning. Photoshopped, embellished, and modified, they suddenly look better than we ever could. Viewers begin to feel like they are the only one struggling while everyone is doing "awesome." Sadly, today's kids live their lives comparing themselves to the others. We must remind them that social media is only the tip of the iceberg, hiding the reality of most users' lives.

Teachers I have talked with are afraid they've not taught students how to evaluate mistakes or failures. Meeta Kumar, who has been counseling at Penn for 16 years, has noticed this change. *"Getting a B can cause some students to fall apart,"* she said. *"What you and I would call disappointments in life, to them feel like big failures. We've unwittingly conditioned them to think that failure is something to avoid at all costs. Unfortunately, this has cost them greatly."*

I've talked to many people, not only my age but also my children, about coping skills. How did we get them? How are they taught? I don't know, but I believe I have them. Perhaps the beginning of coping skills came when my mother, if I were feeling sorry for myself (maybe my plans didn't work out, or I couldn't go somewhere), would simply remind me to buck up. Our dad would remind us that life is not fair. I believe I taught that skill to my children. However, I do think there are many young people today who don't have them. There's not a class to go to called "Coping Skills." Schoolteachers and also law enforcement are concerned that young people of today are not being prepared for and ready for real life.

The young today seems to think they have more friends—that social media creates those friendships. They have hundreds of friends on the Internet but no real friends that come to their homes, sit with them and do homework, or meet them at the local fast food place where they laugh and talk face to face. They are lonely, and that breeds depression.

"As a species we are very highly attuned to reading social cues," says Dr. Catherine Steiner-Adair, a clinical psychologist and author of "The Big Disconnect. *"There is no question kids are missing out on very critical social skills."*

We didn't even realize that we were learning how to make friends growing up in our little town. We were also learning how to maintain a friendship. We did not agree with everyone but as I write this, I believe we were tolerant of people. As children picked their teams for certain games, some were fast, strong, and great at the sport. Others—not so good, not so great, but everyone was included, no one was left out. I can remember playing kickball with the big kids, and although I wasn't very good at it, everyone still clapped and yelled out encouragement.

There were people with special needs in our town. I think of one boy who was about my age. He could not speak, walk, or feed himself; but he smiled and made sounds whenever we walked into his home. His mom let us take him out in a little red wagon. His arms and his legs hung out, and we hauled him all over town. Everyone was kind to him. Although he was different, we didn't treat him much differently, although we may have been a little more careful with him as we pulled him down gravel roads or across the railroad tracks. He was our friend. He was one of us.

> *"It's never too late to get back on your feet. Though we won't live forever make sure you accomplish what you were put here for."*

—Abigail Adams

CHAPTER 31

EVERY FACE TELLS A STORY

What do you look for when you stop a vehicle?"

Why am I stopping the person? That's the first question an officer has. That dictates the initial plan. He/she looks at the car, truck, or SUV, the license, make, color. Is there anybody in the back? The officer is carefully watching. Are they moving around, hiding something? If there's no one in the back, he/she keeps their eyes looking at the front seat. What are they doing?

They used to walk up to the driver's side They no longer do that at every stop. Now they exit the squad and often walk up to the passenger side. It puts the officer farther away from the driver and also farther away from highway traffic.

Trooper Troy Christianson answers questions in his "Ask a Trooper Column."

Q: Dear Trooper Troy:

When troopers pull over a vehicle, why do they approach it on that traffic side rather than the passenger window? I have observed some other law enforcement agencies approach from the passenger side and thought it made sense from a safety perspective.

A: Trooper Troy says:

Officers are trained in both approaches, and both have their advantages. The side the officer chooses during a traffic stop generally comes down to one important element – safety.

As a Minnesota State Trooper, most of my traffic stops occur on the freeway or on state highways, where high speeds from passing vehicles is a real safety concern.

Passenger side approaches have proven safer for the officer if the vehicle stopped is struck by a passing vehicle. Other benefits to this approach include a greater view of the vehicle's interior in the driver's area of reach, as most people are right-handed. It also gives the officer a larger area of escape if the officer needs to retreat in an emergency.

The advantages an officer has from a driver – side approach includes the ability to detect/smell if the driver is under the influence of alcohol and because it is easier to communicate with the driver.

On most of my traffic stops, I approach on the passenger side because I feel safer from traffic. A few years ago, on a traffic stop, an approaching vehicles passenger – side mirror grazed me while I was on the driver side of the stopped vehicle on I- 35.

In training the trooper is told to have already decided what he's going to do once he stops the car. Is he giving a ticket? a warning? That's good in theory several told me but even though they have decided what they're going to do after they talk to the person, after they've asked more questions, it's not unusual for them to change their minds. It's attitude, the officers tell me. A lot depends on their attitude.

When he approaches a vehicle this trooper/supervisor, knew he must be aware of who is in the vehicle, front and back seats, and if they look like they are uncomfortable. They might be hiding something or ready to open their door and try to hit him. He continues saying he would guess that more than 95% of the people that get stopped are deep down nice persons. He does stress to those that are breaking in with him, that the motorists they stop have not done anything against the trooper. That motorist broke the law against the peace and dignity of the State of Minnesota only. If they did not listen to his message then they were not happy in their career.

Instincts, their training, experiences that they have on the road is what makes their decision and also what will keep them safe. They have a sixth sense about people, about danger. Some feel they had it from the time they were young. Others believe it came with experience.

"When and how they acquired it doesn't seem to matter—as long as they have it. It's in their eyes. You can see it in their eyes." On average, says UCLA research, May 24, 2017 written by Travis Brad Berry *on inc. com/travis,* we hold eye contact for seven to ten seconds. We do it for a little longer when we're listening than when we're talking. If you're talking with someone whose stare is making you squirm—especially if they are motionless and unblinking—something is up and they might be lying."

I'm reminded of Clint Eastwood words in the movie, *The Outlaw Josie Wales.* "How did you know which one was goin' to shoot first?" asks his sidekick. "Well, that one in the center: he had a flap holster and he was in no 'itchin' hurry," says Josie. "And the one second from the left: he had scared eyes; he wasn't gonna do nothin. But that one on the far left: he had crazy eyes. Figured him to make the first move."

Every face tells a story. Body language tells an officer what's going on even when the person he or she encounters says nothing. Anything that gives law enforcement officers an edge can help keep them safe.

"UCLA research showed that only 7 percent of communication is based on the actual words we say. As for the rest, 38 percent comes from tone of voice and the remaining 55 percent comes from body language."

An officer knows words and body language better match. Otherwise, get ready for trouble.

A deputy patrols an area close to 400 miles. He's often in a rural setting. If he's approaching someone in the woods, generally he is assuming this person is a hunter. If possible, he partners up with another officer before approaching someone in the woods. Hunters carry guns and knives. He makes it obvious that he is a law enforcement officer. That may come in the form of announcing his presence, wearing a blaze orange vest, and keeping his handheld very loud. He is not a deer! First and foremost, he looks for a gun. Just as important, he watches the hands. Also, he makes sure his dispatcher knows exactly where he is.

He's always mindful that he never knows who he is about to make contact with. It may be a suspicious person or a traffic stop. The policeman I'm interviewing goes on to say that he realizes that the person he is making contact with may very well possess a weapon and may be intent on hurting him.

His main concern with any interaction is being able to see the person's hands. His challenge with every interaction is keeping a vigilant mindset while still maintaining an outward professional appearance and attitude. Constantly reminded that there is no such thing as a routine traffic stop, he is also aware that it's easy to become complacent and let your guard down. He reminds himself that conducting a traffic stop is one of the most dangerous parts of the job.

An officer doesn't know who he is pulling over and is always at a great tactical disadvantage when conducting that stop. Obtaining as much information about the vehicle, the driver and the occupants before making that stop is always important. He runs the license plate to make sure the vehicle is not stolen or wanted for a crime and also to obtain the identity of the potential driver to ensure that there are no active warrants or suspended or revoked driver's license.

He is always aware of the surroundings. It has become second nature to him to be alert and to survey his surroundings. He looks for potential hazards or suspicious activity, suspicious people. Conducting traffic stops on the roadway with busy traffic is the most dangerous part of the job. When the time and situations permit, he takes great care in picking and choosing a safe location to conduct the traffic stop. He works in a large city and the vast majority of his traffic stops are conducted on busy and often congested streets.

They entered into this profession to help people, that's what they do. The sheriff has a softness in his voice as he talks about his chosen profession. He tells me they are here to serve the public. He knows the public doesn't always like law officers, but the majority knows what he knows—we need laws and we need them.

Expected to have the ability to talk a person out of jumping off a high building, to have a sixth sense of who is lying or telling the truth and what their behavior might be, these men and women are expected to make a decision to end a person's life or die themselves in less than a split second. That decision had better be right. If not, they may lose their own lives or take someone else's. They must have the ability to show empathy, sympathy, incredible self-control, and humor. The officers I spoke to have also seen the smiles, felt that pat on the back, heard the cry of a baby born in a car, the handshake and thanks from helping a person in need.

Mike and I went on our summer vacation in our new 1988 Chevy step side. The pickup box was full of camping equipment. It was a smaller truck than we were used to but Mike was a proficient packer. One of the places we wanted to go was a secluded campground. We drove 50 miles on a gravel road to get there. He had maps of the area and loved to explore.

We left our tent and some camping gear at our campsite but still had many things in the back of our little truck when we started exploring the area. As we rolled down a dusty dirt road with heavy woods on either side, we saw two men standing in the middle of the road. They were dressed in camouflage and looked scary to me.

Mike stopped and rolled the window down. The men said they had been dropped off by an Adventure Expedition and that things had gone wrong from the beginning. They talked of being dropped off in a heavily wooded, secluded area, crossing a swollen creek, everything getting wet, including their matches, and then being lost. One man said his feet were bleeding, and he could feel the blood swishing in his new boots. They begged us to bring them to a resort that they hoped was not too many miles away.

Mike told them we were going to explore the end of this road and would be back. I had hoped at that point that we would not be back and would just keep on driving. However, I soon found out that we were heading down a dead-end road. Now I was really nervous. I was scared and didn't trust them.

"We can't take them with us," I said. "What if they slit our throats and steal our money?" I can still see the look on Mike's face as he turned to me and said, "What if they just slit our throats and don't take our money?" It was a flippant answer and I was irritated mostly because I was scared.

"I can promise you," he said reassuringly. "They are not going to slit our throats." I was actually relieved and asked how he knew that.

Mike replied in a calm voice, "They're each carrying a gun. They'll just shoot us."

"We have to take them," he said. "They're going to be standing in the middle of the road. We'd have to run them over."

It was a long way to the end of that road. I had lots of time to express my fear. My stomach hurt. After we turned around and started back, we were getting close to where we had seen them. Now we saw not two, but eight men blocking the entire road.

Mike looked over at me, shrugged his shoulders, stopped and rolled down the window. They surrounded the truck.

They didn't dare tell us there was this many, one of the two we had encountered on our first meeting tried to explain. The others had stayed in the woods when they saw us coming. We were the only people they had seen and they had been out here for a week. They needed our help.

Mike got out and pulled the tail gate down. The men had large military duffle bags and began shoving them into the box of the truck. Two men got in the cab of the truck. I had to sit on one's lap. It was a tight squeeze, but the other six piled in the back—three in the box and three clinging to the tail gate. Mike looked at his maps and found the resort they talked about.

Down the road we went at a snail's pace. The men cheered as we saw the name of the resort on a sign with a big arrow showing us the way. They had not missed the plane which was soon to leave the airstrip not far from the resort. The owners had no way of knowing the men were in trouble. No one in the party had a cell phone back then.

After the truck was unloaded and the fellows had quickly gathered the rest of their things from their rooms, out came money. Each tried to pay us. We declined. The young man who had told us his feet were bleeding took off his shoes, pulled off his socks, and yes, they were full of blood. His ankles were raw, red meat. After hugs for me and handshakes for Mike, we were again rolling down a gravel road, talking of our adventure.

"How did you know they were telling the truth?" I asked.

Mike had been watching them and listening carefully. The two young men had said they knew nothing about camping. Encouraged by a friend to join the group of explorers, they were soon dropped in the woods, anticipating an exciting outdoor experience. Although young and strong, attempting to cross a fast-moving, swollen creek had left them cold, wet, and without anything to make fire to fix their food and stay warm. All had been plagued with blisters from new boots. They were college kids in their 20s—inexperienced and afraid. *Their* faces told their story. "Their clothes and boots were new," Mike said. "The looks their eyes. They were scared. And I thought, *they're telling the truth.*"

> *"If one tells the truth, one is sure sooner or later to be found out."*
>
> —Oscar Wilde

255

CHAPTER 32

LESSON LEARNED

Barak Obama was born to a White mother and a Black father. When he won the Presidency, many had great expectations, myself included, that he would be a bridge between the races. It was the Democrats turn to win after President's George W Bush's eight-year turn at the helm of our country, following eight years of Democrat Bill Clinton's stint as the leader of our nation. Obama, a senator from Illinois, had no experience in governing, unlike his two predecessors who had each served as governors.

On June 22, 2009, our television broadcasts and newspapers were filled with the report of President Obama's remarks about a Cambridge officer, acting "stupidly." Many officers have not felt supported by their government under Obama. Several believe our own Minnesota Governor Mark Dayton has not been supportive of the police, and most feel President Obama not only did not support them but that he added to the public's distrust.

"Don't fumble yourself" was a statement my father often made to all of his seven children. He never explained exactly what he meant, but we all knew. President Obama fumbled himself into quicksand when he made hasty comments before knowing all the facts. He did say at one point that he realized his remarks ratcheted up the rhetoric. CNN reported on July 23, 2009, that Cambridge police have demanded an apology from President Obama over "stupid" comments.

According to the police report, Crowley arrived at the scene, went up to the front door, and asked Gates to step outside. The officer was investigating the report of a break-in in progress. As he did so, Gates opened the front door and said, "Why, because I'm a Black man in America?"

Crowley's report states that he believed Gates was lawfully in the residence but that he was surprised and confused by Gates' behavior, which included a threat by Gates that Crowley did not know who he was "messing with." Crowley warned Gates that he was becoming disorderly. When Gates ignored this warning, persisted in his behavior, and ignored a second warning, Crowley informed him that he was under arrest.

"Mr. Gates' supporters have condemned his arrest as racial profiling," said the AP.

Police representatives insisted race had played no part in the incident and that the President should retract his "disgraceful" comments and apologize to Sergeant James Crowley.

At a hastily arranged White House press conference July 24, 2009, CNN reported that the President said:

> *"In my choice of words, I unfortunately gave the impression that I was maligning the Cambridge Police Department or Sergeant Crowley specifically. My words didn't illuminate; they only added to the media attention."*

At the press conference the President also admitted that he did not have all the facts.

Dennis O'Connor, Chairman of the Cambridge Superior Officers Association, accused the President of blundering into something he knew little about. He said, "When you don't have all the facts, your next words should be *I have no comment.*"

President Obama's comment on the issue, without knowing all the facts, and admitting that Prof. Gates was a friend of his, has left a "bad taste" in the mouths of law enforcement—one that most have not been able to get over.

Sergeant Crowley said he made the arrest after Professor Gates overreacted and refused to end a stream of invectives and accusations of racism that had followed routine questions and procedure.

I guess that Gates was angry, but quite possibly he was embarrassed. One of his neighbors had called the police. Although Gates was angry it would be reasonable for the officer to ask for his identification, he could have been the person breaking in. The officer would have been in trouble had he not made sure the man in the house was the owner, and also that Gates was safe.

There was a new security system set up in the store where I worked. I had been told the code to disarm the alarm and also that I had only seconds to do so. I was confident that I could handle it and said the code over in my mind as I walked to the door. As soon as I turned the knob, the buzzer started telling me it had been activated. I quickly put the code in, but the buzzing didn't stop. Soon the alarm was sounding throughout the huge area, and I knew it was also sounding off at the police station. I called my boss and he told me the *correct* code. I had transposed the numbers. The noise stopped, and a policeman stood outside the door. I walked into the large entry way, opened the door, and told him I had set the alarm off but assured him all was fine. I was embarrassed and knew Mike would soon hear all about it. The officer, who I of course knew, asked if I was OK. I laughed and said, "I am fine. Please go." He did not. He stood looking at me for a few more seconds and then asked if I would step outside. I did, and we talked another minute before he left. He was being cautious, making sure I was safe and that someone inside didn't have a gun pointed at me.

Obama invited the two persons involved in the Gates and Crowley kerfuffle and also Joe Biden to what was called a "Beer Summit" in the Rose Garden at the White House. Obama hoped that the meeting would dial back the controversy and create what he called a "teachable moment."

A New York Captain talks of a turning point with the police in our country when politicians got involved and offered opinions in cases, especially in deadly force situations, way before any real facts were known. He thinks they were reacting to media broadcasts and, much like many people, made judgements about the case before all the facts were in. He's disappointed that even President Obama took this position and sent in the Justice Department immediately. This was premature and suggested there was corruption, incompetence, racism, or other big problems with the department. Sadly, in his opinion, this political interference and implied wrongdoing eroded the public perception of the police and the entire criminal justice system. The officer blames incompetent politicians for the terrible situation we are in today with police officers being ambushed all over the country as well as a tendency for people to resist the police.

The holder of the highest office in Minnesota didn't get good press either. News channel KARE-11 reported on July 10, 2016, that Minnesota's largest labor union, serving law enforcement across the state, is calling his recent comments following the shooting death of Philando Castile "unthinkable, irresponsible, and reckless."

"Would this have happened if the driver and passenger were white?" Governor Dayton asked. "I don't think it would've. So, I'm forced to confront and I think all of us in Minnesota are forced to confront that this kind of racism exists."

Do you think our previous leaders, state and federal have supported law enforcement?

I will quote others to give my readers an idea about the thoughts given by most law enforcement officers.

> "Never underestimate the power of stupid people in large groups." –Unknown

> "A typical vice of American politics is the avoidance of saying anything real on real issues."—Theodore Roosevelt.

> "Suppose you were an idiot, and suppose you were in congress. But I repeat myself."—Mark Twain

> "Sometimes I wonder whether the world is being run by smart people who are putting us on, or by imbeciles who really mean it." –Mark Twain

> "One useless man is a shame, two is a law firm, and three is a Congress." —John Adams

On Sunday, Sean Gormley, Executive Director of Law Enforcement Labor Services, released the following statement:

> *"Last week's tragic shootings in Dallas, Falcon Heights, Minn. and Baton Rouge have tested our emotions, our faith, and our resolve as a community and a nation. Difficult issues are justifiably being confronted and tensions are running high.*

> *Thorough and impartial investigations of these incidents are essential to ensure and preserve the public trust in law*

enforcement. Indeed, the families and loved ones personally affected by these tragedies deserve no less.

However, the fact that Minnesota's political leader would disregard this investigatory process and use the power of his office to share a premature and unsupported conclusion about the shooting of Mr. Castile just hours after his death is unthinkable and irresponsible.

Police officers have a duty to protect and to serve all— including those who dislike or distrust cops. The comments have only deepened the divide between these groups and made our jobs more difficult and more dangerous. We expect a great deal more from the holder of the highest office in the State of Minnesota."

Is the media painting a correct picture of law enforcement?

The majority of law enforcement officers don't trust the media. They do not trust them to tell the whole story. Officers believe the media for the most part is not pro law enforcement.

Sadly, officers believe the media loves the sensationalism. They also believe it's what their viewers want.

I will use others' quotes to relay the feeling of those I interviewed.

> "Do not fear the enemy, for your enemy can only take your life. It is far better that you fear the media, for they will steal your Honor."—Mark Twain

> "If you don't read the newspaper, you're uninformed. If you read the newspaper, you're mis-informed."—Mark Twain

"Get the facts first, then you can distort them as you please. –Mark Twain

"A lie gets halfway around the world before the truth has a change to get its pants on." —Winston Churchill

We now have a new leader in Minnesota. He has a new slate to write on and hopefully will be supportive of the Minnesota Law Enforcement community.

"Be careful when you blindly follow the masses...sometimes the M is silent."

—Mark Twain

CHAPTER 33

DON'T TAKE YOUR GUNS TO TOWN

The streets of Chicago are bleeding. The blood of young men and other bystanders spewed onto the streets and sidewalks of Chicago August 7, 2018. The horror of the weekend filled newspapers and television channels. It's not that young Black men hadn't died on those bloodied streets and sidewalks many times before. It just hadn't been that many in one day. Chicago, along with other large cities, has seen their young men killed in record numbers. The dead are mostly young Black men. Television showed the violence of gangs, roaming the streets where families used to live, families with a mother and a father, where intact families used to live in the homes and apartments.

Who is killing these young people? It is young Blacks killing their own young Blacks. Newspapers and television channels reported on the carnage of that fateful day. It was, however, not really different than what has been going on for a long time.

Emotional officials called for increased accountability for gun assailants after at least 11 people were shot and killed and about 70 others were wounded in a spate of shootings over the weekend. The violence peaked early Sunday, including one shooting on the city's South Side that wounded eight people," according to CBS Chicago, written by their Crimesider Staff.

Police on Monday attributed the dozens of shootings to gangs, the illegal flow of guns and sweltering August heat that drew more people outside. No arrests had been made in the wake of the violence.

Chicago Mayor Rahm Emanuel condemned the violence in a press conference, broadcast on all the major networks. He said, "We have a heavy heart." Both Emanuel and Chicago Police Superintendent Eddie Johnson called for increased accountability for shooters and a broader community effort to decrease violence.

Emanuel decried what he called a "shortage of values about what is right, what is wrong" and said, "Anyone who knew the identity of a shooter has a moral responsibility to speak up."

I heard the news reports that shootings took place at a block party and a funeral. There were victims from the age of eleven to sixty-three. I cannot help but wonder when—when will the sane people from Chicago finally say ENOUGH! Will they finally take back their communities? Will Black Lives Matter call their protesters to protest what is happening in their neighborhoods to their mothers, sisters, and brothers? Can they enlist all the people who so willingly protest on the streets and bring all the people who rant on social media to come with their tools of building, their cleaning rags, brooms, buckets, and a little elbow grease to clean up the streets and help their fellow blacks for something good?

"A violent weekend in Chicago is shining a spotlight on another issue some don't talk about: Who is killing the Black victims?" KARE 11, TV August 7, 2018.

"You don't see these killings in mass numbers like this in other races," Tanisha Taylor Bell told KARE 11, TV August 7, 2018 from her Atlanta office. "How can we expect someone else to respect us if we don't respect ourselves? The Black-on-Black crime that is plaguing cities across the nation? You have to start at home."

Chicago native Tanisha Taylor Bell owns a public relations firm, Perfect Pitch Media Group. But for nearly 13 years as an executive producer at CNN, Bell found herself writing stories about gun violence in Chicago.

On August 31, 2018, an Atlanta pastor delivered controversial remarks during Aretha Franklin's funeral, criticizing Black-on-Black crime. I watched some of the nine hours' coverage and taped the rest to watch later. Franklin's family was not happy with the comments made by Rev. Jasper Williams, Jr. Williams, who is Black, said "African-Americans kill the same number of Black people slain by the Ku Klux Klan throughout history in a matter of months." Speaking of black-on-black crime, he continued, "There's got to be a better way."

In his eulogy, Williams spoke on the state of Black America, saying it had lost its soul and that Franklin was calling on her race to turn its direction around.

Addressing criticism of his eulogy at a news conference given before the Franklin family released its statement, Williams stood by his words, saying Aretha Franklin had chosen and trusted him to speak and that he wanted her life to continue beyond the funeral.

Addressing Black Lives Matter, Williams echoed the comments he made in the eulogy:

> "I'm saying that when we as a race sit back and get mad, if a police officer kills one of us, and we don't say anything when 100 of us are killed by us, that something is wrong with that. I'm not saying that Black lives do not matter in terms of the worth of a Black life, but what I'm saying in essence is that it does not matter, ought not matter, should not matter, cannot matter until Black people begin to R-E-S-P-E-C-T, respect Black lives. Only then will Black lives matter."

Asked whether he thought Franklin would have approved of his eulogy, Williams said:

> *"Because of the great contributor that she was to the civil rights movement and all that she gave, I would think that if I'm doing something to turn Black America around, that she would be pleased."*

With the unending violence in Chicago I was reminded of Don Lemon's (a Black, CNN anchor) somewhat famous and controversial comments following the George Zimmerman acquittal in 2013.

He was highly criticized for his comments. Newspapers and television stations were quick to broadcast his statements many times.

"Black people," Lemon said, *"If you really want to fix the problem, here's just five things that you should think about doing.*

> *Number 5—Pull up your pants.*
>
> *Number 4—Stop using the N-word.*
>
> *Number 3—Respect where you live.*
>
> *Number 2—Finish school.*
>
> *Number 1, and probably the most important, just because you can have a baby, doesn't mean you should, especially without planning for one or getting married first.*
>
> *More than 72 percent of children in the African-American community are born out of wedlock. That means absent fathers. Studies show that lack of a male role model is an express train right to prison and the cycle continues."*

David Clark, Sheriff of Milwaukee County and a Democrat, criticized the growth of the welfare state on several television stations after the riots in Milwaukee. "Rioters exhibit underclass behaviors."

Just the fact that so many children are born without a father in their lives should scare all of us regardless of race. In Heather MacDonald's book, *The War on Cops*, Heather warns that race-based attacks on the criminal-justice system are eroding the authority of law and putting lives at risk. And goes on to say that a straight line can be drawn between family breakdown and youth violence.

We have all heard about the problems with living on welfare. Self-esteem is gone and generations seem to follow down that same path. When you don't have to work for what you get in life, you don't appreciate it. I am reminded of a quote by Jane Austen "There are people, who the more you do for them, the less they will do for themselves."

Having jobs when I was young gave other young people and me feelings of self worth. Young girls baby sat for 25 cents an hour. The job included washing dishes (sometimes making supper and washing dishes from several meals), folding laundry, and giving Saturday night baths for the children. There was little food to eat, but sometimes there was baloney and bread for a sandwich and vanilla ice cream with Hershey's chocolate topping for a treat.

There were only so many babysitting jobs to go around, and I loved getting the call. It was usually for Saturday night. I don't remember sitting for others during the week. When I was fourteen, I was offered a job working at a Drive-In, thanks to my older sister who worked there at night. I worked the day shift and earned 65 cents an hour. I thought I was rich and was excited when I got a W2 form. I actually had taxes taken out of my pay, although I got them back. Many young people worked for the farmers in our community, cutting corn out of the beans or detasseling corn. It was hard hot work but the pay was pretty good for children.

Manners and proper behavior start in the home. Please, thank-you, excuse me: those few simple statements of civility should begin while the child is just learning to speak. My parents, extended family, and a community can help to instill that. However, it must be a concerted effort.

When I was young, the children in our small community had many mothers. Any woman, even those without children or those with children already grown, did not hesitate to step in and involve herself in parenting us. One's mother did not have to see you misbehaving. Any number of women would tell you to stop what you were doing if they happened to see any skullduggery or hear any inappropriate language.

I sat in a restaurant with a friend one Saturday morning drinking a Coke. I blew into the glass with my straw to created bubbles. A mom stopped by the booth and told me to stop that. She also said my mother wouldn't like that. So, I stopped. I prayed she wouldn't tell my mother or I would have been in big trouble.

Sometimes today, if a mother disciplines her child in a store or in some kind of public view, she may be the one who is chastised. If her tactics are severe enough, social services may be called to check her out for child abuse and she could even possibly go to jail.

When my friends and I gather over coffee and talk about our children and grandchildren, we all agree that we would be in jail if we disciplined our children today as we did back then. Remembering one particular incident where my friend and I went up into our attic always brings a smile to my face. From a metal blue trunk, we took out my mother's wedding dress and a couple of dresses that she had worn in others' weddings. We tried them on. I think I was in her wedding dress and my friend in a burgundy satin dress, parading around, when my mother came up. She scolded us both, told us to take off the dresses, and, before leaving to go down the stairs, she gave each of us a swat on our back side. I don't remember that it was particularly hard, but we were upset and frightened by the tone in her voice and the swat on our behinds. I spent the rest of the day in my room and my friend was sent home crying. Although we never talked about it, I am quite sure that she stopped crying before she reached her home and never told her mother about the incident.

"The strength of a nation derives from the integrity of the home."

–Abraham Lincoln

CHAPTER 34

FRIENDS NEVER SAY GOOD BYE

He always respected law enforcement but didn't think he was smart enough to ever be a part of it. He had a very bad education—a great big red F stapled on his report card when he was in eighth grade.

I interviewed a retired police chief. He said he could always do things but didn't have much of an education and didn't think he could even pass a test. Harvey was about 23 years old when he got the job as a policeman in the mid-50s.

His family was very broken up, but he did have his wife to talk about it with. His wife convinced him that he did have the brains to do the job.

Officers didn't go to school for law enforcement at that time. They just put you on the job. (Formal training didn't come along until 1967.)

So, Harvey bought a blue shirt and blue pants. The police chief gave him a .38 pistol and put him on the street. He had been in the Korean War, had grown up fast, and was pretty mature. A fellow went to bat for him. The chief hadn't really wanted him as a patrol officer, but the friend did.

He went on to share his experiences with his wife, and he was not a worrier. He grew up in the welfare system. He worked on a farm for a couple of years and would come home to his mother occasionally.

He had spent some time in an orphanage near Como Park. Lying about his age, he went to work for the Great Northern Railroad at age sixteen. In the summer of 1949, Harvey's brother came to pick Harvey and his twin brother Harry up on a farm where they were working. His brother told them to get their clothes, he was taking them home. Harvey again went back to his mother for a while.

Harry died about 22 years ago. He had been accidently shot in the head years before by a friend who was practicing a fast draw, leaving shrapnel in Harry's head. He eventually died from taking coumadin.

Harvey got along with people from all different agencies. He plans a gathering at times to renew friendships with old friends from the other departments.

He doesn't think his children were teased at school, although they might have taken a little heat because their dad was a cop.

The police chief doesn't know how to answer my question about ever fearing for his life. There were incidents throughout his working years that could have turned dangerous, but that's a part of being in law enforcement.

Harvey saw little police brutality in all the years he worked. The majority of the time, the people he worked with, or worked for him when he became police chief, showed extreme restraint in dealing with people.

When asked about the use of cameras, he thinks it will be detrimental to solving crimes. He believes most crimes are solved by talking to people, and if you're talking to people with your cameras rolling, they're not going to tell you anything.

He smiled as he tells me his interrogation technique. Harvey sits down with the guy and gives him a can of Mountain Dew. He calls it truth serum. They start to tell him what he wants to know. Officers usually know less than they think, but if they trust you, they'll talk to you.

He tries to adhere to the advice that he gave others. Treat people the way you want to be treated.

Yes, he missed family life, especially early in his career. There was only so much staffing power, and he was expected to be on the job. He believes God was shining on him when he got that job. Yes, he'd take the same job again today. He liked the challenge of the work, and he would do it again in today's world as well.

If you're there to help, he thinks people know it. He told a story about a Christmas some 40 years ago. He and his wife stopped at a house and gave a woman $20. Many years later, he saw the same woman in a store. She told him she had never forgotten what he did for her and that she had really needed it. He came from an orphanage, a broken home, and hard times. He had seen it in his own growing up years, but he has not become hardened.

October 29, 1981. Itasca County Sheriff's Deputy Robert ("Beefy") Lawson was on vacation. Beefy Lawson was a workaholic but that day he might have relaxed and enjoyed his time at home had there not been a call from the sheriff's office that changed his day—his world—his family's existence forever. Instead, a man named Audie Fox fatally shot him during an 18-hour standoff.

Audie's estranged wife asked Beefy to go to Fox's parents' home to assist her with picking up the children. Deputy Lawson agreed to go. Upon entering the home, he found the two children sitting at the kitchen table with Audie's aunt. Fox then emerged, pointing a .357 at Lawson's head.

Fox demanded that Beefy give him a phone number for his ex-wife, but Beefy said he did not have it. Audie made Beefy lay down on the floor, again demanding the phone number. After counting to three Audie put the gun to Lawson's head and pulled the trigger.

Audie Fox perpetrated one of the Iron Range's most shocking crimes. Fox, who reportedly felt persecuted by police, said during telephone negotiations that he had placed X-marked targets on the children's heads and planned to kill them if police came in the house.

Over the years, Fox has filed many unsuccessful appeals of his conviction and life sentence. He was denied parole in 1995 and 2005. He was again up for parole in 2015. His potential release has been publicly opposed by the Lawson family and Itasca County law enforcement officials. His parole was denied.

Harvey Dahline, retired Police Chief, writes in his book, *Dedication to Duty*, about his friend Beefy Lawson.

He was a special friend over the years having worked many criminal cases together. His work ethic was beyond comparison. Getting onto a case, he thought the workday was 48 hours.

Honest, admired, and respected, he helped send many a criminal to prison. Yet one of the first persons they would look up when they got out was Beefy.

You will always hear fine things said about someone after they are gone. But I worked with the man. I also spent 40 years as a policeman in Grand Rapids. Robert "Beefy" Lawson and another deputy would be in the top three investigators in all that time.

What follows is information I gained both before and after the 18-hour standoff on the morning of October 29, 1981, when Itasca County deputy Robert Lawson was shot to death in the home of Audie Fox's parents.

Fox, who was separated from his wife, and had been living in Colorado, had demanded to see his son, a five-year-old. His two children were living in the area with their mother.

Lawson had been called by his wife to see if he would pick up the children at Audie's parents' home and she was hesitant to do it herself. The deputy was on vacation at the time called in and volunteered to take the call.

A deputy that I interviewed had gotten a call from Beefy that morning, asking if he would go with him to the Fox home. He had to say no, that he had an interview for a job as a probation officer. That was his first love and he wanted that job badly. He and Beefy were dear friends, and the fact that he could not be with him that day has haunted him.

Another deputy said he had gotten a call about it from dispatch but he also had something else that he had to do so could not take it. This deputy's family heard that an east end deputy had been shot and they were worried that it was he who had taken a bullet.

Harvey's story continues in his book.

Fox's girlfriend, said that when Lawson walked in the door, Audie Fox came out from behind a partition, holding a .357 revolver with both hands. She said he twice ordered Lawson to get on the floor and Lawson refused both times. Lawson finally complied when Fox cocked the hammer of the gun.

It is said Fox asked Lawson where his wife was, but Lawson refused to tell him and was given the count of three. The girlfriend said she took Fox's daughter into the living room and heard Fox count to three and then heard a loud noise.

Deputy Beefy Lawson was to lie in the entryway of the Fox house, deceased, for some time. The Sheriff and Chief Deputy had negotiated by phone with Audie Fox, the shooter. Then another officer, without weapons and alone, was allowed to enter the entryway to remove Deputy Lawson's body, bringing it out to his squad car and placing it on the trunk of his car while driving it out to the main road. This took place in the early afternoon.

Excerpts of the Investigative report by Officer Dahline:

Officer Harvey Dahline doing an investigative report on one, Audie Fox, today's date is 11, 2, 1981. This incident took place on October 29 and 30th, 1981 in the Pengilly area.

At approximately 11:00 AM on October 29 I became aware of the fact that officer Beefy Lawson had been shot in the Pengilly area. As the day wore on, we realized this might take some time, but we (the Grand Rapids Police Dept.) did offer our help.

At approximately 8:00 PM I went over to the Pengilly area where I met a deputy at a house that was set up as the headquarters for as long as this incident was to take place. I did talk to the deputy and he gave me the general layout of the land, the houses, and so forth. An idea of what was going on, and what they were trying to do at the time. I asked him where I could be of assistance to him at this time, and he told me that there was a point of the house that was possibly a little weak where no one could see the basement windows very well. He did take me over there and showed me the area where he would like me to watch. With me was a Deputy Sheriff from the Hibbing office and his partner. We did place ourselves in an area where we could watch two sides of the house and also the basement windows.

Around 11 PM I went back to the headquarters area to get a blanket and some gloves and some jackets that I had in my vehicle as some of the guys around my area were getting pretty cold. When I came up to the main road, I walked with Audie's mother as she was going back to the house. On the way up to the house she said that she thought she would need God's help to make these things turn out right and I wished her luck. She then proceeded on down the road back to the house.

At about 4 AM on October 30, the word was coming out that there would be no shooting and that Fox was supposed to be coming out with his children and his mother. About this time a deputy arrived in my area and with him was a BCA agent. They told me there was to be an ambulance going around to the front into the driveway. About this time an ambulance did drive down the main road, turned into the driveway and parked facing the house, approximately 50 to 60 feet away from the house. Getting out of the ambulance was two officers, both in blue uniforms. They both walked up into the driveway towards the front of the house until they got about 20 to 30 feet from the steps; this was in a lighted area. They at this time spread their clothing and showed Audie's mom that they weren't armed. I believe that a deputy did go into the house momentarily and then came back out.

The standoff continued:

We then held a conference around the corner as to whether to break off contact or not because of the demands that he was starting to make and the frame of mind that he was working himself into. It was decided during this conference not to break off contact because this was as close to the door as we have been able to get, and as long as we had contact, we would see what we could do. We then talked over the possibilities and a deputy then gave me the go-ahead to see if I could talk my way to the door. If I thought I could then proceed, I was to do so, but if I thought I couldn't, I was to break contact. Two men were to back me up and were to be close to the steps. Two others were to be close by the corner, and they were to follow me in as soon as possible after I went in. The key at this time was whether we could get Audie's mother to stand in the doorway with the door open and talk to me.

As I was standing in the doorway about five minutes, she came out and said, "He does not like you here because he thinks you have a gun. I told her that she did not have to worry as I would show her that I did not. I then removed my hunting jacket and placed it on the ground along with my gun belt and empty holster. I then proceeded up the steps, spreading my light coat so that she and Audie could see my waist. She was holding the door at the time. I then took a step past her and pivoting, putting my back to Audie, raising my coat in back so that he could see that I did not have a weapon. At the same time, I continued to pivot and dove for him; I caught him around both arms with the two children squeezed between us. Within a second or two, four officers were all assisting me. Audie at this time was still resisting and trying to break free. We were all carried outside, away from any weapons. He was searched and handcuffed. I removed his boots and socks, someone else removed his shirt in *a search for any weapons. The Chief Deputy then took over on what he would like done.*

Fox was no stranger to Lawson or many other law officers. He had been found guilty of two counts of felony theft in August 1976 and sent to two consecutive terms of 0 – 5 years at St. Cloud State Reform School, serving 1 1/2 years. Beefy Lawson had been the investigating officer. Most recently Fox had been wanted for the theft of a $5000 motorcycle. Again, Lawson was the investigator. Fox was also wanted in the Twin Cities for theft, assault with a gun, and possession of stolen property.

The sheriff reported on Monday, November 2, that the search of the Fox house resulted in the seizure of 41 guns. One firearm belonged to Officer Lawson and had been found in the sump pump. Another was the alleged murder weapon found in the chimney. Also found were 3100 rounds of ammunition. Fox was convicted of murder by a jury of 10 women and 2 men on Monday, April 26, 1982. Judge Warren Saetre sentenced 27-year-old Fox to life in prison in the Stillwater State Penitentiary. In 1995 Fox was to come up for parole hearing. Many others and I wrote letters of opposition. The following is my letter to the parole board:

Office of Adult release
Ref: Audie Fox

In 1981, Beefy's Lawson's life was taken in a deliberate execution. He was on the floor face down, a gun put to his head by Audie Fox, threats were made, and a trigger was pulled.

Left dead was a police officer and a personal friend of mine. Beefy was known throughout the area as a friend to everyone and an honest, hard-working deputy who went beyond the call of duty to help not only citizens but also lawbreakers to get back on the right path.

Beefy would work hard to send someone up for breaking the law, but the first person they would look up when they got out would be Beefy and then thank him.

I have been a police officer for over 40 years and it seems inconceivable to me that the State could even consider parole for Audie Fox. This execution was planned and deliberate. Fox got a life sentence, but he deserved more. I think this is a good illustration of what is wrong with our judicial system.

Don't you think it is about time we start meaning what we say: 40 years is 40 years and life is life? What kind of a message are we sending? Audie Fox should never see the light outside of a prison. I know Beefy Lawson never will.

Respectfully,
Harvey Dahline
Chief of Police
40 years in the Justice System

★ ★ ★ ★ ★

"No person was ever honored for what he received. Honor has been the reward for what he gave."

—Calvin Coolidge

CHAPTER 35

COMING TO AMERICA

We moved to our new lake home a few miles out of town in the middle of October 1992. I had not changed the address on my license from our house on the edge of town. I called our new polling place and was told I could bring someone along to vouch for me. I asked my neighbor if she would tell them where I now lived, and she said she would. I asked her when she was going to go and vote. She couldn't vote. She was not a citizen. I knew she had lived in the United States for 30 years. She was from Germany and had married a United States soldier. I expressed my wonderment as to why she was not a citizen after all this time. She said she just haven't taken the time. And also asked me if I had any idea how hard it is to become a citizen? She went on to say she wasn't going to tell anyone about this but had been working on getting her citizenship for some time. She believed she would soon be able to pass the test. She also told me that although she had been in this country for many years, she never quite felt like she belonged because she wasn't a citizen.

Mike, had, of course, changed his license, and he vouched for me at the polling place, predictably reminding me to get mine changed.

Mike was working a day shift shortly after we had moved to West Central Minnesota. I drove the 45 miles to visit my parents. He was getting off at 5 o'clock. I loved to spend time with my parents, and he knew I would not leave their home with any extra time to spare before he got home. In other words, he knew I would probably be driving too fast.

My children were riding with me—one in the front and one in the back. As I got closer to home, a squad car pulled out from behind a billboard with lights flashing. Since he was driving close behind me, I could see the car through the rearview mirror but couldn't get a good look at who was driving. I did not stop, and, for the first and only time in my life, I flashed an obscene hand gesture to him in my rearview mirror. As soon as I had done that, I remember thinking, *Jeepers, I hope Mike's the one behind me and not someone I don't know.* I still did not stop but slowed down as I entered the city limits. Now though there were lights flashing, the short sound of a siren, and a squad car angled right in front of me. (I almost hit it.) People were walking and driving by. I'm sure they wondered what in the world did that woman do. Mike got out of the car and walked over to me.

"Can I see your license, Ma'am?" I said, "Get away from me." "Your license, Ma'am," he said again, with a sterner voice. I grumbled, reached for my purse and took my billfold out. "Please take your license out of your wallet." I made some sassy remark and moaned a little. The kids were waving to him, smiling; they were little and of course didn't have a clue what was going on. He took a long look at my license and asked, "Is this your current address?" By then I remembered: Oops, I had not changed it. I said, "Yes, Officer, that is my right address." "It seems to me," he said in a feisty voice that you live with me at …. I said, "Not for long." He laughed, gave me a warning ticket, and wrote on it that I had lied to the officer. Then, with a smile and a twinkle in his eye, he said, "I'll be home in a few minutes. Put a pizza in."

Immigration has become a dividing force in society. My great grandparents came from Norway and settled on the Minnesota prairie. There was no system set up to help them. They struggled on their own. There was farmland to be had, but if they starved to death on that land or if crops were swept away by ferocious prairie fires, too bad. They were on their own.

Immigration policies seem to be in a boggled mess. The influx of immigrants from Central America is not the first time that the United States has struggled to deal with those from other countries.

Friday, August 18, 2018, *The West Central Tribune* reported that approximately 20 new citizens would hopefully be able to swear their allegiance to the United States of America next spring. I had never actually seen what that entailed. I thought of my neighbor and the love she had for this country but who never, until she actually passed her citizen test, really felt she belonged.

At the ceremony, they recite the Oath of Allegiance in front of a district judge. The Naturalization Oath reads:

> *I hereby declare, on oath, that I absolutely and entirely renounce and abjure all allegiance and fidelity to any foreign prince, potentate, state, or sovereignty, of whom or which I have heretofore been a subject or citizen; that I will support and defend the Constitution and laws of the United States of America against all enemies, foreign and domestic; that I will bear true faith and allegiance to the same; that I will bear arms on behalf of the United States when required by the law; that I will perform noncombatant service in the Armed Forces of the United States when required by the law; that I will perform work of national importance under civilian direction when required by the law; and that I take this obligation freely, without any mental reservation or purpose of evasion; so help me God.*

Presidents have grappled with the dilemma for years. Leaders have struggled with finding a solution and have yet to come up with an answer that our congress can all agree on.

Theodore Roosevelt on Immigrants and being an AMERICAN. www. liveabout.com.

"In the first place we should insist that if the immigrant who comes here in good faith becomes an American and assimilates himself to us, he shall be treated on an exact equality with everyone else, for it is an outrage to discriminate against any such man because of creed, or birthplace, or origin. But this is predicated upon the man's becoming in very fact an American, and nothing but an American...There can be no divided allegiance here. Any man who says he is an American, but something else also, isn't an American at all. We have room for but one flag, the American flag, and this excludes the red flag, which symbolizes all wars against liberty and civilization, just as much as it excludes any foreign flag of a nation to which we are hostile...We have room for but one language here, and that is the English language... and we have room for but one sole loyalty and that is a loyalty to the American people."

In 1986, President Ronald Reagan signed a major immigration law that gave amnesty to people in the country illegally who arrived prior to 1982.

1980 GOP presidential hopeful and future president, George H.W. Bush, was asked by an audience member if children in the country illegally should be allowed to attend U.S. public schools. Bush didn't hesitate, saying he doesn't want to see 6- or 8-year-olds being uneducated or made to feel that they're living outside the law." I am thinking of George H. W. Bush as I write. He would become our 41st president and died at the age of 94. I watched his coffin being placed on Air Force One in Houston, Texas, on his way to Washington, D.C., where his body would lie in state until a service was held. I love all the pomp and circumstance that goes with a state funeral.

President Bill Clinton, in his State of the Union Address in 1995 said, "All Americans, are rightly disturbed by the large numbers of illegal aliens entering our country. The jobs they hold might otherwise be held by citizens or legal immigrants. The public service they use impose burdens on our taxpayers. That's why our administration has moved aggressively to secure our borders by hiring a record number of new border guards, by deporting twice as many criminal aliens as ever before, by cracking down on illegal hiring, by barring welfare benefits to illegal aliens. In the budget I will present to you, we will try to do more to speed the deportation of illegal aliens who are arrested for crimes, to better identify illegal aliens in the workplace as recommended by the commission headed by former Congresswoman Barbara Jordan. We are a nation of immigrants. But we are also a nation of laws. It is wrong and ultimately self-defeating for a nation of immigrants to permit the kind of abuse of our immigration laws we have seen in recent years, and we must do more to stop it." C-Span Jan. 24, 1995

President Barack Obama, in his State of the Union, December 12, 2013, said, "Real reform means strong border security. And we should continue the work of fixing our broken immigration system, to secure our borders, and enforce our laws, and ensure that everyone who plays by the rules can contribute to our economy and enrich our nation."

In a nationally televised address from the White House, in 2014 the president warned about an "actual humanitarian crisis on the border" prompted by a surge of migrants from Central America, and urged Congress to take action on his immigration agenda. Like the current White House, the Obama administration struggled to find the right response to a dramatic increase in the number of migrants fleeing violence and poverty in Central America.

"Obama talked of a pathway to earned citizenship, passing a background check, paying taxes, and a meaningful penalty, learning English, and going to the back of the line behind the folks trying to come here legally." PBS August Oct. 23, 2016.

Our congress for so long has begrudgingly glanced at the immigration problem and then ignored it. There are such difficult problems to try to overcome because of the enormously long neglected complications in tackling this long festering wound.

Pictures of young children, exhausted frantic looking immigrants tug at our hearts. As do the other thousands of homeless who are already citizens here, living on our streets, many under our bridges, many in culverts. Veterans who have served our country with pride and bravery cannot find a place to live. Their addictions and mental illnesses are already stretching the resources of our counties and cities to the breaking point. The old saying, "Talk is Cheap," comes to mind. Everyone seems to be talking about it on the news, in restaurants, bars, and local gathering places. All seem to have opinions but no solutions.

I have asked many who are not in law enforcement their opinion as well. All want secured borders. They are saddened by the plight of those wanting to come into our wonderful country and distressed by the pictures on numerous television stations and on the front of newspapers. However, they have expressed their belief that they must come in legally. The media shows pictures of the women and children, and the scenes are sad. However, I hear the words *secure borders* and *legal entry* from those I know. I also asked the women I have breakfast with once a week how they viewed the problem. The women at breakfast and the other group had stern words for those trying to charge our borders. It was simple. *Come into our country legally.*

Native Americans were sleeping in tents in downtown Minneapolis, Minnesota. We had, of course, heard it all and seen the people camping on MNDOT property in the heart of the city. There are serious health issues with this problem—drug use and the smell of the area. Let's take care of these people first. Let's take care of our own.

Another man told me that he and his wife are very liberal but they want the law obeyed. He went on to say that he has heard many discussions from people who came here legally. They too believe there is a right way and a wrong way—and these are people who came the right way.

A retired high school principle has been subbing for Minneapolis Public Schools for the past eight years. He has taught in many English Language Learner classes. The teacher has yet to have one student who causes any problems at all or doesn't know how lucky they are to be in this country. He asked a student what he liked best about this country. The student told the teacher that he and his family have been here two years and they haven't seen ANY poor people. His family sends money home to relatives in Africa so they can eat.

When I asked the question to law enforcement about immigrations, there were varying opinions. Many simply stated that it is the law. If we don't want the law, get rid of it. That reminded me of Abraham Lincoln's comment, "The best way to get a bad law changed is to enforce it strictly."

Captain in New York City:

Enter the country legally and he would welcome you. Enter illegally and you are in violation of the law and should be detained, arrested, and sent back where you came from. He believes local law enforcement should have the tools to arrest anyone that they encounter who is in our country illegally (probable cause).

The officer also believes that once detained, the Feds should promptly take custody and initiate the process to deport. Second offense should begin a more difficult process and more harsh detention and deportation.

He does not believe that politicians at any level should have the power to enable unlawful entry into our country or to unlawfully remain in the country.

If someone is truly seeking asylum, he thinks a process should exist to legally apply, seek temporary secure shelter, and allow a reasonable time to verify identity and circumstances. This process should not be allowed to circumvent the law by anyone.

A policeman told me that he doesn't look for illegals but if he stops them for an infraction, certainly, he will turn them over. Another officer said he doesn't deal with them and lets the Feds handle it.

Although this country is made up of immigrants, a police officer from a large city feels strongly that the border needs to be controlled; and for the safety and security of the people who reside here, access into this country needs to be closely monitored and controlled. To him this is not unreasonable.

Even though he believes in a secure border, he agrees and understands that there is a need to allow immigration into this country, though it needs to be done in a controlled way where the immigrants are properly vetted. He likes the idea of a big wall with a big beautiful door.

He also believes that if someone entered this country illegally, they should be deported back to the country that they came from. This seems like common sense to him, and he has a hard time understanding the argument for allowing illegal immigration. If local police officers come across any illegal immigrant during their duties, they should be able to turn them over to the Feds.

A seasoned law officer believes the constitution must be followed by all branches of the government. He believes all who enter must do so legally. Another officer suggested facetiously, that they should simply ask the public which laws they would like enforced and which ones they would like law enforcement to just forget about.

Law enforcement officers suggested people remember that we have laws. Many wanted judges to rule on the law and not try to make law. One retired trooper sees that judges sometimes seem to feel sorry for the violator and put obstacles in the way of those who follow and also enforce the laws.

I was asked if I knew what the word illegal means? The question was directed at me by a retired officer. "Yes, I sure do," I replied. Then, he wondered, why I asked his feelings about it?

We spoke about a mob storming our border. The BBC reported on November 26, 2018, that Mexico said it has deported nearly 100 Central American migrants a day after they tried to storm the US border. He spoke of Gandalf in the movie "Lord of the Rings" and also made the motion with his arms, You shall not pass!

Newsweek, Nov. 27, 2018, Chantal Da Silva reported:

"The group, among thousands of migrants heading towards the US, was rounded up after trying to cross the border "violently" and "illegally" on Sunday, said the interior ministry. Video footage shows dozens of people running towards the border fence near the city of Tijuana. Tear gas was used to suppress the crowd.

Under President Donald Trump, The Case Processing Centre's use of the substance has hit a seven-year record high, with the agency deploying the substance a total of 29 times in Fiscal Year 2018, which ended on September 30, 2018, according to the agency's data.

However, the data also showed that the substance was deployed nearly the same number of times in Fiscal Years 2012 and 2013 under former President Barack Obama, with CBP using the substance 26 times in fiscal year 2012 and 27 times in Fiscal Year 2013".

The Washington Examiner November 26, 2018, along with Fact Check and Snopes, reported that yes indeed, several presidents including Obama, along with Jimmy Carter, Ronald Reagan, and George W. Bush have used tear gas to stop illegal people from crossing our borders.

We have the privilege of living in the United States of America. I haven't talked to anyone who didn't want immigrants to be a part of this melting pot of diversity. They do, however, want those wanting to live here to come legally, speak English, get a job, be a part of the solution, not the problem, be productive and an asset to our society.

> *"A simple way to take measure of a country is to look at how many want in... And how many want out."*
>
> —Tony Blair

CHAPTER 36

TROUBLE ON THE LINE

"911, this is Anne. Where is your emergency?"

As the operators answer their calls, these questions can be heard. It becomes a frantic conglomeration of voices staffing their phones.

"Is the baby breathing?"

"How old are you?"

"Are you alone?"

"Is there somewhere you can hide?"

"Can you lock yourself in a room? Maybe the bathroom?"

"You shot your wife?"

"Calm down."

"Stay on the line."

"Help is on the way."

"Put the gun down."

"Where are your parents?"

"Is he breathing? What is his color?"

"Keep pressure on the wound."

Men and women keep a fast and frantic pace answering calls for help. The woman I am interviewing told me that nobody gets it, until they sit in that chair.

The people answering the 911 are our first call for help. They ask a series of questions that annoy us in our panicky frightened state of mind. The questions they ask help them establish what we need—who we need. Their steady voices telling us to calm down are an irritation and often invoke angry responses.

They have heard the desperate screams of a victim as she is being attacked, the desperation in a man's voice telling where to find him before his family gets home, then the gunshot.

They field dozens of calls when the weather threatens. A traffic accident can result in many 911 calls from cell phones, but the operators answer each call as if it were a new emergency. It could be a call for help for a heart attack or any other long list of emergencies. They are taught not to assume. No matter how much training or how much experience, the dispatchers review whether they did everything fast enough and right. They do the best they can.

I visited a friend on a beautiful fall weekend. I had arrived on Friday and my intention was to leave Sunday. She talked me into staying another day. Sunday evening, we gave her husband a break from our talking and laughing. The night before we had all sat in the den, while she and I tried catching up on the latest goings on in our lives. He had tried, without much success, to watch college football.

We settled into the comfortable living room, She, lying on the couch facing me and I, facing the large windows looking into the moonlit night with a clear view of her daughter and son-in-law's large white house across the pasture. My phone rang and I walked outside to get a better cell phone signal.

After our conversation, I settled back into the wing back chair, putting my feet on the ottoman. My friend and I were enjoying a glass of wine when suddenly the white house across the pasture erupted in flames.

My *calm* voice said, "That house is on fire!" As my feet found their way to the floor, half sitting, half standing, I struggled to my feet while saying again louder, "That house is on fire!" My friend leaped from the couch sending a glass on the coffee table tumbling to the wood floor, breaking as it hit the floor and her screaming her husband's name. There were seconds of chaos as he ran into the room, not knowing what the emergency was. For a split-second I thought the occupants of the burning house would die. She was on the phone to 911 as he yelled that they were sleeping in the basement. He ran out the door, started the six-wheeler parked in the driveway and roared away. Hearing the words, that they were sleeping in the basement gave me hope as the upstairs of the home totally exploded in flames.

As the frantic grandpa made it to the end of his driveway, a young man had parked his car and was standing in the road calling 911. Grandpa called for him to come with him to help him, telling him there were people sleeping in the basement. Pounding on the door with no response, grandpa had a rock ready to throw through the window as he asked the young man if he could kick in the door?

Yes, he could...and did.

The son-in-law, now waking and thinking someone was trying to break in, was ready to fight.

"Get out! The house is on fire!"

Grandpa's words sent his son-in-law running to scoop up his six-year-old daughter who was still asleep. As they ran out the basement door, the doorjamb was burning.

As the sound and sight of flashing lights filled the cool night, the hysterical grandmother, pleaded with the 911 dispatcher to save her granddaughter and son-in-law. I could hear the dispatcher calmly telling my friend that they were out and safe.

In no time, a quivering little girl was lifted out of Grandpa's six-wheeler and placed safely into the waiting arms of her Grandma, who would ask me later why I didn't take the phone away from her. There were two reasons: She was on the land line, and, also, no matter how much she screamed or cried the dispatcher would know her location and she would have fought me for it.

The six-year old's worry is for her bunny, her dog, and her cat. Before long, her dad walks in the front door, carrying the bunny in one hand, the cat in the other, and the dog following close behind. The bunny is soaking wet, the cat has a sooty face, and they all smell like smoke. Smiles abound along with whispered voices saying, "Thank you, God!"

While grandma snuggled with granddaughter, I walked to the end of the driveway to view the scene. The flashing lights of fire trucks, rescue vehicles, and squad cars filled the picture. My thoughts turned to Mike—to Ken, my present husband, whose work brought them to these images—to other people in crisis. In my mind, I thanked the volunteer firemen. Later I would learn that the young man who kicked in the basement door was a state trooper's son. As calmness came over me replacing the fear of the past hour, the events played over in my mind, and I could almost hear Mike saying, "It was not their time."

That incident was also a reminder not to assume that location will automatically be known. Landlines are more easily traceable—tracked with better accuracy. This is not always so with cell phones. The cell phone call for help could be routed through the nearest cell phone tower to a neighboring 911 system. In 2018 when cell phones can tell Uber, Facebook, or even video games *and* designated contacts where you are located with amazing accuracy, 911 operators often cannot.

You can improve your chances of being located. If you're calling 911 from a mobile phone, most factors determining whether your device will be located by the dispatcher are outside your control. Here are a few tips to help emergency responders locate you: if you can get outside do it. The biggest challenge in locating cell phone calls is when they are indoors, subject to more interference between the phone and cell phone towers. Don't assume 911 can find you just because you dialed your phone. Be prepared to tell 911 as much as you can about your present location.

Tuesday, April 3, 2018 Arizona central.com writes an article about the 911. And it says that a new service is being provided. It will enable people to text 911. This will help the deaf or hard of hearing speech impaired but it will also help anyone who can't speak out loud without putting themselves in danger. A homeowner might be hiding in a closet from a burglar or domestic violence victim doesn't want an abuser to overhear their call. Those who need to text 911 are asked to keep their messages concise, provide an exact location and the nature of the emergency in the first message. They are also asked to avoid text abbreviations.

If you are in a tall building, make sure to tell the 911 operator what floor you are on or what room number you are in, ideally both. Even when it transmits your location, your phone does not transmit your altitude. In a tall building, that could cost responders time.

"It is now easier than ever for victims to reach 911, but harder than ever for responders to reach them," wrote David Shoar, the sheriff in St. John's County, Florida, and president of the Florida Sheriffs Association to the FCC in November 2016.

"Early one morning three young men headed out to go duck hunting on a lake outside of Duluth. One of the men soon realized that the boat was sinking. He swam toward shore using a bag of duck decoys as a flotation device with one of his friends, while the other friend clung to the boat filled with water. He dialed 911 for help. Remaining calm, he was able to give clear answers to the St. Louis County 911 dispatcher." *Duluth News Tribune*, March 10,2017.

They don't have a lot of happy endings. As the dispatcher took the 911 call, she was instructing the young man and asking questions until she could no longer hear him...but he could still hear her."

"People should look around and know where they are in relation to the shore so they're able to give directions if necessary," said St. Louis County Search and Rescue Squad Captain Rick Slatten, in an interview for the *Duluth News Tribune,* March10, 2017. "Many people say they're on the lake when calling 911, but a dispatcher needs a land location in relation to where a person is on the lake." The operator's longevity on the job means knowing what to say to people who are panicked. A calm demeanor during the emergency helps everyone stay calm.

March 27, 2018 the *Arizona Republic* reports that a Phoenix television station put live video of a cat stuck atop a power pole on Facebook, and the areas emergency 911 system was flooded with calls. Phoenix Fire Department dispatchers' activities nearly came to a screeching halt Monday morning amid an avalanche of emergency calls regarding the cat. It drew more than 319,000 views in the following hour. 11 dispatchers fielded at least 100 calls demanding a rescue unit, according to Phoenix Fire Capt. Rob McDade. McDade said "I love animals;

however, we have human lives we have to save at the same time. People with medical emergencies were forced to wait on the phone." Officials from the Salt River Project utility company are tasked with rescuing the cat. A spokesman for the SRP said a resident climbed a ladder and brought the cat down before the company's troubleshooter arrived.

There are a few things the 911 dispatchers would like you to know:

- Please don't call asking for phone numbers; we are not "Information." If you are on speakerphone, we can't hear you if you are speaking; our voices will electronically override yours. We know you are upset, but we can't help if we don't understand where you are or what type of assistance you need.
- Do not assume that our computers can pick up your location. We can get an idea of where you are, but there is no guarantee that information is accurate. Every question we ask is important.
- A dispatcher's job is also to keep our responders safe. When people who abuse the system tie up our lines, we are unable to help those in dire need. We spend our days dealing with high stress situations, and we do our best to guarantee a safe outcome for everyone involved. Please respect the 911 emergency system and call only for true emergencies.

Trooper Sergeant Jesse Grabow answers questions in his "Ask a Trooper Column."

Question: When on a freeway, and an emergency vehicle is approaching from the rear but not in the same lane, is it the law to pull over and stop? Stopping on the freeway can be very dangerous.

Answer: Minnesota state laws says that upon the immediate approach of an authorized emergency vehicle, the driver shall yield the right of way and shall immediately drive to a position parallel to and as close as possible to the right – hand edge or curb of the highway clear of any intersection, and shall stop and remain in this position until the authorized emergency vehicle has passed. If on a one – way roadway, the driver shall drive to the closest edge or curb and stop.

Every situation varies when emergency vehicles are responding to an incident and how much room there is to yield and move over and is there enough time for this to be done in a safe manner?

In my experience in responding to emergencies, I have seen drivers that had not seen or heard me behind them and this created a very dangerous situation. Some drivers noticed my presence translate and apply the brakes very hard at freeway speeds. Other dangerous situations that I see are lane changes as I am about to pass them on the left.

I talk about driving with 100% of your attention on the task of driving. By eliminating distractions, you will be able to see and hear an approaching emergency vehicle and other potentially dangerous situations that you may encounter.

If you find yourself with an emergency vehicle approaching you very quickly, safely slow down and move over as soon as you are able to and yield to them. Also watch out for the vehicles in front of you in the event that they break abruptly.

Law enforcement understands that there are some situations where motorists are not able to come to a complete stop, like on a freeway, so officer discretion will come into play.

Anne

She started working for the Robbinsdale Police Department, chalking tires. The hospital parking lot had a one-hour parking regulation, and they wanted it enforced. She drove a squad car and wore a uniform.

The woman telling her story is a retired 911 operator. She has heard the frantic screams of a wounded person and the terror in the voice of a parent whose child has been harmed. The manner of injury is diverse, but the drama taking place on the phone is similar. Someone is in a crisis, and she is their first call for help. She has also been the 911 caller needing help. Now retired, she has had time to reflect, to come to terms with a career that evolved rather accidentally.

Anne has an infectious laugh and a twinkle in her eye. Her goal was to be a stewardess. Her Godmother, a TWA stewardess with beautiful red hair, seemed larger than life, an Auntie Mame of sorts, and Anne wanted to be just like her.

Born and raised in Minnesota, Anne worked in a restaurant and drove school bus after graduation. She met her soon to be husband Earl the Friday before Thanksgiving, and they were married in February. After their marriage, he worked as a mechanic and she went to work at the courthouse in Family Court Services, bringing all the files needed for a particular case to court. She's not sure how she got that job.

They became parents in 1971—a baby girl. Anne stayed home for 10 months and then went to work dispatching for Brooklyn Center PD.

She wishes people knew how important the questions that she asks are. Even though the questions take a few seconds, help is not delayed. She tries to remember also that this may be the first time they have called 911.

She learned on the job. There was no official training for dispatching when she started. The dispatchers did everything. They took the calls, dispatched squads, ran license checks, took pictures of those brought to jail, gave them clothes, ordered their food, and helped the public at the window, and that names just a few things that they did.

Anne worked many places dispatching, and her husband, too, worked for different police departments and also for different counties. They ended up in Annandale. Their children were all in school. Brooklyn Center was hiring, and she got a job with them. She worked the dog watch from 11 p.m. to 7 a.m. or sometimes 7 p.m. to 7 a.m. When she got home in the morning, the kids were either getting ready for school or had already left, and that seemed to be working well. They left a lot of Post-it notes so people knew what was going on.

November 18, 1988, Anne walked in the house, and things didn't look right. Her husband's wallet wasn't where it should be. Something was wrong. She found Earl downstairs in cardiac arrest. Her children were home from school but she doesn't remember why. Calling 911 was different then. One just dialed, and then, if one hung up, they had a one-button pushback and would call back to the house.

They did CPR but could not get his heart beating. Her children were 17, 13, and 12.

Trying to spend time with her children, she would often be at a sporting event they were in but having to leave early to get to work. Sometimes questioned by someone at a championship game, wondering how she could leave, she knew there was someone sitting in a chair after a long day of frantic calls. They wanted to go home. She needed to be to work on time.

Anne learned to do a lot of things. Learning to pull a camper trailer, she and her children enjoyed the outdoors. She was 38 when her husband died. She sighs and reminds me that life goes on.

In 1990 she went to work for the Minnetonka police. She had a friend there, and he made sure she had nights.

Later she made the move to dispatching for Hennepin County. When dialing 911 for an emergency came into practice, she thought it was a mystery for many. She also encountered people who thought there was a charge for using it. There was a whole learning curve to the new emergency phone system. In the beginning, she thinks they respected it more. She knew from being somewhat on the administrative side, that 911 did not become what they intended it to be because they got calls for a barking dog or for someone stealing their recycling.

Taking the job for Hennepin County was a hard move. Hennepin county was the embodiment of a dispatch center. Uniforms are not worn home, so the first thing to do when arriving at work was to put the uniform on. Her drill? She sits down and the phone rings. Hennepin County Police and Fire or 911. This is Anne. What is your emergency?

She hears many hysterical people on the other end of the line. The people who cannot speak English well are difficult to understand. This was the number they were given if they needed help. They would call 911 if their baby was choking or if the mailman didn't come. It was that far apart with the help they needed.

To calm people when they are hysterical, she would drop her voice an octave and keep asking the same question until she got an answer: "What is your address? I can't help you until I get your address."

"Did you find yourself acting like a dispatcher with your family and friends when you weren't working?" I asked.

Of course, and it's still with her. The biggest thing she shares is that she interrupts people and asks so many questions. She bites her tongue and reminds herself she is not working, that it's not her turn to talk.

Anne had kept in contact with a man she drove school bus with years ago. He was working for the Minnesota State Patrol and had been promoted. She called to congratulate him, and he told her about a man he thought she should meet. He had lost his wife from a heart attack.

DJ to Dispatch

He wanted to be a radio announcer. He relaxes in a chair when our interview starts. He grew up in North Minneapolis, listening to the popular radio stations. I smiled as he talked of the radio stations. I had listened to the same ones. Graduating high school in 1970, he was called into the military and spent 1971-1973 serving his country. When he got out, he attended Brown Institute to learn how to be a disc jockey. He got his first on-the-air job in a city in South Dakota. But, $400 a month and the perks of being on the radio (young female listeners wooed him) weren't enough. He went back to the cities and got a job playing polka tunes. That quickly changed when he interviewed for a dispatch position with the Minnesota State Patrol. When they heard he was a disc jockey and knew the area, they hired him on the spot.

He started in 1974, working in what was called The Dungeon. A bit nervous on his first day, he was a fast learner, and dispatching was fairly easy. A desk man answered the traffic law questions. Bruce answered accident calls. At that time, there weren't that many.

There was no official training—just OJT. He rode with the troopers in the air and on the road. It helped him do his job. They were the link to everyone. The dispatchers got to know the troopers personally. They visited him in the dungeon.

He wore a uniform every day, was asked a lot of questions about the law, but stopped wearing uniforms when a trooper was killed. He looked sad, and the tone of his voice changed. He didn't know his friend had died. No one told him. He heard it on the radio and almost drove off the road.

The trooper had been shot and killed early Saturday morning June 2, 1997. He was assisting county deputies who were responding to a shooting call. As they approached a car, they saw the suspect lying on the front seat. The man sat up and began firing, striking the trooper in the chin. He died about an hour later. He had been with the Minnesota State Patrol for fifteen years.

The dispatcher continued with his story. He wasn't married yet when he left the radio station, but his mother had heard about this woman at the church circle. She was an LPN. He didn't like that she smoked but she was really cute and they eventually tied the knot. Christine died at age 42 from smoking and heart bypass surgery. She had already had surgery twice and died having the third surgery. When he arrived at the hospital, the doctor told him she wasn't going to make it. He had about ten minutes to be with her. He had two young sons, eight and eleven, to raise and learned how to cook with help from his mom. His parents also helped with the kids. The boys were missing their mom, and he needed to work a day shift. He was disappointed that it took so long for him to get that schedule; but, when he finally did, things got easier.

Bruce met his second wife, Anne, through a trooper who used to drive school buses with her. She worked as a 911 operator. They married and lived in his house for a year, then bought a lot and built a new home.

Bruce worked from 1974 to 2009—35 years. I asked him if and how things had changed since he started. They had fun in the old days. They can't have fun anymore. Troopers would call, ask what the dispatchers wanted to eat, and bring them meals.

He received many calls and letters from people, thanking him for his help. Strange as well as sad phone calls came in. One man called to report a man spitting on his car. Bruce said they would keep an eye out for that person. His worst call was a murder/suicide. The man just got home; his family's been killed. His son's still in there.

He went on to say he never knew what kind of a call he would get. Any call could be an emergency.

He decries political correctness, and believes it has become extreme. Everyone has to careful what they say and there's no camaraderie like there used to be. But yes, all in all, it was a good job, and he would go back to it again today. He sees it's getting more dangerous every day to be in law enforcement, and they'd better be scared for their safety.

Incidentally, his children, who thought his work was normal and looked up to him, now have related careers.

> *"The purpose of human life is to serve, and to show compassion and the will to help others."*
>
> —Albert Schweitzer

CHAPTER 37

THE SOUNDS OF SILENCE

The involvement of crime is difficult. Especially if it is an intrusion into your personal life. Someone stealing your car or breaking into your home is a frightening disturbance of your sense of safety, your feeling of control. Suddenly you are vulnerable. You call the police and they make a report. At times it may seem mundane. They hear it, write it, go to court and testify about it.

However, there are law enforcement officers who listens to the brutal words of an abuser or to the heart wrenching story of the abused. It might be physical, sexual, or both. They are trained to hear the horrible wounding one person can do to another. They try hard to develop a separation from what they hear but it affects them immensely.

She has to listen carefully. Sometimes the voices get so soft she can hardly hear them. The woman turns up the volume and listens as hard as she can. It has to be right. She has to transcribe the words that are said. As she told me about her job, she talks in a soft voice herself. She listens to interviews with victims and perpetrators of crimes and types what she hears for the court transcript.

I had never thought about the fact that someone interviews and of course someone types those interviews. The victims of crimes are sometimes reluctant to talk. Spouses who are beaten by the person they love find the words hard to say out loud. They often feel a sense of shame that they contributed to this abuse or at the very least shame that they did not leave a long time ago.

Some secrets hidden away are difficult to drag into the bright light of knowledge. Sexual abuse of a child is heart wrenching as the child struggles with words to describe the fear and exploitation. Sometimes they are too young to know the words to describe what has happened to them.

The interviewer is a professional, a member of the police department, or a social worker. They are trained—seasoned veterans. It doesn't make what they're hearing less sad or difficult to hear but they have heard it so many times before. They have seen and heard the seamy side of life already too many times. They've toughened to the heartache brought too often by people close to the victim—often it's family members—the persons we should be able to trust the most.

It's so hard for her to hear what someone can do to a child. She's typing the cruel behavior of one human being toward another. What do you do someone will ask? She types for the city or county. This woman can't tell anyone what she actually does. She can't talk about it. They think she types letters or something. This soft-spoken woman can't say that she is typing the anguish and torment one person has done to another.

The person typing the information is a stranger to the people whose voices they hear on the recorder, but it is also a human being listening to the terror or the admission of brutality that has been perpetrated on another. *She thought she couldn't do this anymore. The pretty woman has tears in her eyes. She's heard too much... knows too much. Is it her age, is she getting too old? She has to hear it right. Some would talk low or high or didn't want to be heard. She had decided that she couldn't do this work anymore, but then they needed her to help again, and she couldn't say no.*

Sexual assault and molestation have become almost common place. In the *West Central Tribune*, Saturday July 28, 2018, the paper reports that a 74-year-old was charged with felony kidnapping and false imprisonment after he tried to pull a ten-year-old girl into the men's restroom at a store. It seems that almost daily the television news or an article in the paper has yet another story of attempted or actual sexual assault.

West Central Tribune Friday, September 8, 2017.

"Three men were charged with a total of 12 felonies Thursday for allegedly kidnapping and assaulting a 15-year-old girl over a 29-day period until the girl escaped and they were arrested."

Smaller towns in rural Minnesota no longer escape the crime normally found in bigger cities. Local police departments are dealing with larger more brutal crimes. Longtime residents are asking themselves why? What's happening in our society?

Colleges are also finding themselves trying to search through individual accounts of what happened—really happened, between students behind closed doors, often with alcohol involved in the encounters. Booze, young women and young men always has and always will make for a volatile mix. The usual *he said/she said* runs into a quagmire when sexual assault is the charge. Some feel that the charges by women is often remorse when the drug wears off and in the bright light of day reality hits.

"Colleges are struggling to find fairness. An article in the *Star Tribune* September 25, 2016 says a student at Gustavus Adolphus College in St. Peter, Minnesota wrote on Facebook that another student had raped her and that the college had punished him with a 500-page essay. That started off a petition drive demanding that campus rapists be expelled and touched off changes that are reshaping the campus today."

Newspapers and television have been filled with the horror show concerning the sexual assault on more than 150 young American girl gymnasts and former USA gymnastics. Dr. Larry Nassar will spend the rest of his life locked up after a judge sentenced him to 42-175 years in prison.

Priests in the Catholic Church have damaged the image of their religion so intensely that it will take years to fully recover. Several people I have talked to have asked themselves, *how can I stay in my church?* They are praying that the Pope will take aggressive steps to stop this once and for all and a recovery will take place. Faithful Roman Catholics worldwide wait to see whether changes will be made.

Her town celebrated what was called an "All-night Sing" always the Saturday closest to July 4th. "A young man asked if he could sit by her. He was so sweet and so nice. He asked if he came the next year would she go out with him? She said she'd have to ask her mom. The next year she bought fabric and a neighbor sewed a new dress for her. She had told her mom about the man and her mom had said that he could take her home. She wore the newly sewed white dress. Instead of taking her home he took her into the woods, raped her and then took her home. She wadded up the dress and put it in the bottom of her dresser. She doesn't know whatever happened to it.

The #MeToo movement has again brought to the forefront the tragically ignored truth—women in all walks of life and of all ages are sexually exploited and harassed at times by men.

In the *USA Today*, Dec 18, 2017 the headline reads: "Sexual Harassment Cases Have Congress Flailing."

Allegations of sexual harassment and misconduct have increased on Capitol Hill. It seems as if congressional leaders not sure of how to handle this are flying by the seat of their pants.

Leaders in both parties seem to be scrambling to get to the bottom of allegations on a case-by-case basis, looking over their shoulder to see if they're next, even urging some members to step down before the ethics committee finishes an inquiry.

Accusations of rape against Harvey Weinstein, longtime movie mogul, have been broadcast and published in newspapers. He has responded over and over again: any allegations of nonconsensual sex are unequivocally denied.

Power plays a role in this, just going along with something doesn't necessarily mean consent. One actress said in dealing with Harvey Weinstein that she had just froze in fear. She guessed it would be considered rape, because she didn't want to do it.

On November 29, 2017, Savanna Guthrie announced at the top of the Today Show that her former co-anchor Matt Lauer had been fired. Shortly after that announcement, Garrison Keillor, the radio host of Prairie Home Companion, joined Lauer on the list of men accused of sexual harassment and assault. Keillor was also dismissed.

Earlier Charlie Rose, CBS morning show host, had been fired amid charges of sexual harassment. One has to ask how many and for how long people that worked with him knew. I dare say if the truth be known coworkers in every aspect of putting on the television morning show had heard that gossip. I watched Charlie along with the others on CBS in the morning and I liked him.

West Central Tribune reports Tuesday, May 1, 2018 that the University of Minnesota paid $282,000 to resolve sexual harassment complaints against Athletic Director, Norwood Teague. Teague said he had entirely too much to drink and behaved inappropriately and communicated inappropriately towards his colleagues.

Beloved entertainer Bill Crosby who we all thought was the perfect father figure falls from grace amid not just accusations but the conviction of being a rapist and now spends his time locked in a cell.

Will this really bring about a much-needed change, or will it be like the 1990s full of thunder and then slowly relegating itself once again to a flash in the pan? Will it be trendy and fashionable for a while, then back to the usual behavior, and the acceptance once again of that behavior?

The 1990s began as a feminist decade. Clarence Thomas had been nominated to become a Supreme Court Justice. Anita Hill testified, claiming that Thomas had sexually harassed her when they worked together. Her testimony was compelling but either not believed or they simply didn't want to hear it. I watched the hearings on television and was ashamed of some of the legislatures I had previously held in high regard.

Just a year after Anita Hill's testimony, Democrats chose Bill Clinton as their presidential nominee. What started with Hill leading nightly newscasts suddenly became the scandal of Monica Lewinsky and many others accusing President Clinton of affairs and sexual harassment.

Mike and I were spending the winter in Sarasota, Florida and watched the proceedings play out. On January 26, 1998, Clinton told the nation, "I did not have sexual relations with that woman, Miss Lewinsky." I remember those words and his finger wagging at the camera. I believed him, I wanted to believe him. He was my president. I had voted for him. Clinton later confessed that he did indeed have an *improper* physical relationship with Monica Lewinsky.

Our former president is getting attention again, all these years later, with a special on A&E "The Clinton Affair" and also his interview with Judy Woodruff on PBS.

I recorded the interview and have watched it many times. He was our president and his lack of empathy for Monica was inexcusable.

Judy said "Al Franken has resigned. Do you think that's a good thing?"

Former president Bill Clinton replied "Well in general I think it's a good thing, yes." He continued "I think it's a good thing that we should all have higher standards. I think the norms have really changed in terms of, what you can do to somebody against their will, how much you can crowd their space, make them miserable at work."

Woodruff also asked him if he owed Monica an apology. He said "No."

In a CBS interview Sunday October 14, 2018 correspondent Tony Dokoupil asked Hillary Clinton if she thought her husband should have resigned after his affair with Lewinsky, then a White House intern, became public.

"Absolutely not," Clinton said. Clinton also said the relationship wasn't an abuse of power on the former president's part. Lewinsky was "an adult."

Gloria Steinem told the Guardian on February 6, 2017 that she would not mount the same vigorous defense of Bill Clinton today that she offered in a controversial 1998 article.

"We have to believe women. I wouldn't write the same thing now because there's probably more known about other women now. I'm not sure," she said on the red carpet of an annual comedy benefit for the MS Foundation for Women.

"What you write in one decade you don't necessarily write in the next. But I'm glad I wrote it in that decade."

"If all the sexual allegations now swirling around the White House turn out to be true, President Clinton may be a candidate for sex addiction therapy," read Steinem's 1998 essay, titled Feminists and the Clinton Question.

Clinton is not the only United States President that has been known for his inappropriate sexual behavior, including our President Donald Trump. President John Kennedy's long time inappropriate sexual behavior was widely known by the media but no one ever asked him about it at a press conference.

Maybe the climate has changed. Maybe thoughts and feelings have changed about women. Saturday Night Live—once home of our now former Senator Al Franken—became a standard against which comedy is measured. Franken made his reputation before his political career as a rude, foul mouthed Saturday Night Live comedian. Franken's views on women as sexual objects were clear. Voters seemed to not care who he had been or what he represented years ago, and voted him to be a United States Senator from my state of Minnesota.

"Jane, you ignorant slut," became a catchphrase by capitalizing on the stereotypes that have harmed women. Women gathered around the television for decades to laugh at the insulting rhetoric SNL served. I was one of them.

We, the women today, are the other half of the population that empowered our descent into crudeness. Women have gone along buying into the stereotypes—and fashion—that diminish them and their daughters. I watched the 40th anniversary of Saturday Night Live and laughed out loud. I laughed so hard tears came during the three and a half hours special. We must ask ourselves what we have contributed to the climate of conflict concerning our treatment. Have we giving mixed signals and do we continue to give those same signs even today?

Sexual violence affects everyone. Someone you know—your mother, your sister, your son or daughter, your spouse, friend, neighbor or co-worker—has been a victim. You also may know someone who has perpetrated sexual violence.

> *"All I insist on, and nothing else, is that you should show the whole world that you are not afraid. Be silent, if you choose; but when it is necessary, speak—and speak in such a way that people will remember it."*

> —Wolfgang Amadeus Mozart

CHAPTER 38

EYE OF THE STORM

With the sun just rising and a cool wind on his face, he started his trek through tall grass. This is his idyllic place—his job—his life. Soft spoken, he seemed shy when our interview started, but that characterization was quickly dismissed. He was reserved but friendly and forthcoming. His love of nature was in his blood. At the prospect of my interview, he had scrolled through his mind, dragging up memories of life growing up in the outdoors.

His father had also been a game warden and, as such, was rarely home. His recollection of his father's work began when he was about six. They were living in southern Minnesota. The house had no running water, kerosene lamps, an outhouse, and a chamber pot. Cars were not provided by the state at that time, so his father drove the family car for work. A brother and sister were also a part of the family. They all rode along with dad at times. Since his father was out checking hunters and fisherman, his mother was often called on to answer questions from the public and also to do some of the actual work of a game warden. She knew the answers. Men came to their house; well-dressed hunters would stop by with their big American Pointer dogs. When a hunter or trapper brought a fox in to collect the bounty payment, she grabbed an axe, walked up to the stump, and cut off the feet. This prevented the person from going to the next county and getting paid again.

The now retired game warden continued his stroll down memory lane. Pheasants were dropped off in crates at their home and his dad would release them into the wild. He recalled his dad working in the northern part of the state during deer hunting season because there was not a hunting season in southern Minnesota. He had told his dad to bring him back a bear cub.

The love and respect he had for his father and the profession each had chosen was evident in his words and the expression on his face as he talked of his father. "Were you proud of him, I ask?" Yes, of course he was proud of him. "Did he know," I asked? Well, he never said that to him.

Later after moving to Southern Minnesota, he remembers a game warden coming to his house and said that he and his dad had to go and look for stranded hunters. He thought the man had said "strangled hunters" and it scared him.

There was no television so of course no weather channel. In 1940 people walked outside their doors, looked at the sky, and tried to read the signs of weather. My grandmother felt a storm coming when her arthritis acted up. There was also the WCCO radio signal, which had what passed then as a weather forecast. The local newspaper also contained information about the weather. It was, however, just a guess as to what kind of conditions may lay in store.

November 11, 1940, began sunny and mild with a warm temperature of 50° across Minnesota. Waterfowl hunters headed out wearing perhaps a light jacket and short sleeve shirt. They were enjoying the unseasonable conditions and unaware of what was churning on the western horizon. An extended Indian Summer had duck hunters longing for blustery, wet, miserable, cold weather. Change was overdue. Sloughs, secluded bays, and marshes called to the hunters scanning the skies for the great flocks of ducks coming from Canada.

One can imagine the hunters getting their decoys, shells, and shotguns ready along with their boats. Food for the day was packed and Thermoses were ready for hot coffee.

In his book, *Where the Sky Began: Land of the Tallgrass Prairie*, John Madson describes the genesis of a Midwestern blizzard as "a temperature marriage of cold, dry Polar air sweeping down from Canada and warm, moist subtropical air welling up from the Gulf of Mexico."

My dad was 25 when the ferocious November 11, 1940, blizzard hit the Minnesota prairie. He spoke often of the infamous storm. He and my mother had been married for two years and had a baby girl who was almost a year old. He talked often of the wide-open spaces with nothing to stop the unrelenting summer winds that roared across the prairie nor winter blizzards that came with unstoppable voracity.

He spoke about what was then called Armistice Day (now Veteran's Day) storm differently. It was still fall. The first part of the month had been warm. This blizzard had been wide spread: Livestock perished by the hundreds of thousands; losses to wildlife, especially pheasants, were spectacular; many found themselves in trouble hunting ducks on that fateful day on Lac qui Parle Lake, which was close to my parents' farm. The few communications and power systems they had in the area at that time were disrupted, and moving about was brought to a standstill. Towns and villages close to a main road became shelters for stranded travelers as they sought refuge from the storm. People opened their homes to strangers, providing protection from the deadly forces of early snow and freezing weather.

For some there was no shelter, no refuge. Motorists stuck in snowdrifts on remote stretches of road were buried alive in their cars, their frozen bodies not found for days.

My dad told of farmers who, after checking on their livestock, could not find their way from the barn back to their farmhouse. The general savagery of winter storms on the prairie, not just the Armistice Day storm, had disoriented many a farmer. A rope tied between the house and the barn kept them safe, but they were not prepared this early in the season.

According to weather.gov. the National Weather Service Reports, when it was all over, about 20 hunters had drowned or frozen to death after being stranded mostly along the Mississippi River. Many stayed out too long because the hunting was great as waterfowl tried to escape the storm.

In all, the blizzard killed 154 people in the Upper Midwest, including 49 in Minnesota. The highest snow total was 26.6 inches, which was reported in Collegeville. The storm caused gales on Lake Michigan that wrecked ships, killing 59 people.

The storm took many lives. It was known as the day all hell broke loose—the day ducks flew and men died.

Willis Kruger, a Minnesota Game Warden had made plans that morning to team up with another warden and spend the day checking the numerous waterfowl hunters scattered throughout the backwaters of the nearby Mississippi River.

Willis was born on May 26, 1907. He started his career as a state game warden on July 29, 1939. He was a game warden for 15 months when the storm hit. He was 33 years old when the blizzard came roaring down the Mississippi River Valley.

For waterfowl hunters, November is the month they have been waiting for. The anticipation of the hunt brings thoughts of alarm clocks going off early in the morning, motoring on the river, northwest winds, putting out waterfowl decoys, and the whistling of wings from ducks that can't be seen yet. Maybe there's a hot cup of coffee before legal starting time, and then the first ducks come into the decoys.

November 9, 1940, a Sunday, was a routine day according to the entries Willis made in his daily report at the end of the day:

> *November 9 – went by car to West Newton Bottoms. It was raining hard but patrolled part of this area by canoe. Then went to West Newton near Fisher Island. Patrolled this area checking hunters for over limit licenses and unplugged guns. Ducks were flying good and a hard rain continued all day. Stayed in slough until dark. Missed two late shooters on account of poor visibility. I was not so certain who they were so could not make an arrest. Patrolled nearly all of Weaver slough and one main camp where most hunters go out from.*

Willis returned home, but, as in the case of today's conservation officer, he was never off duty.

He wrote:

> *The two fishermen from Alma, Wisconsin called at my home at night. After questioning, I gave them back the gill net, which I had found with no tags on. In a telephone conversation with the Wisconsin warden, I found out they were good, honest fishermen and that the tags no doubt were stolen from the nets. I believe this is the best way to settle this minor trouble as long as Wisconsin would be involved with it.*
>
> *November 10 – Went by car to Lake City. Checked on gill netting belonging to a fisherman. He does not have his nets out so returned to Waukesha. Went into West Newton Bottoms. Checked a few hunters here then went into Weavers Bottom. Patrolled this area the balance of the day, watching for open water shooting and so forth. Shooting stopped a few minutes after 4:00. Had trouble getting out of slough on account of fog but found my car about 5:30 and returned home.*

That would be the end of his routine patrol for several days. The next day he would be caught up in the middle of the Armistice Day blizzard.

November 11 – Met another warden. We decided to check hunters all day and try to find a hunter whom we believed was hunting in Weaver Bottoms. A very big wind came up so we warned a few hunters to leave the area. Arrived home about 5:30 PM and immediately went to sheriff's office and reported bad storm. A call came in that one man had drowned and another in very bad shape at Pughs Point... We found roads blocked but finally got to Pughs Point. Conditions were terrible, waves 4 to 5 feet high and any attempt at rescuing hunters would have resulted in death for us. We drove around locating cars and missing hunters.... Went to Nelson, Wisconsin to answer a call sent in earlier in the evening.... Both hunters there were found dead, three rescued alive.

November 12 – Rescued two Rochester hunters alive, aided the Sheriff in other rescue work...took my car and patrolled West Newton and Weaver Bottoms area. All hunters appear to have gotten out safely in this area. Stopped at hunting camp to inquire about missing persons.... Sheriff aided me with all this work. We searched the area below Waukesha for 3 St. Paul hunters believed to have drowned. Found overturned boat in Robinson Lake. Waves were very high yet... rescue work very dangerous. All hunters alive are saved.

November 13 – Went by car to Burrichters slough. I got across ice on Robinson Lake, patrolled islands for bodies of St. Paul hunters. Ice is unsafe to put many people on... Patrolled this area until 11:00 a.m. then went to Pughs point to look for Waukesha hunter who had drowned. We used boats and pike poles trying to locate his body... Bodies of two hunters found at Robinson Lake near shore. I walked past them at least four times but did not see them. Also was near them Monday night... Sheriff and I drove to Weaver's slough. Report of car still parked at West Newton. When we got there, it was gone. A Lake City hunter had spent night at farmhouse after spending the entire night in the swamp on Monday. We returned home at 9:30 p.m.

November 14 – spent most of morning below Wabasha searching for St. Paul hunter in Robinson Lake. At noon went home, ate dinner, but before I went to Waukesha drove to Pugh's point. Tested ice and took soundings in bay. Ice was safe so got pike poles, ice chisels and went back to Pugh's point, chopped holes all afternoon, and searched for body of Waukesha hunter. Returned home at 10:15.

November 15 – went to Pughs point. Helped with rescue work in recovery of Waukesha hunter. Received a call St. Paul Police Department was sending an expert down to recover body. Met him at Burrichters. He stated we were using the only right method to recover body... Spent entire day on recovery of bodies.

Kruger was still participating in searches for missing hunters but five days after the storm began his usual law enforcement duties.

November 16 – went to Pugh's point. Worked all morning on rescue work. Dragged river for body of Waukesha hunter... Made trip down river looking for hunter's equipment. Caught a man shooting ducks in open water. Took his gun and license and when I looked at his license, I saw he was only 16 years old. Told him he was under advisement but gave back gun and license. Will investigate later as to age as he certainly looked over 16 years.

Went to boat landing at Waukesha, helped unload seine and then returned home. Had calls to answer and several parties called at home for information about hunting. I have several investigations to make but have had no time to spare. They are minor charges so will take care of first part of the week.

November 30 – It snowed all morning and I stayed home. At noon patrolled out towards Thielman. Watched for pheasants to get a better check on them. Issued some retaining tags there... Patrolled part of the area for pheasant signs but drifting made this work useless and no hunters were out. Returned to Waukesha about 5:30 and worked on monthly expense account. Completed daily reports for mailing. Body of Waukesha hunter never recovered.

Willis Kruger retired in 1970. He had worked for the Department of Natural Resources for 31 years as a Game Warden. He received many honors for his work as a warden. The Kruger Management Area of the Richard J. Dorer Memorial Hardwood Forest near Wabasha is named in his honor.

When Game Warden Kruger's son was in ninth grade, he got a job working in a printshop. Later he went to Dunwoody and learned more about printing, received his certification, but didn't know if this is what he really wanted to do. He got a job in Wildlife Management. His superior there told him to get his degree. He did and went to work with his dad for two weeks and also trained with other officers. When he started, the title of Game Warden was important to him. Later, that was changed to Conservation Officer. It took some getting used to. Even after the change, people still referred to them as game wardens—introduced them as game wardens. This Conservation Officer thinks they wanted the change because at that point they had more duties protecting wildlife in many different ways. He took a job in Minneapolis but stayed only three months.

He met a young lady at the St. Paul office. She was a secretary and he was smitten.

When they married, her husband drove a state car and she had her own. They moved to Mankato and she was hired at the state office downtown. Six weeks later she was pregnant. Their baby boy was born the same day John F. Kennedy was killed; the priest said she should name her son John. Her parents came down from Minneapolis. They had heard the news of the president's death on the radio and her mother spent the whole time in the hospital chapel praying for the Kennedy family.

Ten months later another son was born and they bought a brand-new tract home. Eleven months after the birth of their second son, a girl was born, they moved to a larger house in a different neighborhood. The neighborhood was full of young people and children. The move was wonderful and she felt like she truly belonged.

Her husband was gone the majority of the time, day or night—she, home with three little ones. Calling the game warden was calling their home. His work number and home phone number were the same and was freely handed out. The phone rang day and night. Calls came from people wanting to know the laws or from a bar to settle an argument about the law. Sometimes they wondered if people called to ask a question or just to see if he was out there working.

His wife would answer questions on the phone with only what was in the "Synopsis" a booklet explaining the rules. It was up to date and she didn't have to worry about giving the wrong information. Her husband couldn't be there for school functions and other family things, as he was dedicated. If he actually wanted to have time off he had to leave town, otherwise people would come to their house or find him in town someplace.

The State of Minnesota decided the Conservation Officers were going to work a forty-hour week. They were not happy—felt they couldn't do their job—didn't have time to educate as well as enforce the law.

Being alone much of the time made the young mother self-sufficient and self-reliant. When the children were all in school, she became a part-time manager of the officer for fundraising at the Y. She met many people, and they also got to know her. Mankato State University called, there was an opening in the Athletics Department. She got a part-time job and loved it. With that job she was eligible for free tuition classes and took classes for six years eventually ending up with a degree in Business Administration and was promoted to Office Manager.

The pride this wife has in her husband is evident. She talked of his integrity. If he saw a father who had a child with him while breaking the law, he would send the child to the car. He did not want to reprimanded the father in front of his child.

The last year he worked, her husband got a cell phone, a promotion, and had a downtown office. This new position meant he dealt more with the guys and wasn't out in the field. He missed a lot of school activities but there were a few perks for his children. People often brought newborn animals to their door thinking the babies were abandoned. He brought one of those little fawns to school. It was exciting when the baby started crying as they walked down the hallway. School room doors opened. It was a great time until the little one pooped all over his uniform.

He taught a course on Game and Fish and safety with boats and snowmobiles at Mankato State University for twelve years before he retired and for another two years after retiring. Retiring at 59, he also worked as a Bailiff for eight years.

"I go to nature every day for inspiration in the day's work."

—*Frank Lloyd Wright*

CHAPTER 39

THE LONG AND WINDING ROAD

His mind made a promise his body can't keep. The retired Chief of the Minnesota State Patrol talked of getting older and remembering his remarkable life. He had no intentions of going into the law enforcement field. Married and the father of two children, he was working as a representative of an insurance company selling memberships and automobile insurance. His goal was to sell a hundred memberships in one month, and he did just that. After reaching his goal, he found himself losing interest. They offered him a district manager position, but he had decided it was not for him. He told his wife that he just couldn't put his heart into it anymore.

He saw an ad in the St. Paul Pioneer press. They were hiring for the Minnesota Highway Patrol. He was still working for an insurance company and was in the cities. He asked if there was a place in the metro that he could take the exam. Yes there was and they gave him the address. There wasn't an empty chair when he walked into the packed auditorium at 9 a.m. He decided he wasn't going to take that exam; he still had a job. As he walked down the hall to leave, a gentleman came around the corner and asked him if he was there for the test. The gentleman told him that people were bringing extra chairs. So, he went back in, sat down, and took the test. If that guy hadn't come around the corner, he would have walked. He was at the right place at the right time.

Roger was 28 and one of the oldest rookies. He had talked it over with his wife, and she was supportive. His ambition in life at that time was to make $10,000 a year. That was a good wage in the 60s. The Highway Patrol paid $224 a month while he attended Rookie School. When he graduated, the patrol sent him to Erskine, Minnesota. They had not had a trooper there before. He doesn't remember being particularly nervous but was excited his first day at work. He patrolled heavily traveled highways 2 and 59 and was there for 18 and a half years. He felt camaraderie with the people he worked with and went on to say he had great partners. He eventually became Sergeant and then Captain but had never had any aspirations of being Chief of the Minnesota State Patrol.

He was promoted to the rank of Sergeant (now called Lieutenant) and that meant a move to Mankato. His wife wasn't excited about that. Their children were in college and they were living on the lake. He had a friend, a doctor, and told him that his wife didn't want to move. The doctor said he should take the promotion. After the move he wrote to the doctor and said that if he didn't like it, it was his fault.

They hadn't lived in their new town for a week when his wife got a call, asking if she liked to bowl. They needed her to substitute. His wife went and she loved it. Summer came, and she was busy with golf. Mankato was where the Minnesota Vikings football team trained and she liked watching them practice. The players on the team soon knew her by her first name.

Then came the promotion to Captain and a move to Virginia. When he got promoted this time his wife was agreeable. They had moved once and that worked okay. He then attended the Northwestern Institute of Traffic Investigation.

I asked if he thought law enforcement officers are scared today.

He hopes they're not scared. He thinks they should be cautious. They take a physical test and a psych test to make sure that they are physically and mentally able to do the job.

He talks about the process of hiring for the Minnesota State Patrol. Applicants are upset if they don't pass a psych exam and are passed over. They say they're not crazy. Of course not. It's just that a psych evaluation lets them know if they are ready to be a police officer.

A trooper also does an investigation on the person applying for the job. The trooper talks to the local police department, the sheriff, to neighbors, and to anyone in the community who knows the person applying for the job. The trooper does a thorough investigation, and, by the time he/she is finished asking questions about the applicant, the trooper knows a lot about this person.

I asked about cameras. He's in favor of them. He tells me that the individual can explain what actually happened, but the camera tells it exactly. There are two sides to the story—always this and that, but the lens in the camera sees it all.

I ask about car chases.

He knows if you don't chase, it gets to become common knowledge, and they'll run from you every time. The supervisor will help the troopers involved decide if they should continue with the chase. If the motorist takes off, the trooper doesn't know if he might've just killed someone or stolen that vehicle.

He's a policeman not a politician is how he answered when the commissioner asked him if he would like to be Chief of the Minnesota

State Patrol. Then he was asked who he thought would make a good chief. He mentioned a few names—who he thought would be good—their strong points—their weak points.

The commissioner said he had received over 250 letters from people who express their opinions as to who they thought should be Chief of the State Patrol. No one mentioned his name. Nobody knew him. That's why the commissioner wanted him.

The commissioner wanted Roger in his office the next day for pictures and press. He was to wear a class A uniform. He'd be meeting the Governor.

Roger considered himself an anomaly. Normally those positions are very political. People thought he might be eaten alive, but he lasted 10 years. He was non-political, and was the longest-serving chief in the history of the patrol.

When he became chief, he made getting drunk drivers off the road a priority long before it was popular to do so. He talked of the time when, if someone had been drinking, the police just brought him home.

It had to distance him in some situations, in some way, was his answer when I asked if he felt a distance from the troops, first as a sergeant, then as captain, and lastly as the chief.

He continued with his revere: sometimes on a Friday night, he would get in his car, grab a cup of coffee and ride with one of the troopers until about 10 p.m. when the dog watch car came. Then he would jump in the car with him. He got a call from a trooper in Forest Lake, asking when he was coming to ride with him.

The Chief spent time on public relations. He was often featured on WCCO's radio's popular morning show. He wanted to enhance the public opinion of the state patrol. The patrol had an extraordinary friendly relationship with the public because of him.

Mike's mom listened faithfully to WCCO radio and would often comment that she had heard the chief.

When Mike's father passed away suddenly at the age of 67, the chief came for the funeral. I told him that we were honored that he took the time to be there. He wanted the troopers to know that he appreciated their work and that they and their families were an important part of this organization.

The popular men of WCCO's morning show were the emcees at the chief's retirement party. He told people who attended, that 90 percent came to his party to see the emcees, and the other 10 percent came to make sure he was really leaving.

Roger had lots of friends outside of law enforcement – all through the years he worked and today as well.

He was not ready to retire. He had a mandatory retirement because of his age. He still had things that he wanted to do and was capable physically and mentally to do them. One of the things that's difficult is that in any leadership role, there are things some of the people would not understand. He couldn't say that the commissioner said this is what we have to do. Roger couldn't pass the buck. Some decisions he didn't agree with either, but it didn't matter, it was going to happen.

Roger is alone now and talks of his wife. He believes that being the spouse of a state trooper must be one of the toughest jobs there is. They were on the night shift a lot. He would have never made it without her. After he retired, his daughter said that her mom never closed her eyes until he drove into the yard. He always knew his wife and children were proud of him.

No, he would not want the job again. Not with the circumstances that exist today. But, if he could live it all over again—just the way it was, then absolutely!

"Retirement is not the end of the road. It is the beginning of the open highway."

– Author unknown

CHAPTER 40

THE LONG ARM OF THE LAW

Distrust. Aggression. Confrontation. Law officers are seeing it all. Drivers ignoring attempts to stop them and flee. People are more brazen and want to fight with the police. Law enforcement is walking on eggshells. They feel more scrutinized, second guessed, their life threatened more than ever. Officers are trying to keep their communities safe while the people are often questioning their methods.

Police do not want to kill you and they will go that extra mile to try and keep you alive. In interviews a police department does their best to weed out anyone who would not be a good fit for a job in law enforcement. Do some wrong people get into the law enforcement arena? Yes, of course, just as in every occupation, every field of work, has its problems with people who should never have been hired or could not stand up to the pressure and expectations of their employers.

As I write this, I am remembering a trooper who worked with Mike… A hard-working trooper and dedicated family man. However, he threw up at accidents and soon found another job. Not everyone is cut out to see the sights, hear the sounds, and handle the odor of a fatal car crash, or a person who has committed suicide and not found for several days.

The public has a right to expect people in all jobs to be honest and up standing citizens—that is not going to be. We do however have a right to expect good behavior from certain people in certain professions. Police officers are not the only ones we can and should expect better of.

When I board an airplane, I should be able to trust that the pilot is sober and not psychotic. I expect to be assured that my doctor is not impaired from drug use and is not a pervert. Our teachers impact our young life for nine months each year for a minimum of twelve years. We should be able to expect them not only to know how to teach but that they are not pedophiles.

What are your thoughts about accusations of police brutality?

A group of about 70 people, between the ages of 28-88, not in law enforcement, answered unanimously that they continue to trust the police. Their fingers pointed at the overzealous media hype. As well as the video taping of law enforcement when the altercation was already in progress that didn't tell the true story.

Of course, there are some bad apples that get into law enforcement. However, they are quickly discovered and let go.

The sergeant can only speak from his 21 years of experience working with his police department. During his time, he has been on thousands of calls, witnessed many situations where officers were required to use force ranging from simple escort holds, pressure points, all the way up to deadly force. He can say with confidence that in his experience, 95% of the time officers showed great restraint and used the proper amount of force. He has mentioned before that the use of force never looks good to any citizen. In his experience, the public has a difficult time differentiating between proper use of force and police brutality.

He continued with a common example – the average citizen has a difficult time accepting that it often takes several officers to take a single person into custody who does not want to be taken into custody. He is well aware that as the average citizen drives past, they may witness several officers on top of the suspect using various strikes to certain pressure points on the suspects body in an attempt to get the suspect to remove their hands from the pockets or from a weapon and get them to comply and into handcuffs. To that average person, it may appear that the several officers are exceeding their necessary use of force because the suspect is outnumbered and the officers are using strikes just as they have been trained. Use of force, he reminds us, does not look pretty and is very often mistaken for police brutality.

This is not to say that there are never situations where officers have exceeded their authority in their justified use of force. It happens, but this officer believes that real instances of police brutality are rare and the percentage is very small compared to what the general public has been led to believe. When that does happen, he agrees that the officer should be held accountable.

It is also important to note that good officers do not like bad officers. Personally, he would not tolerate a partner or coworker who displayed excessive use of force. His coworkers feel the same.

Again, his experience with police brutality is limited to the department he works for. He imagines that there are some departments in certain states and regions of the United States where officers are not as educated and as well trained where the instances of excessive force may be higher.

The officers of Minnesota are generally considered nationwide as better educated and better trained which translates to better tactics and restraint and less instances of excessive force.

This police officer doesn't recall the guys that he worked with ever doing something that shouldn't be caught on camera. He remembered the times when there was a knock-down-drag-out fight. It's not a pleasant thing to watch and officers need to get the upper hand. If people took a cellphone of that they would not catch the whole thing. He has never seen anybody doing anything to anybody that wasn't necessary. Officers have to make a lawful arrest. But if the public came in on the end of the struggle, they would not understand what had been going on and how it actually started. He understands that it does get kind of ugly at times. Sometimes, once you got him cuffed and under control sitting in a holding cell, the prisoner would apologize for his behavior and say he was a little drunk and lost control.

An officer finds the idea that police are out of control and lack education and training as utter nonsense. Like everything these days, he feels it has become politized where facts get in the way of truth. He believes he has been fortunate that he hasn't had to use force much. He tries to treat others like he would want to be treated and that respect is often reciprocated; not always, but most of the time.

NPR- May24, 2019

"Civil rights advocates and law enforcement groups have reached an agreement in the California legislature on new rules for when police can use deadly force.

Under the agreement made public Thursday, officers will be able to use lethal force only when it is "necessary" and if there are no other options."

Necessary: Required to be done, achieved; essential, needed, required, compulsory, mandatory, imperative, demanded, inevitable, unavoidable, certain, for sure.

That's widely viewed as higher than the existing legal standard: that the use of deadly force is legal if a "reasonable" officer would have acted similarly in that situation.

Reasonable: A person having sound judgement; fair and sensible. Rational, logical, fair, fair minded, decent.

The proposed law also states that an officer's conduct leading up to the shooting will be considered — but so too will the suspect's behavior. And there's language in the bill that requires police to use other alternatives, such as de-escalation or "less lethal" options, before using deadly force. But these requirements are a statement of intent, not a specific checklist.

"The general idea is, we want the police to see if they can avoid the fatal encounter," said Robert Weisberg, a professor of criminal law at Stanford Law School.

He added that defining the new "necessary" legal standard is going to be very, very difficult for the courts" — and for officers, too."

Law Enforcement Officers are well aware that some officers have made mistakes. It's unfortunate, but they remind me how many thousands of police interactions occur every day. Many of these are violent. The reality is that officers are human and will make mistakes. Perfect does not exist. Our society needs to come to grips with that. Society has placed so many unrealistic restrictions on criminal justice that hiring qualified officers is very difficult.

Officers are confident that more restrictions will only play to the activities of the criminal. Restrictions embolden the people who insist on challenging authority.

The behaviors of some segments of our society cause them to question what they are doing to change their own behaviors and attitudes.

An officer wonders if perhaps some of our leaders should let the criminals be responsible for their safety and welfare. Then let them decide who they want wearing the uniform. He is adamant that our silent majority needs to step up or live in an environment that favors predatory behavior.

I am reminded of the quote: "And maybe remind the few, if ill of us they speak, that we are all that stands between the Monsters and the weak. –Michael MarkLess

I was at a brunch with several women and asked if they had ever been in a physical fight? I had never and all but one of the others said no, they had not. I don't think the public has an inkling what it takes to actually fight.

Mike came home one night having been in a fight with a man he had stopped for driving erratically. Mike said he had fought with him for several minutes. Mike had won but it had been a battle. Mike was strong and I questioned why he had such a hard time controlling the man. Mike told me that I didn't have a clue what it takes to subdue a person, particularly one on drugs.

A Minnesota Cop's Perspective on the Use of Force
by Terry Smith

During most of my adult life, whether working or not, I have seldom been far from a gun. Pistols, shotguns, semiautomatic and fully automatic weapons are at the top of the pyramid of tools that cops use to quell violence or arrest seriously dangerous people. Most of the time, the threat of a gun is all that's needed to make people drop their weapons or otherwise submit. Sometimes that's not enough, and an officer makes a decision that he will remake and relive in his mind for the rest of his life: whether or not to pull the trigger.

There are people who believe that some police officers are always on the hunt for an opportunity to kill someone. Maybe there are some like that, but I haven't met any of them. There's more than one reason that, despite extreme danger or tremendous provocation, most cops will go the heroic extra mile to avoid shooting. One is that all departments nowadays go to great lengths, when hiring, to weed out every candidate who would not be a good psychological fit for the job. Most of the hundreds of officers with whom I rubbed shoulders did not project the aura of trained killers, waiting for a chance to drop the hammer. They were more often people with well-developed social skills who were above-average in their ability to interact with others. There are not many professions that encounter death more often than law enforcement. Cops know violent death for what it is: not something that happens in a video game or a movie but a sad, ugly event that leaves a wake of grief, often for people on both sides of the action. A person with normal feelings and understanding just doesn't want to go there.

Perhaps above all, every officer knows that a decision to shoot will change his life, and never for the better. Moments after a police-involved shooting, for those in the eye of the storm, the world begins to rotate in a different direction—one they've never experienced before. No matter that he may have, moments ago, thought he was going to die. Never mind that he may have risen to a level of heroism that few ever attain. It makes no difference if he placed himself in the gravest danger to save someone else. Now he's a potential defendant in a homicide investigation, his gun seized as evidence, a blood sample taken, possibly read his rights from a Miranda card. He's off the job, maybe for a while, maybe forever, and it's all beyond his control.

In the days following the shooting, the media will demand to know the identity of the officer and will, sooner or later, be given the information.

His family may be forced to go into hiding to avoid camera crews and nut cases. The police department will be restrained in its release of information, not wanting to later find that something that it gave out proved to be untrue. No restraint will be exercised on the other side of the conversation, as interviews with anyone who will talk about the situation are played over and over on cable TV. If the officer is white and the person he shot is a minority, that part of the story will outweigh all others. Every man or woman who pins on a badge and carries a gun knows that all of this will happen if deadly force is used. They also know that it's a decision that will probably come on them unannounced and may have to be made in a few seconds.

Nearly everyone can remember some time in life in which he or she felt threatened and intimidated by another person. For people in some neighborhoods, the feeling is there almost constantly. There's an ample supply of sociopaths in our world, people who don't respond to reasoned words or even the threat of legal penalty. The expectation that most of us have is that when we are threatened with violence, the police will respond quickly to a 911 call and nullify the threat. We understand that a truly out-of-control person may have to be stopped with physical force. The question is how much or what kind of force?

For a number of years, police officers have been taught the concept of the "force continuum." Imagine a line graph running from the lowest form of force (voice commands) up to the highest (deadly force, which usually means shooting). In between the two extremes would be the use of such things as physical restraint; blows delivered by fist, foot, knee or elbow, or the implementation of such tools as chemical irritants, stun guns or batons. The idea is that the officer should move to the point on the continuum at which there is just enough force to overcome the perpetrator's resistance. Nice theory, but not so easy to pull off.

I wish that everyone who wants to weigh in on what constitutes police brutality could at least once experience a really violent struggle with another person. They would find that 30 seconds into the fight, they're already sucking wind. They might be disoriented from a blow to the head or a punch to the solar plexus and be desperate to hang on and recover. They may be unable to create enough space to get at a weapon, even if they now realize they may lose the fight without using it. They'd quickly learn that, in the midst of a struggle, one can't know exactly how much force it will take to win. To not win could lead to the other combatant seizing control of their weapons without the slightest inclination toward moderation.

In recent years it's become trendy to grab your smartphone and hit "record" whenever you see an encounter between police officers and the public. Add to that dash-mounted squad car cameras and "body cams," and there's a vast amount of raw footage of cops doing their jobs—often pretty well, occasionally poorly. Most of the officers I know aren't bothered by the filming except for this: Often it catches only part of the action and misses the rest of the story.

The other problem with videotaped action is that it is used much like instant replay in professional sports. Every Sunday afternoon, we watch terrific athletes do nearly superhuman things on the football field. A receiver leaps high at the back of the end zone, making a fingertip catch as he is hit by a defender. An official crouches nearby, trying to see if the catch was made, whether control of the ball was maintained and if the receiver came down in bounds. It happens with lightning speed, and the official makes the call based on what he thinks he saw. Then the analysts take over, and we all get to see how the official did. We view the play from different angles and, most important, get to see it in slow motion, even frame by frame if that helps. "Look there, Joe, just as his left foot comes down, his heel touches the chalk ... he's out of bounds ... I think they'll reverse the call." In just that way, the luxury of slow-motion review and time to analyze can make the highly stressed decision of a moment seem like a bad call.

According to Wikipedia, in 2008 there were about 765,000 full-time sworn state and local police officers in the United States, with another 120,000 federal officers. Imagine the number of interactions that 885,000 cops have with the public every day. Given the variety of people involved and the confrontational aspects of many of these situations, it should be no shock that some of them are handled poorly, even terribly. The real surprise is that, even with people's impulse to get some good video footage of cop misbehavior, the actual number of events that raise public outcry is a micro-percentage of the total.

We have every right to expect only the best from police officers. We want them to be honest and respectful, caring and kind. We need them to be aggressive, yet capable of holding back, brave but not brutal. We'd like them to rush to interpose themselves between us and danger, even at the risk of losing their own lives. During the 37-year span in which I was on the job, I saw all of these things manifested over and over by many of those I worked with. I must admit that once in a while, I saw something that didn't make me proud. I was working with humans, after all.

Terry Smith served as a police officer for 37 years, first as a uniformed officer with Bloomington, Minn., Police Department, then as a special agent with the Minnesota Bureau of Criminal Apprehension. For the last 17 years of his career, he was the special agent in charge of the BCA's regional office in Bemidji. He drew his gun numerous times while confronting violent offenders but pulled the trigger just once, to fire a warning shot.

> *"Down these mean streets a man must go who is not himself mean, and who is neither tarnished or afraid."*
>
> —Raymond Chandler

CHAPTER 41

LATE NIGHTS, EARLY MORNINGS

Did you share your worries?

Trooper: He was young and naïve and likely didn't have many fears. In a rural area they were so often alone. Backup was rare at best. He didn't like that.

Suburban officer: He did. It was a severe shopping center fire.

Trooper: She didn't really share much of it even when there was shop talk by the other troopers she worked with. She loved to sit around and hear their stories but didn't share hers.

Trooper: He never shared his worries and fears with his wife because he didn't want to worry her. He walked the beat with Minneapolis cops for at least a month. He was never fearful and felt it was his duty to help his partners.

BCA officer: He shared some but some things were too gruesome and would have make his wife worry too much. He kept them to himself.

Trooper: He rarely brings his work home or shares it with his wife. He has kept a journal of interesting encounters (comical or sad). He wishes he would have started the journal on day one. Encounters that he would have thought really interesting his first year are commonplace now.

Deputy: He certainly would not share his worries and fears with anybody at the sheriff's office. At least not when he first started. He typically would talk to friends who were just starting out in law enforcement but in a different department. Eventually he realized they all shared the same anxiety that goes with the territory in law enforcement. During the last half of his career he would often share experiences with his brother-in-law who is a Minneapolis police officer.

Trooper: His wife was always concerned for his safety. He rarely discussed his job with her. If she heard stories from friends or read it in the newspaper then he would answer her questions and try not to alarm her.

Police officer: He tries not to take the job home with him. He always tries to make it a point to keep his worries and fears at work and not discuss them with his family members and spouse. He never wanted them to know how dangerous the job really was. The officer never wanted his family to have to worry about him while he's at work. Luckily his spouse grew up in a law enforcement family and already had an understanding of what the job was about.

How much family life did you miss?

So much that this retired officer looked back and felt selfish. Selfish for doing what he loved—his dream of being a policeman and felt that should not have come first. His family should have.

Policeman: He missed many events over time. It was sometimes easier to just skip the event than to burden someone else with his absence. Yes, he would want the job today if it were the same as when he started. But he would not want the same job in today's world. It's getting harder. Respect for each other, for the general good and even for the individual himself is in jeopardy.

Deputy: For about the first 10 years of his career he felt like he was missing out on some good times with family and friends. He'll never forget the time that instead of sitting in a man cave basement watching the Vikings game, he was dealing with the trespass complaint out in the middle of nowhere. He felt pretty sad and started to realize this is what he had signed up for. As the years went by and he gained seniority the schedule got better. In patrol he was working five days on with four days off. Investigations was also a better schedule working four days on and three days off.

Trooper: He missed a good amount. He knew he had to be out there on the road during snowstorms and holidays when everyone else was safe at home with their kids and spouse. He missed sporting events that the kids were in. He thinks the kids understood but can imagine they were not happy about it.

New York City Officer: He definitely missed out on a lot of family life, especially when he was on nights, which was more than half of his career. His first 8 years was on nights and the next four was on the 8 p.m. - 4 a.m. He was promoted to Sergeant at about the time he would have been able to get a day job but went back to the bottom of the seniority list and got a 3 p.m. – 11 p.m. shift. He had felt more human but was still away from home when the kids were growing up. The officer tried hard to get off for the Christmas holiday and would trade with others officers who were more interested in being off for some other holiday. As for school functions and many other family functions, he was working.

Minneapolis Police Sergeant: He soon knew law enforcement is a 24/7 profession that does not take holidays off. He knew when he became a police officer that he would be working nights, weekends, and holidays for a good portion of his career. As his career progressed, he realized that he was missing a lot of family time because of the job. It really occurred to this father when his oldest son was 16 years old, potentially 2 years away from leaving home, how much he had missed.

He goes on to name some of the things he missed: School conferences, sporting events, family gatherings, reunions, holidays, helping with homework, and family dinners. He along with others had a long list of what they had missed. Family communication became notes to one another. Many talked of going days without seeing their children or their spouse.

Police officer: Her first ten years were the hardest. The rookies and low seniority members work a lot of holidays.

Trooper: He knew he wouldn't have banker's hours anymore when he changed his career. It hasn't been much of an issue and he actually liked the schedule over his bankers' hours.

Was your marriage affected by your job?

The answer from many officers: Absolutely!

Policeman: He thinks it was at times because of the mental dedication to the work. He goes on to say it is the kind of work that requires a great deal of commitment or it will spit you out. It will not work without total involvement and that can be hard on your spouse.

Trooper: Probably in some ways because he was gone a lot and worked many holidays and weekends. They lived in his work area so he could stop home occasionally when he wasn't busy.

Trooper: Yes, in some ways it was. Her marriage didn't last; but she says it was not a good match to begin with. They were very different.

Trooper: He took a pay cut joining the patrol. He wasn't a very good husband; he told me rather matter-of-factly. He continued that the lack of money played a big part in his wife's unhappiness and also that he was gone much of the time. She was young and wanted to be a part of the young set. They soon had three children, no money, and he worked weekends, nights, and holidays. He missed much of family life. His son was in sports and most of the time he could not attend. His early marriage did not last.

Trooper: His marriage was somewhat affected, as schedules changed many plans, especially for kid's birthdays, anniversary plans, and time spent together.

Many believe that law officers have a large percentage of divorces, but with the data compiled and analyzed researchers found that officers actually had a lower divorce rate than the national average. The national average for all occupations was 16.96 percent compared to 14.47 percent for the average law enforcement. www.livestrong.com

What did you like about your job?

Trooper: He liked the freedom of not doing the same thing every day. The ability to go where he wanted when not answering a call. This officer believes in safe and sane travel on our roads and he enjoyed taking action on those who didn't believe that.

Police officer: She loves the fact that when she went to work, she never knew what was going to happen. It was never the same.

Sergeant: There are many things he liked about his job. There's job security, good pay, good pension, and the job itself can be fun. He also liked responding to a variety of calls throughout the shift and that every shift is different. He also liked the autonomy of the job. There is a certain amount of freedom that an officer has throughout their shift. Aside from responding to dispatched calls the officer has the luxury of being as busy as they want to be. The training is also exciting—the shooting range, emergency driving, etc.

Deputy: The two things he loved most about working were narcotics investigations and being a patrol sergeant. He talked of working in narcotics as a crash course in law enforcement and the Constitution. They would build up a case, write up a search warrant, and crash through doors. After making arrests, they would conduct custodial interrogations and bring suspects to jail. They also had to make sure charges were filed and bail was set within 48 hours. He remembered it as so much fun!

He continued, that thankfully for about half of his 26 years at the sheriff's office he was also able to work as a patrol sergeant. He enjoyed working on the front line while at the same time keeping his distance from administration. Generally getting along with everybody at the department, he also, at times, learned to be very cautious around some of the more ambitious deputies. Some patrol sergeants like to spend the majority of their shift in the office. He avoided the office like the plague. With new technology he was able to perform the majority of his responsibilities remotely.

Officers had many of the same feelings about their job. They were helping people, responding to their needs. They had a great sense of camaraderie of coworkers, they enjoyed the thrill of the chase, and catching bad guys.

What didn't you like about your job?

Policeman: Paper work, being on call, boring shifts, and politics, were some of the parts of the job that were his least favorite.

Troopers: Many didn't like court testimony. Arrogant selfish drivers also made the list. Having to resolve ugly situations alone. Icy roads and fog, and the constant neglect from lawmakers. Being on call, especially in the middle of the night, and winter, and working in rural Minnesota. There's no help out there.

Policeman: He hated to go to court. He would do his best arresting, processing and preparing everything for court and people would get away with a lot of things. He arrested a woman for DWI. She went to court and a bleeding-heart judge fined her $25.00 That same day a guy was in court for a stop sign violation and the judge fined him $45.00. But what do you do? He had judges that would fall asleep on the bench. If you had court after lunch some judges drank their lunch. His wife was on jury duty, and couldn't believe it. The judge actually fell asleep.

Trooper: He hated to get up out of a nice warm bed to look for a crash scene. He also did not like blizzards. He had a new partner. She came to him for her last week's training. One evening they left the police station where they were doing reports and it was starting to snow those big flakes. She thought it was beautiful. He didn't think it was beautiful as he knew some careless person will not slow down and then go in the ditch or worse. They'd be driving in that mess to help them with their problem. A month later it was a repeat of the same conditions when they left the police station. She looked up and remembered that blankety-blank snow He agreed!

Deputy: He was sick of dealing with Drug Dealers, and calls them the biggest rag asses in the world.

What is your feeling on gun control?

Policeman: He doesn't believe we need assault weapons but, knows a gun needs an operator. He is adamant that our focus should be on values and mental health. There are also strong feelings about more laws and better background checks.

Deputy: This officer felt pretty sure he is not in the majority with law enforcement when it comes to gun control. He believes we need more gun control especially handgun control.

The odds of a homicidal, suicidal, or accidental shooting with a handgun far outweigh the odds of coming to the rescue with one.

Trooper: He is a life member of the NRA, and donates about $1,000 bucks a year to them to fight what he calls the gun grabbers. He has a concealed carry permit in South Dakota, Arizona and a federal concealed carry. He still does a lot of pistol shooting and has a range set up in his garage in South Dakota. Both his daughters have a concealed carry permit too.

Trooper: He has many guns and wouldn't mind having them registered.

New York Police Captain: He believes gun control should be handled locally as much as possible. He thinks there also needs to be coordination between states and that is where the federal regulations come in. Federal law needs to be the fall back in cases where the states fail to deal with issues. He believes there have been many times when federal law was a better fit than state law. In those cases, it would involve the FBI and use the federal system of justice.

Sheriff: He has dreams about pulling out his gun. He wants people to remember that guns don't kill people. People with guns kill people. It's people that kill people with bats, guns, knives, fists, and many other objects. He's also a big advocate for gun safety taught in schools.

Police officer: He is worried as jails have become mental health holding tanks. This law enforcement officer believes they are not equipped. They serve and protect but are not physicians or nurses.

Most believe there is a need for better background checks and no need for assault rifles. They also talked of the mental health issues that seem to plague our society more each year, and the need for more mental health professionals to try to get a handle on those problems.

Do you think the public understands the job? What do you wish they knew?

Police officer: He knew there were things they don't understand? They don't understand that an officer is not a machine. That he might still get mad, lose his temper much as he tries not to, he's still a human being. He has to make decisions in a second. The media might have a week and a half to pick a part what an officer did, but an officer has only a second to decide.

Trooper: She thinks some might understand but for the most part, not really. She knows the public gets a taste of it from the media and also from some shows on TV. But in actuality, she doesn't think they really know what's going on with officers.

Trooper: Rarely, yet for the most part people respected him. When people had questions, they came to him or called him. He thinks the state patrol is still the most respected agency in Minnesota because of the training.

Police officer: He did not think the public understood the danger of police work. He said that police are out on the streets and often the first people to get to whatever is going on. If it's an accident or a shooting, they're the ones that come first, the paramedics come later. They see and experience a lot. Their mindsets change after they've seen a few suicides. The officers have to become tough. That's how they cope. When they go to a really gruesome accident, they have to work their way through it. They can't fall apart, express grief or any other feelings or opinions, at least not at that moment. They have to do what is expected and handle it. That's why *they* have the job.

He went on to tell me that a friend working in a large city felt demeaned, like he was just a human garbage collector. Some people in big cities seem to act that way. Officers have trouble finding anyone who would even be a witness to any incident. Even if they saw something, they won't help the police. Most cops are relatively fair and impartial. All they're trying to do is keep a lid on things and keep people's lives peaceful.

Trooper: He said he knows they don't understand. One has to be there. He talked of a high-speed chase in the dark. It was scary enough, but when he knew there were a lot of deer on that piece of road, it added to the excitement. He thinks the public should ride one shift with them to understand what they do. Of course, one shift would not be enough, but it would be a start.

Deputy: He hoped the public would gain a better understanding of what law enforcement is all about. With technology such as body cameras and social media, he hoped such understanding would improve.

Trooper: It seemed to him that most people think that all state troopers do is patrol the highways and write tickets. That is not the job. Yes, they write tickets, but he felt sorry for the people he had to ticket. He wrote a lot of warnings for speed, and also with a smile on his face, reminded them to slow down.

Police officer: He wished the public knew that without law enforcers, their world would be chaotic and dangerous.

Trooper: She wished the public knew that they, too, are ordinary humans just like they are. They have families, pay bills and taxes, but have chosen a dangerous career.

Police officer: He knows that the public has no idea what a street officer goes through. He talks of split-second decisions, hours of boredom, and sheer terror in some situations. He remembers the frustrations of dealing with so-called experts who have never done the job, yet are telling officers how it should be done.

Trooper: He wished the public would get smart and quit watching news commentators and listening to their opinions. He thinks it's a bunch of BS. He wants the public to quit believing all the so-called experts who don't have a clue.

Trooper: She wants the public to realize that officers have compassion. She herself has sleepless nights thinking about the people she has come in contact with.

BCA Officer: He told me he cared deeply about people while dealing with them, but had to step away emotionally when the job was done. He did CPR or first aid on some people and never found out what happened to them after the ambulance left.

Trooper: He wished the public knew he is just out there, doing his job just like they are.

Minneapolis Police Sergeant.: There is a lot he wished the public knew about him in particular and law enforcement in general. He believes that if the public really knew about the difficulties of the job, there would be much better understanding and far less criticism for law enforcement. He would also like it to be possible for every citizen to ride along with an officer at some point in their life—to walk a mile in their shoes to see the reality they face every shift.

He wants the public to know that the overwhelming majority of law enforcement officers are caring, compassionate professionals who contribute valuable things to the community they serve during every shift.

He wishes the public would realize that the overwhelming majority of law enforcement officers are truly colorblind and base their actions solely on behavior and not race. He believes it would be nice if the public would make the important distinction between racial profiling and bad behavior where the actor happens to be black or some other minority.

He is really bothered that much of the public believes that cops are inherently racist. He wishes the public knew that police officers don't go to work every day looking to arrest or shoot a black person at any chance they get.

He wants the public to know that law enforcement officers are not immune to making mistakes and that they would understand that sometimes those mistakes are made while using good-faith judgement, often in split-second, life-or-death situations. Police officers get scared, too.

He hopes the public understands that police officers have families who expect them to come home after every shift. He also wants the public to know that whenever an officer uses force, it never looks pretty. An officer is supposed to use the amount of force necessary to end the situation as quickly as possible. Sometimes it takes four or five officers or more to subdue and control a single person who is hell-bent on resisting and getting away.

He wishes the public knew that the overwhelming majority of good police officers do not like the bad officers who give the profession a bad name.

www.cbsnews.com: July 8, 2019. "Starbucks is apologizing to an Arizona police department after six officers were apparently asked to leave a store on the Fourth of July. This was because a customer said the officers made him feel unsafe.

The coffee giant faces a growing backlash online. It includes the hashtags: #DumpStarbucks and #BoycottStarbucks."

Starbucks released a statement calling the incident "completely unacceptable" and mentioned that it has actually in the past partnered with the Tempe police to host the community outreach event, "Coffee with a Cop."

The association for the Tempe, Arizona, police department, says on the Fourth of July, six officers were enjoying their drinks at a Starbucks ahead of their holiday shift when a barista asked them to leave because a customer complained their presence made him feel unsafe.

After the officers left, the association tweeted, "Several of those cops are #veterans who fought for this country! #ZeroRespect."

I asked some people how they felt about what happened at Starbucks. These are some of the remarks.

They like to see the cops in places... any place.

They don't think anybody would like that comment—to tell police that they can't come in and get something to eat.

They wonder what's the matter with that guy? Is he nuts?

We'd better appreciate and thank the police for protecting us.

We have to respect our police. What would we do without them?

I'm thinking of the day Starbucks get robbed or someone working or sitting in their restaurant gets beat up. Maybe it's the person who said the police made him feel unsafe. Who you gonna call? Ghost Busters? You'll call the police and pray they get there soon.

I am reminded of the quote in the movie *Sea of Love*. Al Pacino, plays the part of a New York City Policeman. "Come the wet ass hour. I'm everybody's Daddy."

"We face what you fear."

—Anonymous

CHAPTER 42

ONLY THE STRONG ONLY THE BRAVE

Did you know your family was proud of you?

Trooper: Yes, his family was proud and participated in law enforcement Memorial events. He was a member of the Law Enforcement Memorial Association Honor Guard. The family often attended ceremonies. They also expressed their support verbally.

Deputy: He knew his parents were proud of him and actually he was very proud of them. They were a law enforcement family. His dad worked for the Minnesota State Patrol.

BCA officer: His family was proud and very supportive.

Deputy: He knew they were proud of him. They never said it in words but he knew it.

Trooper: Yes, his family was proud of him. Their actions and what they told their friends made him feel good. He retired in 1995. When he was working and his family got called to jury duty they were excused because they did not want law enforcement people and their families on jury duty. He got a call this Christmas from his oldest daughter. She told him she was sent home from jury duty because of what he did for a living. She thanked him.

New York Captain: He is pretty sure his family was proud of him. Whenever there was a promotion they were there. His mother always put an article in her local newspaper when he was promoted. His wife put up with the job for all these years and stuck with him through it all. She always supported him. As he looked back, he's not sure how she did it.

Did you feel a camaraderie with your partners?

Trooper: Yes. His partners were like his brothers. He is still friends with so many, even from the Academy. They have an annual retired trooper get together. The other departments have said that since he retired, they realized how well they all worked together.

Policeman: Yes, a very tight bond. He has kept in touch.

Deputy: Yes, he got along really well with partners in all departments. He doesn't see them much anymore – doesn't have time.

Trooper: Yes, he has always had a good relationship with his partners and the law enforcement community in general. His last station was a little more isolated and he didn't have that much contact with the past partners.

Deputy: Yes, he felt great camaraderie with his partners. They treated him well and yes, he has kept in contact with them. The job they had – they had to rely on others, and besides the troopers, the local police department was very supportive of him too.

Trooper: He has a great deal of respect for his partners and officers who work in law enforcement. He worked a brief time as a deputy with Anoka County before accepting a position with the state patrol.

Police Officer: He did, and still does feel camaraderie with his old work partners and academy classmates. Still he does not spend much time with them outside of work. Though there are rare occasions, he tries really hard to keep a separation with work and personal time. He has noticed and also been told by older officers that the camaraderie nowadays is not what it was like in the old days. It was common for work partners and shift mates to hang-out with each other after work on their personal time.

Trooper: There was strong bond between partners when he was working. Nowadays, from what he hears and sees, it appears that today's troopers don't have the bond that they once had.

Do you think officers today are scared?

Policeman: He thinks there's many reasons to be.

Trooper: Some are, but he doesn't think most are. He believes if you are scared you should not be in that job. He was never scared. He just did his job. That's what he had to do. He helped people when they were in trouble. He had to contain, apprehend, and go through the court system.

Officer: He understands they are scared of the unfair treatment by the media. Officers are scared of the sector of the public that feel so entitled and want to employ the media to help.

BCA officer: He thinks they are just like law enforcement officers were when they were young. They are ready for anything and waiting for their next jolt of adrenaline.

Deputy: He doesn't necessarily think law enforcement people are scared in this day and age. He does think there is less interest in going into law enforcement. Several years ago, he remembered how tough it was to get a job in law enforcement. The Oakdale Police Department once had 500 applications for one position. He doesn't think that's the case anymore. People are noticing how challenging the job can be not to mention dangerous. People are finding there are much better paying jobs and benefits out there.

Trooper: He thinks those who are up to no good or involved with criminal activity have been emboldened to disrespect any kind of authority. He believes it stems from the not so distant political climate, media and Hollywood that have made the "good guys" the "bad guys."

Police officer: He knew there are evil and crazy people that officers encounter every day. Drugs are everywhere and violence is the normal.

Trooper: The officer believes law enforcement are scared of spineless spokespeople in government positions who are more concerned about selfish ambitions rather than the greater good.

Have you feared for your Life?

Trooper: Yes, he came door-to-door with a 17-year-old from South Dakota with a handgun. The officer had him stopped in a plowed field after he stole a squad car and kidnapped a man at gunpoint. He put the gun down. Another time the trooper slid off the road during the pursuit. The last thing he saw before the snow enveloped the car was a bunch of big trees while sliding sideways.

New York City Captain: He surely feared for his life from time to time. However, he was pretty well trained, well equipped, and had help nearby if it was needed. He had a few incidents with *man with gun* calls which turned out to be a man with a gun but he never had to fire his gun except in training and no one every fired on him—that he knows of.

Trooper: He had a guy threaten to shoot him; he pointed a gun at him. The trooper hit the ground and exited the left door; the guy was in his face with the gun. The suspect pointed his gun at the trooper who fell to the ground, and came up with his gun pointed at him. The suspect threw his gun on the ground and his hands in the air. He had a 9mm German luger. The man came to court, plead guilty and got a piddly fine. The police recorder later told him that this guy had fired a shot over the top of the patrol car. The trooper never heard that shot hit the ground.

He continued. There was a weigh station where they would go to fill out reports, etc. When they pulled up the dispatcher would give out the auto report which was stolen vehicles and license plates. They got it twice a day and he wrote them down every day religiously. He always had it in front of him. He drove in late one night and there was a car sitting near the weigh station building; this car was sitting with the left driver's door open. The light was on in the outdoor bathroom. The officer checked and sure enough that license number was on his list of stolen cars. When he got out of his car, he was prepared for something, but didn't know what...he had his hand on his weapon. The trooper told him to come out with his hands up. All he knew was that the car was stolen. He called for help from his partner.

The guy came out of the toilet with his hands in the air. They searched his car and found stolen guns and juvenile girls in the back seat. They admitted to burglarizing several places. He said he had put the gun in the toilet. The next day the trooper went in there with a long wire and flashlight and pulled the gun out of that toilet. That gun had come from the burglary of a Minneapolis cops' residence.

Deputy: Yes, he has feared for his life. Although he told me he really didn't realize how close death was until it was all over. He listens to his senses. That's what will keep officers going home safely after their shift.

Trooper: Late night call outs. She's all alone out there and never knows what to expect.

Suburban Police officer: In-progress calls with weapons involved. He had several close calls during cases, domestics, mentally ill folks.

Policeman: He had more threats on his life than you could shake a stick at because they didn't like suddenly seeing law enforcement in their area. The area he worked in was clannish. He saw them force people out. The officer had a guy pull a gun on him in a traffic stop because he was tired of the policeman arresting his friends. When that man got out of prison, he stopped to say hello and see how the officer was doing. There were no hard feelings and he apologized.

Deputy: With the benefit of 20/20 hindsight, he knows of occasions where he really dodged a bullet. His last two DWI arrests took place on rural roads where the driver not only crossed the centerline but was heading straight for him.

During the first one, thankfully, he had plenty of time to react and there was not a lot of traffic on the road. It took place just after lunch and the driver had a .30 blood alcohol concentration.

The second one also took place during the day on a roller coaster road also known as Highway 50. The drunk driver was westbound and the officer was eastbound and for some reason, he turned off of the highway and seconds later dispatch advised of a serious crash on Highway 50. The driver had crossed the eastbound lane, went into the ditch and was launched airborne at a driveway embankment. The vehicle flew about 150 feet into a large tree killing the passenger.

Minneapolis police officer: Yes, many times in his career he recalled fearing for his life. Having worked in Minneapolis for 21 years, he has been in many situations where he thought how the situation could turn out tragically for him and/or his partners. Vehicle pursuits, foot chases in dark alleys with suspects who were thought to be armed, building searches on in-progress burglaries, responding to any call that was in-progress where the suspect was armed or was known to be armed, officer involved shooting, the 35W bridge collapse. That just names a few situations.

He talked about a fight that he had with a drug dealer who was looking at spending a considerable amount of time in jail. The officer was in a foot chase with the suspect when he caught him in a dark alley. The drug dealer outweighed him by 80 pounds. He remembered fighting with him and thinking if he lost the fight, there was a good chance that he would be killed with his own gun. The officer exhausted every option short of using lethal force during the fight. The officer was exhausted, fighting, struggling to get the guy in handcuffs and hanging on to him. He could hear the sirens of his backup getting closer, praying for them to get there quicker. The officer was sharing just one example of several situations where he has feared for his life.

A seasoned veteran of law enforcement shares this: He has been shot at, fought with some fearsome people, been on countless high-risk raids, arrested murderers, armed robbers, dope dealers...but was always so intent on the action that there wasn't much opportunity to be afraid. After the fact, he often wondered how close he may have come to being killed.

"Bravery is not the absence of fear but action in face of fear."

—Century writer John Berridge

CHAPTER 43

TAKE IT EASY

What did you do on your day off?

Fishing and hunting were the answers for many. For others, woodworking and making things was another, along with shoveling snow, and mowing the grass. A day off or even two in a week wasn't much time. There were chores around the house and yard to handle.

Many talked of camping as family time in the summer. A retired suburban officer told of just trying to spend time with family. He enjoyed cycle riding and, if there was time, he liked to just relax. Another trooper talked of riding bicycle with her spouse. Outdoors seemed to be many of the ways law enforcement used to unwind and relax. Their children's school sports also took up much of their time off.

In addition to hunting and fishing, another officer had extra property where he could be by himself and do whatever he wanted to do. He trimmed trees to open a trail and cut brush. That was his relaxation.

Moose hunting had been a bust this year for a trooper. It had snowed and rained for eight of the ten days of the hunt. The lakes and rivers were four feet higher than usual, and the woods were full of wolves. The hunting party could hear them howling over the noise of the boat motors. At the end of the hunt, it snowed 12 inches. They had to stay four more days before the float plane could come for them. He called this hunting instead of shooting.

When Mike started with the patrol, many of his days off were spent working for an electrician. Since he often worked weekends, days off during the week were perfect. He could work a couple days for a busy man who had only one other employee. Mike had worked for the phone company and was used to wires. He was also meticulous. His wiring was perfect.

Many law enforcement officers had part-time jobs. Pay is much better today, but in the old days, several took pay cuts to be on the patrol. Many questioned if they could afford to go into law enforcement.

Mike also found time to hunt with a good friend he had met while employed by the telephone company. They worked on the line crew. He and Dave hunted ducks on a lake in southern Minnesota. They would arise early in the morning and lie in mud and other wet areas along the edge of the lake. At times, there was snow coming down or else a drizzly cold rain.

While the guys were *suffering*, Dave's wife Sharon and I would be preparing for dinner out at a special restaurant, in a town about an hour away. It was one of the rare times we went out. It was always on a Saturday night when duck hunting was over for the year. I would hire a baby sitter, and Dave and Sharon would spend the night with us. I tried on many dresses or skirts before settling on the right one. In those days, dressing up for a night out also included nylons and high heels.

Sharon would be dressed up as well. One particular evening Mike questioned whether we should be wearing a dress, nylons, and heels. He said, "A snow storm is coming It's going to be cold and could turn into blizzard conditions." Well, if he thought snow and cold weather were going to stop us from looking beautiful for that special evening, he was wrong. As he put on his winter coat and then his gloves, boots, and stocking cap, and crawled into Dave's car, we teased him just a little.

The meal was delicious. It was the only time during the year I had cold shrimp, cocktail sauce, a salad from salad bar, then steak and all the trimmings. We laughed and talked as the night slipped away. When we walked outside *the real world* was waiting. Heavy snow and ferocious winds welcomed us. We were downtown and could quite easily navigate getting out of town, but soon the darkness of the rural road was upon us. Mike knew the road, so he rolled his window down and helped Dave stay on the pavement.

Sharon and I had to endure the cold wind and snow coming into the back seat. We didn't say a word and felt totally frozen when we finally got home. We got no sympathy from Mike who reminded us that we had been warned but didn't listen. "I tell you what is going to happen and you don't believe me," he just had to say. My children have often asked why their dad was always right. We laugh about one of his favorite sayings although so true. "I tell you, be ready for a rainy day... and here it is...it's raining."

We traveled with Sharon and Dave for many years. At first it was tent camping at a campground in northern Minnesota. We also traveled with them to the Black Hills and stayed in a camper we had borrowed.

Mike's first cycle was a classy 1968 Harley, royal blue and white with white leather seats. He and Dave traveled without Sharon and me one summer. On their way home, the owner of a campground wanted to buy the Harley. Mike quoted him a huge price, and the man said "yes" and would come to Minnesota within the next week. Mike was shocked but arranged for pick up as soon as he got home.

Mike and his Harley starting out for a trip to Colorado with Dave.

Our next motorcycle, a 900 Kawasaki, was really fast. Mike liked it, but it had a small gas tank. Sharon and I loved it—more bathroom breaks. We also bought a bright yellow trailer and could pack more.

Sue, ready for their two-week vacation.

One of our camp sites.

My in-laws and parents would take the children for a week. Sharon's mother would keep her three girls. We would eventually have two weeks when we traveled by motorcycle. My in-laws and my parents would each take one of our two children for a week and then exchange. Also, each enjoyed special treatment, having a set of grandparents to him or herself.

We headed either north or west on our vacations. Eventually we bought a Honda Gold Wing, which came with a larger gas tank. The ride was comfortable, but it could go too many miles between gas stations. Sharon and I were at the mercy of the men.

Our cycle travels were exciting. Misery loves company and misery is sometimes what we endured. Rain, sleet, and icy windshields were not uncommon, especially in Canada. But it was inexpensive travel and we were young. We carried a small pup tent, a one-burner propane stove, a camp kit with four plates, four plastic coffee cups, a spoon, fork, and knife packed tightly in a small box, and a collapsible water pail.

We sold our trailer so were back to just our cycle, which had two saddle bags and a trunk. We each packed our clothes and toiletries in a saddlebag and the trunk held camping equipment. Sleeping bags were held on top with bungee cords. It is amazing how little we actually needed.

Our longest trip was a three-week excursion. We rode across Canada to Prince Rupert and boarded a ferry to Alaska. Cycles were the last on but also the first off. We arrived in Juneau to spend four days at a campground not far from town.

Our ferry to Alaska.

Mike and Sue on the ferry.

We set up camp and hadn't been there long before a park ranger stopped by. With his long hair pulled back into a ponytail, he looked like a throwback to hippy days. (He belonged in the woods.) He told us grizzlies were in an area about two miles away, eating berries. He made it perfectly clear that we were in bear territory, that we were the intruders, and stressed that we follow the rules or we would be the ones to suffer. He told us a story of two campers being mauled by a bear. They had apples in their tent. They lived, but he had no sympathy for them and stressed that we should have anything that smelled— good or bad—stored in a bag high in a tree. Thinking of what we had with us, the list was quite long. Fortunately, Mike had a large bag that he tied high up in a tree far away from our campsite each night and we had no unwanted intruders.

The highlight for the guys was salmon fishing. With a guide, they were off on an adventure. The guide, keeping an eye out for grizzlies, stood guard with a rifle while the men snagged salmon. Later, the guide and his wife also cleaned the fish. Mike always kept a journal of our travels and wrote that we had a delicious meal of salmon that night. I myself don't remember that it was good, so recently, I called Sharon and Dave to ask about their thoughts. All these years later, neither thought it was good. So much for that!

As I was writing this chapter, I read an article written by E. J, Montini of *The Arizona Republic* about the sighting of a mountain lion in a retirement community outside of Tucson. The headline said, "Mountain Lion sighted in retirement community." He said the headline should have read: "Retirees sighted in Mountain Lion territory."

That's of course true. We live in the animal's territory. Houses, stores, restaurants, golf courses, and all the other trappings of a community are in *their* territory where we expect them to accommodate *us*, acting as if they are the invaders. Much like the park ranger in Alaska,

Montini has the same belief, that we, the people and civilization, are trespassers.

> *"Sail away from the Safe Harbor. Catch the trade winds in your sail. Explore, dream, discover."*
>
> —Mark Twain

CHAPTER 44

ARE THE GOOD TIMES REALLY OVER

March 13, 1990
Kelliher, MN.

Dear Chief,

After chasing cars for thirty-three years, I have decided to terminate my position as a trooper for the Minnesota state patrol, effective May 1, 1990.

It was no easy decision to make, but sooner or later, it has to happen. It seemed to come much sooner than I had expected.

In horse racing, when a horse runs his last race, and if he was any good at all, they put him out to stud. In a sense, I have run my last Race/ Chase so being put out to stud did kind of appeal to me until my wife informed me that we are strictly a one-horse family. So much for that idea!

I have always been, and will always be, very proud to have been a part of the Minnesota State Patrol. I can't imagine doing anything more rewarding or to have been associated with a more tremendous group of people.

I've had some of the best Partners a person could ask for and I can truly say it's been fun. There is no doubt in my mind that I would do it all over again, given the choice between this and another career.

If you decide to proceed with a written history of the state patrol, I would like to assist and would be honored to help with such a project. Thank you.

Sincerely,
Richard P, Florhaug, Badge # 235

Mike retired in 1999. He had been a Minnesota Trooper for 26 years.

Mike graduates from Rookie School.

Mike retires.

Mike's last squad car.

Today's squad car.

Were you ready to retire?

Many said they were ready to retire, that they were just tired from years of conflict: too many sights, sounds, and too much drama. A policeman's wife told him he needed to get out, that he had to retire. A trooper was ready at 55 to get out. He knew law enforcement is a young man's job. He was having trouble driving in snow storms, roaring down the highway on his way to crashes, wrestling with drunks, and getting called out in the middle of the night. It was time!

A small-town policeman recalled townspeople saying that he must be glad he wasn't a cop in a big city. He talked of not having the volume of a big city but that officers there have close back up. He was out there all alone and went on to say he should have retired five or six years earlier. He found it particularly disturbing that there were fifty-or sixty-year-old men and women in his town arrested for drug use. He said he had become hardened. He had worked crimes against people he knew that had been perpetrated by people he knew. He had seen too many dead bodies. He was offered a job as a bailiff when he retired. But when he told a good friend, a trooper, about the offer, the trooper wondered if he was crazy and told him to take that uniform off and find something to do.

A retired sheriff believes he has been blessed. I haven't seen the man I was interviewing for many years and was grateful he had time to talk to me now. Although retired, he is extremely busy. With a wide smile on his face, he wanted me to know that he started at a good time. He is grateful he got to work with the old timers—dedicated lawmen. The look on his face told me he admires those longtime friends, as he named the old guard who taught him, advised him, took him under their wing, and educated him by example. He spoke about the times we are living in now, that we are the most connected yet the least informed we have ever been.

After he retired many people thanked him for treating them with respect, treating them fairly, and for the job he did. A retired deputy was telling me about his job, that he now knew he was appreciated. He probably knew it in his working days but didn't think much about it until he retired. His life was different. Law enforcement officers are held to a higher standard, and should be.

A BCA officer I interviewed retired at 60 because it was mandatory. He said he would want the job as it was then, he thrived on it, and that he would also want it as it is today. He started pre-Miranda. (You have the right to remain silent. Anything you say can and will be used against you in a court of law) He was issued a .38 caliber revolver, a flashlight, a set of peerless handcuffs, and a nightstick. No body armor, no portable radio, no mace, no stun gun, no cell phone, no baton... just a big old hickory nightstick.

Once retired he realized it was probably time because the job had worn him out. In his job he got the first call from local departments on any homicide in the top half of Minnesota. Once he received three calls about three different homicides in one night. He sleeps much better these days.

A suburban cop said that with political correctness and a different culture out there, he would not want the job today. He also talked about violence with armed 'gang bangers', that with the liberalistic court and penal systems, the job is nearly impossible. He doesn't miss the uniform but he does miss the people on the street—street cops and investigators.

One policeman said he'd rather sell pencils on a street corner than go into police work today. A trooper said he was tired of always having to be on the lookout for something wrong. So yes, he was ready to retire. He wanted to end his career where he lived before having a major incident with someone in the area.

An officer summed it up when he said that after thirty years, most cops are ready to retire, that bureaucracy is what wears them out.

A trooper hesitated but he left. He had the option of an extra job if he needed because he had to keep busy. He had enjoyed what he had been doing most of the time but he retired because of the early out. The state paid his medical and hospitalization insurance until he was 65. He left at 55.

Another trooper was ready, that even after changing from road trooper to District Investigator the daily grind wore him out.

One deputy was not ready to retire, and hadn't seen that door close yet, but his wife wanted him to retire.

Until about 7 to 8 years ago, before retirement, one said he could see himself back on the job and a much better police officer based on much more life experience. But his night duty had made him cynical and it had taken him many years to recover. The last eight years, it seemed that all he dealt with was the underbelly of society, which had a damaging effect on him.

Major Michael Asleson was the youngest person to be hired by the Minnesota State Patrol. He was 18.

Sept.14, 2012

Letter from Major Michael Asleson

Dear friends and colleagues,

I am concluding my final shift as a Minnesota State Trooper; 35 years and two days. I will soon go 10-7 with the West Metro District where I had my first assignment. The word surreal doesn't even come close to describing these last couple days.

It has been a wonderful experience and I will be forever grateful to have been part of this fine agency that continues to be made of dedicated and talented public servants.

Let's face it; while some of our duties are difficult and distasteful, being a state trooper is enjoyable! It has to be one of the greatest jobs. We have a front row seat to some of the most amazing experiences.

Yesterday I gathered my issued equipment for turn-in this morning and checking items off the inventory list.

It really did seem like yesterday that I was issued those tools of the trade.

The past two weeks have been quite emotional (as it probably is for most members when they retire) for I love this job and in so many ways hate to leave. But the next chapter is about to begin so it's time to move on.

I was so honored last week at the many people that attended the retirement coffee and cake in classroom #4 of the training center. It was wonderful to visit with officers from other agencies (current and retired) members of OTS and MnDot that are amazing partners of the State Patrol, classmates from 1977, former partners, and current colleagues.

What a fabulous turnout last night at my retirement social hour and dinner in Eagan. I was honored and humbled by the remarks. But as I told the group, as much time could have been spent discussing those times when I was wrong, or made a mistake, or needed course correction by a supervisor (or caring partner).

Today Colonel Daly issued me my 35-year service bar. I'll of course not be able to wear it as my blouse has been turned in, but it is funny what a simple piece of fabric and threads mean symbolically. Thanks Chief.

As I mentioned to the group last night, this agency has an incredibly important mission. We help those in need, assist other law enforcement agencies, enforce and educate to prevent crashes, deaths and injuries, and fully investigate crashes when they occur. We made incredible progress over the years but 368 dead bodies from 2011 is reason to stay the course. And 111 dead bodies resulting from alcohol related crashes is reason to keep DWI and seatbelt enforcement a top priority as we work towards Zero Deaths. Most of our youth die in their cars—not in schools or drive-by shootings. The work you do each day is so critically important to protect our most valuable treasure—our kids.

Much has changed since my class of 21 rookies graduated. We didn't have portable radios until 1985. We had no idea what an MDC would be. We were using low band radios with tall whip antennas, with many locations around the state were no radio coverage existed. Although technology, weaponry, devices such as ASP's and Tasers have really enhanced our profession, the basic job has remained the same and we do what we do one stop at a time, one discussion at a time and one call at a time.

Thank you for your friendship and support. It has been an honor and pleasure to serve with you. I am looking forward to watching this fine agency excel as a proud former member.

Sincerely,
Mike Asleson

"For retirement brings repose, and repose allows a kindly judgement of all things."

– John Sharp Williams

CHAPTER 45

MAY THE BIRD OF PARADISE
FLY UP YOUR NOSE

Jokes are a part of life for law enforcement. I would hope anyone reading this would not think… *What—they played jokes on each other?* Yes, they sure did. Mike loved to play pranks but so did others. When his squad car went in for servicing, he would usually find something strange left in it. They were comical, but my favorite as of many others was The Monkey. I was reminded of that by a trooper last week at our usual Thursday gathering of troopers, spouses, and friends when we are in Arizona.

After the squad car had been in for an oil change, someone belted a large blow up monkey into the passenger side of the squad car. Looking regal and important, it sat on the passenger seat for quite a while.

Mike received an invite from the captain of the district to come over to *talk*. The monkey in the front seat was gaining notoriety. Although it was strongly suggested that *the item occupying the other half of the car* should be removed, it did not happen immediately. Hence, another trip to the wood shed. Into the office walked Mike without his hat on (another no no). When asked where his hat was, he answered, "It's the monkey's turn to wear it." Shortly thereafter, the monkey sat in a corner in our living room until eventually the air came out. The story of The Monkey was worth a chuckle at many Christmas parties.

Pranks and good-natured kidding were a big part of our lives. While living in Mike's first station, I picked up a box at the post office, paid for the needed postage, and brought it home. It was a box of dirt. Mike had told the guys he had really wanted to be a farmer.

Another time, after Mike complained to the volunteer fire department that they blew the fire whistle too long, they and their loud siren found their way to our driveway early one Saturday morning while on a training run. That siren blasted us—and all our neighbors—out of our beds. We were new to the neighborhood. The little ones in the area thought it was great fun and Mike didn't complain about the long siren any more.

A Christmas package delivered by a policeman did not raise my suspicion. He said it was meat and that I should put it in the freezer. I did as I was told. Later, my telling Mike about the present put a wide smile on his face. He brought the package up from the freezer and opened it. It was a package of large cow pies.

A deputy and Mike were involved in a variety of pranks. A call to a game warden asking for the whereabouts of the worst smelly dead animal, preferably a deer, could be found. There was one down a deep ravine. The guys worked feverously to retrieve it. Between bouts of gagging and noses filled with Vicks, they managed to bring it up. A member of the posse lived out of town and had a large locked metal gate. They hung the deer on the gate knowing he would have a hard-smelly time getting a key into the lock. Alas, his wife beat him home. She was not happy.

A deputy had a new truck. He was taking a friend out to lunch to show off his new purchase. A deputy and Mike jacked up the wheels just enough so it was actually off the pavement. They watched with glee from around the corner as he struggled to get the truck to move, exiting the vehicle many times trying to see what was wrong.

It was Christmas. Mike was the station sergeant and decided he should buy the women at the Clerk of Court office candy for the holidays. I bought what I considered a nice box of candy. Mike brought it to them. From what I heard about it later, they were pleased with Mike's kindness and generosity.

Someone from the Sheriff's office heard about the candy. He called the Clerk of Court's office and told them he had heard that Jurgens brought them candy. He warned them about eating it. That's all it took. Several of the ladies had eaten the candy. They began to feel nauseous, thinking maybe he had put something in the candy. Maybe he injected something through the box. They threw the rest of the candy away. Oh, the power of suggestion.

Mike wasn't the only one who played tricks. Something would arrive in the mail, sometimes at the courthouse, sometimes at our home. One of them was the letter addressed to Mike with PERSONAL PERSONAL PERSONAL and AIDS TEST RESULTS stamped all over it.

An anonymous letter rejecting his sex organ for an organ donation/transplant had the following as a return address:

> Sexual Research Institute
> Organ Donation Division
> Donor Card Enclosed
> For your Unused Sexual Organ

The letter from the Sexual Research Institute said they were sorry but would have to reject his offer as they had determined that it did not function well.

An anonymous card read, "How are men and government bonds different? Bonds mature!"

A greeting card Mike received just prior to our leaving for Florida was a holiday wish signed "The other 13 women in your life."

Mike walking down the hall of the courthouse would set off an alarm with the women. Jerky's coming... better get ready.

"Were you always mad at him?" I ask.

No! They liked it. It lightened their day. The court system brought hard work and anxiety to them also. She continued saying they tried hard to get the best of Mike but still believe he bested them every time. They loved to hear somebody say "You know what I did to Jurgens?"

They tried, especially at Christmas, to best him: getting a huge box wrapping it filled with smaller boxes and smaller boxes until there was the bottom with nothing. And yes, they missed him when he retired. She trusted law enforcement people knowing the pranks and the jokes lightened their life as well. As much as Mike could joke and fool around, the people that worked with him knew that he was a professional in his work and they could count on him.

As Clerk of Court, Mike always referred to her as "Queen Diane." While we were in Arizona, he bought her a tiara, intending to give it to her at Christmas time—sent, I'm sure, anonymously to the court house. I gave it to her after his death.

Now retired, she keeps in contact with some of the women she worked with though doesn't spend time thinking about the court system and the workings of it. The joking and fun between them and law enforcement made their work easier. They had camaraderie and understood each other.

She talked of Mike's resolve, his courage facing death, and that it was a lesson to all. He lived his last months with dignity, and with laughter and joy.

I had received a letter from our county, telling me I would be on jury duty starting January 1st. We were leaving the end of December to spend three months in Florida. I went to the Clerk of Court office and told them that if I couldn't be excused from jury duty, one of them would have to go to Florida and be Mike's woman for three months. A stay from jury duty was quickly signed. It was legit, and I would fulfill my obligation when I came back.

As I write I am thinking of my time serving on a jury. I was often called to the courthouse to be a part of a jury pool. However, I was excused many times because the case involved law enforcement. I did serve as foreman on a jury concerning a case of suicide. I think everyone should serve on a jury to see the workings of the court—listening, observing prosecutors, defense attorneys, and the judge. Our judge walked into court, announced that he had gout, pulled out the bottom drawer in his bench, and rested his foot. He paged through a book as the case started. I thought *Is he listening? Does he hear what's being said?* Oh yes, he was and, yes, he did. As the civil lawsuit continued, he occasionally scolded both attorneys. I was amazed how much he heard and saw, even though at times, he seemed not to be paying attention.

We were having dinner at a popular restaurant one evening when one of the women from the Clerk of Court office came by to say that the Clerk of Court was furious with him. A prank had been played on her, and of course she thought it was Mike. I asked Mike, "What did you do now?"

"I didn't do anything."

"Then why didn't you defend yourself? Why didn't you tell her you didn't do anything?"

He said it wouldn't matter and that no one would believe him anyway. The actual perpetrator eventually admitted the prank.

We had been gone for the weekend. As we drove into our driveway in Grand Rapids, we were met with a huge sign on our garage door. It said "House For Sale By Neighbors." It was not our neighbors that had put it up.

The gas shortage of 1974 encouraged people to pump their own, partly because it was a little cheaper and to help eliminate long lines. I worked in a lumber yard across the street from a station. The helpful young attendant was used to me. We visited a little while he pumped my gas, washed the windows and checked the oil. It was also the patrol's contract station. Mike had pulled in and was pumping his own as I drove in to the full-service pump. The young man came out and I said "fill it up."

Mike walked over to my window and said, "I'm glad you have so much money that you don't have to pump your own gas."

"I have a rich husband."

He replied, "Some poor guy is out there working his tail off so you don't have to pump your own gas?"

"Why aren't you out catching criminals instead of picking on a poor defenseless woman. Get away from me."

I paid the young man and drove away. I had not been watching the look on his face as we bantered back and forth but Mike had. The young man's head kept going from Mike to me then back to Mike, then me. When I drove away, he said "I don't know why she talked to you like that. She's a really nice lady. Mike said he laughed and said, "That's no lady, that's my wife."

Mike's gallbladder flared up and needed to come out. The guys wanted to play tricks on him in the hospital but the nurses nixed a blowup woman in the bed next to him. Mike was leery as he recovered. I spent many hours sitting with him in his hospital room. He had a roommate, an elderly man who had also had surgery.

When the nurse brought in a bouquet of flowers, Mike asked in an alarmed tone, "Who are they from?" They were from his mother. The nurse wondered what he was so worried about. She didn't know his friends.

He had recently had the IV taken out of his arm and commented on how comfortable that felt. Before long a nurse came walking into the room with an IV bag hanging on a metal stand. She said she was sorry but he was running a temp and she had to put the IV back in. I didn't pay much attention to it until the old man in the other bed said, "There's a fish in there." Indeed, there was a goldfish swimming around inside the IV bag. The nurse commented that there had been many things that the police wanted to do to Mike. She had kept things under control but did allow the fish in the IV. Luckily, it did not have to go into his arm.

A man knocked on my door to tell me not to look outside, and telling me that what I didn't see I wouldn't know about. I had a simple request—that it not impact me in any adverse way.

I finished changing beds and then glanced out the window. There, tied to a tree, was a stuffed animal...half cow and half deer. It had the front of a deer and back of a cow. Attached to one of the horns was a ticket from the city with a fine of $500.00 for having livestock in town and no license for wild animals. It stayed tied there for the entire day. Drivers slowed down, squinting to make out what it was. When the school day ended, I heard squeals of laughter and excitement from the children walking by. Later the strange animal made its way into many yards.

The half deer / half cow tied to our tree.

The 1953 Packard convertible that Mike had bought when he was stationed in Florida was coming to our home. Mike's grandma's house was to be sold, and her garage could no longer store the old vehicle. Borrowing a friend's flatbed trailer, Mike traveled the five-hundred-mile round trip to pick it up. Arriving home late at night, he was off to work early the next morning.

I was not working that day and was sleeping in when a hard knock on the front door woke me. There stood a man wearing a uniform I did not recognize. I told him I had been sleeping. Half-awake, I asked what he wanted. He was there to serve me a Blight Notice from the city. I asked, "What's a Blight Notice?" He wasn't quite sure but said it was a complaint about something unsightly on the property. "So, what's unsightly?" I asked, beginning to realize it might be a ruse. He didn't know exactly. It might be that car. He asked me how long it long it been there, and pointed to the Packard on the flatbed trailer in the driveway.

I laughed and told him it had arrived late last night. He asked if I thought it was funny? He had a stern look on his face. I said, "Of course it's funny. It's a joke, but I'm not too amused that you woke me." He turned a bit red in the face and handed me the paper he was there to serve. Now I was irritated, tore it up, and turned to go into the house. He told me I might have to pay a large fine or even go to jail. His voice was much harsher and he was even more red in his face. "I think I'd like to go to jail," I said. "I could use a vacation from cooking, housework and kids—and they'd probably even send me to college." He looked as if he would have a heart attack, and I thought, *He's a really good actor.* I went into the house still angry about being awakened. Shortly after the man left, Mike stopped by. He now knew about the ruse...the joke. He knew, I knew, but the man delivering the Blight Notice did NOT know. He was newly hired and not a part of the joke. Mike said the man wanted me tarred, feathered, and jailed immediately.

1953 Packard parked in our driveway.

Friends leased a cabin in Canada. Mike occasionally joined them on a weekend or sometimes longer for fishing. They often flew in, as one of the guys had a plane. I joined the group once and we snowmobiled to the cabin. Mike received this anonymous letter in the mail:

Loonhaunt Sportsman Society
Eelpout Airlines Terminal Building
Airport Road

Michael T Jurgens

Dear Jurkman,

As anticipated, the Board of the L.S.S. (Loonhaunt Sportsman Society) held a special meeting to discuss your probationary membership for 1991. After a lengthy discussion concerning your performance in 1990, such as whining, pouting, back stabbing, constant ridicule of fishing experts, it was decided that quite possibly you felt inferior to your fishing companions. That is understandable, considering the number of fish you caught. We also hope this is a temporary condition.

Tentatively, we have decided to give you another chance, and have placed you on probation for a period not to exceed one year on the condition you abide by the rules placed on all probationary members.

These being:

1. Before admittance on any trip, written permission from spouse, girlfriend or boyfriend or both must be received by the L.S.S. no later than 24 hours prior to departure. This permission slip must be witnessed by two people and notarized.
2. All camp chores are to be performed by probationary member or members. (If there is more than one probationary member they will be divided equally)

Chores are as follows:

a. Shovel all pathways.
b. Fetch water.
c. Maintain fire and wood supply.

    d. Wash dishes.

    e. Maintain cabin in a clean and orderly fashion while dressed in sexy lingerie in a color of your choice.

    f. Make fresh coffee in the morning before members of the board arise.

    g. Fuel all equipment (snowmobiles, ice augers). (Members will supply fuel for their own equipment. This is subject to change.)

    h. Drill and clean all fishing holes.

    i. Clean all fish.

    j. In the event that an over the limit of fish has been taken, the probationary member will assume all responsibility with the Ministry of Natural Resources or Border Patrol or both.

    k. Fluff pillows and preheat sleeping bags each night before members retire.

    l. In the event the probationary member cannot make one of the regularly scheduled trips to Loonhaunt, he will voluntarily and graciously provide a member or members of L.S.S. the full use and control of his snowmobile, trailer, sled, truck, and fishing equipment.

In the event of any violation of the above-mentioned rules means immediate BUNGA—BUNGA, and a one-year extension of probationary status.

The annual Patrol Christmas Party was in full swing at a restaurant. I heard a woman's voice in the hallway asking for Mike Jurgens. Dressed in a green pantsuit, white velvet jacket, red Christmas tree bulbs hanging on her ears, a large red velvet bow in her hair, and bright red lipstick, she searched for Mike. I didn't know who she was.

Santa's helper was in great form, and I laughed until I cried. Laughter filled the entire room as others savored Toasting Mike. He blamed many for the set up, but the waitresses finally admitted that several of them had pooled their hard-earned money to give Mike a Christmas to remember. It was also pay back for some of the torture he gave them.

After sitting on Mike's lap and kissing him on his bald spot with her bright red, lipstick-plumped lips, she read this poem:

T'was the month before Christmas and we were all shocked when a smiling Mike Jurgens walked into the shop.

The stockings were hung on the chimney with care. He hopes that Santa Claus would remember him there.

The staff was all buzzin and – busy as can be. Mike said, "Take your time; don't bother for me.

Then we knew that poor Mike was finally trying to be good and generous and extravagant like he always should.

We thought for a minute that he was demented, when all the waitresses he kindly complimented.

We all know he usually shows up very late to parties – which means fewer drinks he must pay.

So, tell me, Mike were you late tonight to this Christmas party with the folks that you like?

We asked all about you, they said for 3 percent you sold your soul to be station sergeant.

We know in the past you'd ask for free leeches at Fred's bait. Now I ask you, does that sound like a cheapee?

In immaculate condition is your state car, your personal car is the biggest MESS by far.

And so, dear Mike, we remember this night, how, for a month, you've tried to set things right.

389

It hasn't gone unnoticed by Mr. Claus so he sent me here with my big red Christmas balls.

To be your Big present and entertain you and acknowledged the month that you were tried and true.

Ten minutes of my time was your generous gift. And now there's only time left for a Christmas kiss.

So, take this [Kiss] big boy, and remember it's true how all year long Santa is watching you!

—Anonymous

Santa's Helper.

"Never regret anything that made you smile."

— Mark Twain

CHAPTER 46

THE CHILL OF AN EARLY FALL

The winter of 1999, Mike and I were excited that we had found a house to rent on the edge of the National Forest in northern Arizona. The rental was a roomy, three-bedroom, doublewide home. Although I had traveled there with a menacing cold, I slept comfortably the first night knowing that Mike would hear every creak and noise in the unfamiliar house. I awoke the first morning to hear Mike already up and making coffee. Being up this early was unusual for him, because he stayed up late and normally slept in. "I'm still on the night shift," he would say.

"What are you doing up?" I had asked groggily.

"I can't breathe," he said with an irritated voice.

Quickly out of bed, I assured him that he had caught my cold, that he would feel sick for a week. By mid-morning he had already been on the roof, making sure the vents were open. His breathing was easier as the day went on. Later in the day we shopped for groceries and roamed around downtown. Enjoying the surrounding area previously on a shorter vacation a few years before, we had decided it would be a good place to spend the winter. When a week had passed, Mike still had problems breathing. He would feel good for a day or maybe just an hour and then have what my mother would call a "spell" where he paced the floor and couldn't quite explain his symptoms.

He tried to give me an explanation of the way his body felt. "I've been sicker, but I've never felt like this. I feel like I'm breathing through my skin." I never understood that description.

On a sunny Sunday morning, Mike, frightened by his body's hourly changes, lay on the bed and asked me to stay with him, to stay in the bedroom. I sat up against the headboard as he restlessly slept. Occasionally awakening, he would tell me he wished he were home. "What would you do if you were home?" I asked.

"I would go to the hospital," he whispered weakly.

I was off of the bed, getting my purse, and stuffing my address book into it. "We can go to a hospital right here; I'll call an ambulance."

He didn't argue and slowly got out of bed. I walked into the living room where the phone was. Mike handed me his wallet saying with a hint of humor in his voice that he didn't know if I could call an ambulance, get the wallet out of his pocket, and give him CPR all at the same time. I assured him I could do it all. We did not go to the hospital.

The Sunday crisis passed as his body fought the dangerous physical changes that plagued him. With the promise that he would see a doctor as soon as I could get an appointment, we each spent a restless Sunday night.

A smiling young doctor greeted us Monday morning. He was new in town and one of the few physicians taking new patients. After a short exam and a few questions, he diagnosed flu as the culprit and sent Mike home with an antibiotic. Flu was raging in Arizona and sounded like a good reason for his problems. The hospital was filled to capacity with victims of the seasonal malady. If Mike needed hospitalization, he would have to be taken to the hospital in Flagstaff.

Mike seemed healthy during the week that followed, and we enjoyed a visit with my sister and husband a couple hours away. By the next week we were back in the doctor's office. For the next eight weeks, we were regulars: Mike's blood pressure spiked to alarming highs, and the change in prescriptions made him dizzy.

An appointment with a cardiologist would put our worries of heart problems at ease. The specialist wrote: Mike is a pleasant fifty-four-year-old man with a strong heart.

We were now well into the month of February and our worries continued. We felt a chill and it wasn't the Arizona winter weather. Mike felt full after only a few bites of food. His legs were at times so weak he could hardly walk. His sense of "breathing through his skin" continued.

My sisters came for a short visit, as did our daughter and husband. The decision was made to return to Minnesota. Our rent was paid through March so we could leave the truck and fly home. Mike didn't like the idea of leaving his new truck in the driveway of our Arizona rental but it was an option.

Another visit to the doctor delayed our trip home by two weeks. Mike's blood pressure was so high the doctor called me into his office and said Mike could have a stroke while he sat there. He wanted to change medication again but Mike had said we were going to Minnesota within the next couple of days. (The doctor wouldn't change his meds unless he stayed two more weeks.) I told the physician I would stay for two weeks and Mike wouldn't go without me. I was right. In two weeks, his blood pressure was under control. His other symptoms, however, had not gone away.

Mike did not let me drive on the way home. Driving had always been a love of his and he assured me he was okay and would get us home. I sat close to him, like I did when we were young and dating.

"Why are you staring at me?"

"So, I can grab the wheel if you have a stroke and die."

"What if I have a stroke and don't die. That would be worse."

Our Minnesota lake home looked inviting as we drove up the driveway. Once we entered our home a feeling of relief from health issues gave us a false sense of wellness. Our family doctor was soon running tests on a weekly basis. A hiatal hernia was found but the doctor didn't think that was causing Mike's symptoms. The doctor did think he might have a bacterial infection. There were many blood tests taken every week—they showed nothing.

"Nothing is more terrifying than a fear you cannot name."

–Anonymous

CHAPTER 47

TELL IT LIKE IT IS

Our world started crashing May 10th, 1999. I came home from work, and Mike said he had been spitting up blood—fresh blood. I insisted that we head for the emergency room. He didn't want to go and talked of going on Monday. We went that evening. In retrospect, there was nothing they really could or would do for him that night.

The doctor on duty took a chest X-ray. I'm sure he saw the tumor. He was not our family doctor, and I suppose didn't see the need to talk about it that night. He told us to see our doctor on Monday and sent us home. We had a long worry-filled weekend. A CT scan was done on Monday with results to be ready on Thursday.

I told the manager at work that I thought the results would be bad. If they were, I would not be back to work. I worked as a building estimator for a lumber company. I took the winters off and returned during the busy summer season. I had the best of both worlds, and so did they. I wasn't needed in the winter and would return when road restrictions were off and the building season began.

I walked in the door, stood in the foyer, and called to Mike, "I feel like I am going to the guillotine."

He came around the corner from the kitchen and said, "So do I."

The doctor's appointment was late in the day. The waiting room was almost empty. Whether true or not, I felt the receptionist had a softer tone in her voice and a more sympathetic smile than usual. The doctor's nurse touched my shoulder as I walked into the examining room.

Mike had asked me to bring a notepad along and write things down as the doctor talked. He knew he wouldn't remember all that was said. That had already been the case with some of our visits to doctors. I had written some questions to ask but really did not actually expect to have to ask all of them. We had a large Mayo Clinic Health Book and I had looked up Lung Cancer after he spit up blood.

I found the little red note book Julie and I had used during Mike's care at home. In the notebook were also the questions I had written down to ask the doctor on the visit after Mike's CT scan.

1. How long without treatment?
2. How long with treatment?
3. What kind and where?
4. What stage is he in?
5. Can he be home?
6. What are the signs as the illness progresses?

Our family doctor walked in, sat down, and proceeded to tell us that Mike had cancer in his lungs and spots on his liver.

Mike's face turned pale and expressionless.

The doctor opened the file and started reading the report of the CT scan. His voice was calm as he talked of the tumors in the lung—lung cancer that had now metastasized to the liver, and how fast this would go.

I couldn't write the words he spoke; my fingers were cold and stiff. I couldn't ask the questions I had written. I couldn't breathe.

Mike and I had felt impending doom since the previous Friday when he spit up blood. We thought we were ready to hear whatever was coming our way. It still hit us hard, and we stared at the doctor in disbelief.

I had to tell myself to breathe. I felt faint. But I finally managed to ask, "How long does he have?"

He couldn't say. It's different for everyone.

"Does he have two years? One year? Months?"

Months. The doctor looked at Mike as he talked. If he did nothing, he thought he should have three pretty good months and two lousy weeks.

"Is there any treatment?" Mike asked, forcing his words out.

Maybe there would be something experimental. He did want Mike to see an oncologist.

What do you need from him? The doctor's voice was so soft and then he put his hand on Mike's knee and took my hand.

"I don't want to hurt," Mike said, as he saw tears fill my eyes.

There was good pain medication. Morphine would keep Mike from hurting, unless it goes into the bone. They still didn't have a good way to get the pain medication into the bone.

It sounded so matter-of-fact to me. I felt numb and as if he were talking to someone else in the room; but there were just the three of us.

As I thought of it later, I felt sorry for our doctor, too, wondering how many times he had delivered that true but sad news to patients and their families.

"I'll need something to help me sleep," Mike said, struggling to smile. "I know I won't be able to shut my mind off when I go to bed."

He asked if I needed something to sleep too? Mike answered that question saying, "No, she can always sleep," before I could tell the doctor that nothing, not happy news or bad news, kept me from sleeping. That was so true. I have always had the ability to close my eyes and sleep, leaving things to God—at least for the night.

We practically had to tell our feet to move as we left the room. We didn't talk as we walked to the car or on the drive home. Mike got in the driver's seat. I wondered if I should drive, but he may have been better at keeping his mind on the road than I. We were in shock. Even though we had expected bad news, we still were unprepared for a death sentence.

Getting out of the car, I felt like I had heavy weights around my ankles and could hardly move. We got into our entryway and stopped. We put our arms around each other and sobbed. I can't even remember what I was thinking as total sadness enveloped us.

We pulled ourselves together and called our son John and daughter Julie. I paced the floor, which is usual when I am feeling stressed. Mike went out to mow the yard, which was also a stress reliever for him. John drove up that night. Julie would bring Mike's mom the next day. We called an attorney the next day, setting an appointment for Friday. We had talked of a will for so many years but never took the time. Now we would *find* the time. A will seemed to be for old people and there had never seemed to be a good time to take care of that.

The attorney was shocked when Mike told him of his impending death and our need for a will. The attorney had been a social friend, and Mike had spent time with him in court so Mike felt comfortable sharing the news.

On May 15, 1999, we began a forced, demanding dance with death. It was at times noisy and frightening. Other times, death was quietly lurking in the corners of our minds—an enemy to be feared and loathed. However, in time, we would welcome it as our friend.

I am not sure the word "shock" is appropriate for what we were feeling, but somehow, it is the word I chose. Even though we felt that we were going to hear bad news, neither of us thought it would be imminent death. I don't think it was quite "denial" but "disbelief" certainly fit.

A biopsy to determine what type of lung cancer Mike had would be done as an outpatient at the local hospital. Mike wanted me in the room when the biopsy was taken. When the doctor asked if I was sure I wanted to be in there, I assured him that if Mike wanted me there, I could handle it.

While waiting for the procedure to begin, an X-ray technician walked through the room. Mike knew him from his many visits to the hospital when a crash had occurred or he had brought a drunk driver in. Mike told him why he was there. The tech gave us the best advice and what we absolutely needed to hear. Mike was not dying today and not dying tomorrow. Don't waste the days that we have. I brought him an Easter basket filled with goodies and a note of appreciation after Mike's death. He had no idea what wonderful advice he had given us.

The doctor pushed a needle through Mike's side and into the liver, since the cancer had invaded that organ as well. I sat with my arms wrapped around my stomach as pain took my breath away. Hearing Mike moan as the needle went in brought tears streaming down my face. He had enormous tolerance for pain, yet I knew it was excruciating for him.

I had never had that kind of pain in my stomach and was thinking I should go to the clinic when this was over. I had also never heard the man I loved groan with such agony. The doctor tried several times, but the biopsy was not obtained.

Ambien was a good friend to Mike. He always had a smile on his face when I said good night to him. We had always believed that a good night's sleep made you ready for whatever came in the daylight.

We found comfort in each other. I knew I could count on him and he on me. Those first days we fumbled around; but as the days went by, we began to come to terms with our fate. Mike had a lot of faith in me. He was constantly telling me that he knew I would be OK without him. That, he said, gave him peace.

I had no doubt that Mike would handle whatever was coming. I had some doubt about my own ability to deal with what was imminent in our life. As we talked things over, he said just the opposite, that he knew I would cope just fine but that he questioned his own skills to handle this.

I would have a wonderful support system. John and Julie would be there for me. I am close to my brothers and sisters, and they would be there for whatever I needed. I had a good job and good friends. I did not have to worry financially.

I knew I was blessed in many ways. However, in the end, Mike would die, and I would be alone. It was an odd feeling at first, and I could understand how denial sets in. Mike still looked healthy. He had a hearty appetite, and food tasted good to him.

When Mike would want to buy, sell, or just need information about something, he would tell me that he "put the word out." That's what he told me to do about his cancer, and that's what I did. I saw two people in the grocery store that I knew would tell others. Within hours, our community had been informed.

Julie's thoughts:

I kept looking at my watch while working the second shift at the hospital. I had planned to call my dad during a break; he was getting news that day about his illness, one that had plagued him for five months. It was a roller coaster of diagnosis with no resolution. For our family, we had never faced something like this. For the most part, everyone had been healthy. I think we all knew it was going to be bad news. We were down patients at the hospital, so I asked the charge nurse, because of our census, if I could take the remaining shift off. Often in a small town hospital, this was an option. I was lowest in seniority, often the one sent home. I never minded. I had three jobs and was a student at the time. I worked at the hospital second shift and was an EMT-I on two ambulance services. One was at a much larger hospital forty miles away, and I was employed third shift and weekends. During the day, two days a week, I was a student slowly working my way to my paramedic license. My charge nurse said yes, take the rest of the night off.

Once home, I looked at the phone knowing I had to call as I was going out of my mind. On the other hand, I just knew it was going to be bad news. I called; dad answered the phone with an unbelievable calm. The first thing he asked me was how my shift was that night. I told him, "Fine, low census, I am home. Tell me about your doctor appointment."

His response is something I will never forget. "Julie, it is bad news. We are not going to be sad or down. We are going to celebrate life and be thankful for the time we have been given. It is terminal lung cancer. I will not survive it."

I told him I was coming home, leaving that night. I was used to being up all night and driving in the dark. It was a 250-mile drive.

He said, "No, I need you to do something for me." His mother, my grandmother, lived fifteen miles from me. She, too, was waiting to hear about his appointment. He said, "Please go to Mom's and tell her the news. I can't tell her this over the phone while she is alone. Go there. Tell her. She will want to come with you here in the morning."

"OK, I will."

He instructed me to call him once I had told her. I quickly packed a bag, called work, and said I needed a few days off. I called both of my crew supervisors. They said they would find coverage for my shifts.

I was out the door, heading for my grandmother's house. All I could think of was *How do I tell my grandmother that her son is going to die in in a short time from cancer?* I did not call ahead to warn her that I was coming. That alone this late in the evening would have made her worry. I just knocked on the front door. She was dressed for bed, sitting in her chair crocheting. I was still in my scrubs from work.

She said to me "You came right from work; it must be bad news." I broke it to her as gently as I could while making sure she fully understood what I was saying and the gravity of the situation. I called dad, told him grandma knew, and that we were leaving first thing in the morning.

Arriving at Mom and Dad's the next mid-morning, there was no one home. A note in dad's handwriting on the table said, "At the attorney's office." I was not surprised. My dad was the consummate planner. I knew my dad would have already started a list of priorities that needed attention.

When my dad walked in the door, he greeted us with a smile. I knew my dad all too well. A smile when a situation was bad meant he was trying his best to put on a brave face and that he was either uncomfortable or scared. This time I knew he was scared, He hugged me tight and said "We are not going to be sad." I remember thinking to myself that this celebration of life routine he was selling was complete B.S. I was upset, sad, and, frankly, pissed off. I wanted to know the plan. He was the strongest, toughest, and most determined man I had ever known. My brother John has often described our dad as if John Wayne had just walked in the room. I would agree with John: Our dad commanded attention just with his presence. He would win every fight, every shoot out, save the damsel in distress, then walk off into the sunset, expecting nothing in return just happy to help and do the right thing. I think of a John Wayne quote: "Talk Low, talk slow and don't say too much."

"And once the storm is over, you won't remember how you made it through, how you managed to survive. But one thing is for certain. When you come out of the storm, you won't be the same person who walked in."

—Haruki Murakami

CHAPTER 48

LEAN ON ME

The first person to come and see us was a former partner of Mike's. It took guts to walk up to our door and join us as we were finding our way. A retired sheriff came shortly after Mike's partner. He put his face in his hands and told us he had been at a garage sale when he heard the news. Mike smiled at me as we both knew the word was out.

We were acutely aware that we would set the tone for our visitors, and it would be up to us to make them feel comfortable. We met our visitors at the door or even walked out on the porch as they drove in. Seeing us standing on the deck made the walk to the door easier. The nicest thing one of the deputies said to me was that he always felt good after a visit with us.

Mike liked his privacy. I knew he would handle this well. I would, however, not have been surprised if he wanted to see only family and close friends. He shocked me and wanted to see people, and for the next three months and three weeks we had company.

Our friends rallied around us. Our home was filled with laughter, tears, and so much reminiscing. The coffee pot was always on, and I baked peanut butter cookies several times a week. I encouraged a call before coming. Mike never said no to a visit but afternoons turned out to be better than mornings. For the next three months, we had visitors almost every day. Friends and colleagues sat at our table, drinking coffee and eating peanut butter cookies. As they remembered the antics, the jokes they had played on others, they too seemed to be mourning together. "We know it could be any one of us going through this," remarked one visitor.

The women from the Clerk of Courts office brought pizza for lunch. They also laughed and talked about the pranks Mike had pulled on them and that they had played on him.

I'm remembering July 1992 when Mike went to his class reunion. The students of 1962 at Montevideo High School were an exceptionally close class. One of his dear friends, Mary, had been with him since first grade. They had, to a certain degree, a love-hate relationship. Mary, somewhat of a tomboy from birth, was tall and strong. I think she could have given him a run for his money in a wrestling match. He would sometimes tell her at gatherings that she should wear a dress or at least a skirt. She'd give him some smart-aleck answer.

The reunion Friday evening was a casual gathering at the American Legion. Saturday night was a dressier affair at the golf club. Mary managed the legion and that Friday evening she brought the drinks to our table. Mike made some sassy comment about her, and she poured his drink into his crotch.

The people at the table roared with laughter. I assumed he would go back to his parents' home where we were staying and change. However, no, he was not going to do that and spent the rest of the evening looking like he had had *an accident*. When Mike related that story to the women from the Clerk of Courts office, they did not believe him. They did not believe that anyone would dare to do that.

Those women from the court happened to be sitting at our table when Mary called eight years later. She wanted to stop by to see Mike. She would not stay long but she had driven up to the North Country to see Mike and also to spend some time with cousins who had a cabin in the area. The women were on their lunch hour, but they decided they would extend it—just a little—so they could meet the woman who dared to pour Mike's drink into the crotch of his pants—at a public gathering no less.

When Mary came to the door, Mike got up and greeted her. He made some smart remark to her, and she said, "Jurgens, you've always been an asshole, and you haven't changed."

Our lunch guests could not believe their ears. They had a good laugh. They left shortly after and our friend stayed awhile. She and Mike reminisced, remembering their longtime friendship, and they admitted that they really did like each other. Mary said, "I'm going to do something I never thought I would do. I'm going to give you a hug." As I write this, I'm picturing that day, Mary hugging him with tears running down their faces. They are running down mine right now. Mary has since passed away after battling her own cancer diagnosis of lymphoma. I'm sure Mike greeted her in heaven with some remark about her attire.

Many friends came to visit us during Mike's illness but strangers came too. A knock on the door found a man standing on our deck with his young son. He had admired the beautiful garden we always had and saw there was nothing planted this year. He went on to say that he had heard that my husband was ill and that was the reason for no garden. He then walked back to his car and brought me a basket full of vegetables from his garden. I don't remember if he told me his name, but I do remember being overcome by his kindness.

A woman who worked as a check-out clerk at a grocery store would ask me how things were going. She had heard about Mike's illness. A few days before he died, she asked her usual question. I answered, "Things are sad at home." I had never answered that way, but I had not thought until that day that Mike's death was coming so close. At the end of the day, she stopped with a bouquet of flowers and a hug.

Our longtime friends Sharon and Dave continued to be close by our side. They were like a quiet fire during those days calming and comforting. Mike was very relaxed around them. They came to us or we went to their home. Mike didn't have to feel embarrassed if his legs got weak and we had to go home. They visited often and I know it was very hard on them as well. It was difficult to see a strong, relatively young man become weak and frail.

Over the years, Mike and I talked about where we would be buried. My preference was the little graveyard outside of the town where I grew up. Mike liked to tease and say if my whole family was there it would be too noisy; he wanted death to be peaceful.

Early in June, of 1999, Mike was feeling pretty good and we decided to make a trip home. We would spend some time roaming around the cemetery. The church had closed many years before but the cemetery was well maintained.

Our family farm, where my aunt and uncle still lived, was just down the road. My uncle walked to the cemetery when he saw our car parked by the church. My great grandparents had donated the land where the church had been built. It was surrounded by state owned land; the noise and smell were wonderful. Mike did not want to be buried close to trees...too many roots. I assured him the roots could not penetrate a vault but he was unconvinced. We did not pick a spot that day, nor did he agree to be buried there. I asked him as we left the cemetery if he wanted to drive to a cemetery outside of the town where he grew up but he said, no.

Mike still looked healthy and was strong with only occasional bouts of weakness. It was hard for my mother to believe he was going to die. She was seventy-nine and had buried my dad when he was sixty-nine.

His sudden death from a heart attack Christmas Eve had been tough to come to terms with. It was hard for all of us now to believe that Mike was dying. I knew the doctor wasn't lying to us, but the ravages to his body that would eventually come were still far away.

Later that afternoon, Mike drove around the block several times where dear friends Lee and Marilyn lived. I was the one who could not compose myself and pull it all together. We knew we would set the tone for how others would handle his illness and inevitable death. We had held ourselves together during that visit and were proud of each other for being tough. However, the moment Mike was ready to park in front of Lee's, I was fighting a terrible battle with sadness and tears. Mike and Lee had been "partners in crime" in their teenage years. There was never actual "crime" but teachers had pulled their hair out over their antics; there had been many trips to the principal's office. They had gone into the Air Force on the buddy system; that had lasted fewer than twenty-four hours. They were as close as brothers. I finally managed to pull it all together so we could spend precious time with them. Knowing this was the last time Mike would see so many of our loved ones was torture. We were tough and hung in there until we left Montevideo, but sadness engulfed us on our way home.

Visiting our parents and friends warmed our hearts. Mike felt good the entire time there and seeing those special people and places for the last time seemed to give him a sense of peace. Again, he told me how glad he was to know death was coming. I knew he was preparing to die and helping me to be alone.

We found comfort in the Bible. Many passages came to mind as we began our unexpected journey. The longer Mike worked for the patrol, the more he encountered the miserable and messy sides of life. He carried the book *New Life* in his squad car. It was a version of the *New Testament* in easy, understandable words. He didn't talk about it but would occasionally quote from it as it pertained to a particular situation he found himself involved in.

Cancer patients who take treatment try to keep a positive attitude. They talk of beating the disease and fighting it with all they have in body and mind. Mike never talked of *if* he would die…he talked only of *when*. I have heard others talk about the deaths of their spouses from cancer. Because they wanted to fight, and never give up, they didn't talk about the real prospect of losing the battle—about the end. Unfinished business leaves regret: words unspoken; issues not dealt with. We agreed to talk about anything either one of us wanted to discuss. We had a lot to talk about. We tried to cover a few subjects almost every day. Sometimes they were simple things: when taxes were due, insurance, his garage full of stuff.

We struggled to maintain a sense of normalcy while accepting his death. According to the doctor Mike's life would end quickly. Without treatment he would be spared the side effects of chemo. We tried to continue our ties to one another, clutching our pain, our memories and our fears. It felt like a knife slicing through our hearts.

We reminisced those last months. We laughed at times and also cried. Mike's sense of humor never left him. Looking at pictures sparked poignant moments as we remembered thirty-five years of marriage and talked of memories. We set up the projector and blew the dust off of old slides, so popular in the seventies. We were without realizing it …working at accepting the inevitable. We were mourning, if that's possible—mourning together.

"Even if you know what's coming, you're never prepared for how it feels."

—unknown

CHAPTER 49

I'M MAKING PLANS FOR THE HEARTACHE. YOU'RE MAKING PLANS TO LEAVE.

Having chosen to forego treatment because the cancer was so aggressive, and grateful to know the end was coming, Mike began to make a list. He had been a list maker since his youth; this was comfortable for him. He wanted to see certain people, go special places, and get his affairs in order for me. He had seen sudden death many times in the past twenty-six years with the Minnesota State Patrol. After investigating a fatal crash, he would come home, lay his clipboard next to the telephone, and say, "He (or she) planned to go home today." He would tell me the survivors felt like they had been hit in the head with a sledgehammer. It had made them unable to think or even move. I had heard him on the phone to a surviving spouse, talking slowly and telling her or him where the vehicle was being stored. He would often ask survivors if they knew who their insurance provider was. Mike was determined to make sure I knew everything I needed to know before he died. This was new territory for us, and we had agreed to talk about anything that either of us wanted to discuss, even if it was painful and made us feel uncomfortable. We kept that pact, although it was heart wrenching at times.

Shortly after the grim diagnosis from our family physician, the yellow legal pad appeared on the dining room table. He often made two lists when making a decision—the pros on one column and the cons on the other. Several times during our almost thirty-five-year marriage, I would arrive home to find sharpened #2 pencils and yellow legal paper on the table: one set for me and one for him. We had arrived at decisions for many things—perhaps a new vehicle or a different home. At times, it was where we had wanted to go on vacation. At one point, it was a long list of things to decide for retirement. However, the yellow pad that appeared in June 1999 was only for him. It was the list he would work on to prepare for his death.

Returning from my walk one afternoon, I sat down at the table while he wrote. He read the list he had made so far in a matter-of-fact tone. "It sounds like you're making a list to prepare for a trip," I said with an almost irritated attitude. "I *am* planning a trip," he answered in a quiet voice. "It's just that I'm going, and you're staying here." I put my face in my hands and sobbed. He continued with his list.

He didn't want me to stay in the lake house. The enormous yard had exquisite green grass, beautiful flower gardens, gravel walkways, an immaculate vegetable garden, and 240 feet of lakeshore. It took constant care, and I was never excited about yard work. Mike and a friend had handled the majority of the yard work. I had been a part of getting the flowers and grass established, but that was enough. Mike was concerned about the upkeep. After trying to teach me the workings of his beloved John Deere garden tractor, he simply asked for my assurance that I would sell it before I wrecked it. I sold it shortly after he died.

A local yard and garden service mowed, trimmed, and raked for me after his death. They did a fine job; however, it would never have been good enough for him. He wanted his huge vegetable garden covered with sod, as he knew a garden was not my *forte*. He encouraged me to move closer to my family when he was gone. I was expecting to go back to work after his death, so I planned to stay in the house for at least another few years. We had lived there seven years, and it felt good to be in a familiar place. When everything seems out of control, the few things that feel normal are embraced. I struggled to hold on to what still felt familiar.

We walked through the garage many times during the next three months as Mike explained what belonged with the items that filled his favorite spot. He was a pack rat and found it extremely difficult to part with his stuff. A piece of tin, a bolt, perhaps a hunk of 2x4 could not be thrown away. There could possibly be a time when that is exactly what he might need. As I walked through the garage with him, I would wonder what he now thought about all the things he had saved. One morning, as if he could read my thoughts, he said, "I know you'll get rid of most of this. I wish I had the time and strength but I don't." Then as if suddenly all these belongings tickled his funny bone, he asked with a twinkle in his eye, "Are 28 gas cans too many?" Several years before, my brother had walked into the garage and in a teasing manner, told Mike there is something wrong with anyone who has 28 gas cans. As we strolled through the garage, Mike said, with a smirk on his face, that my brother was not to get even one of his gas cans.

A paperwork expert, Mike had saved everything. His insurance papers were all arranged with phone numbers and facts noted. His retirement papers from the State were at my fingertips with pertinent information written in the margins. I would thank him for these preparations before he died; and I continued to be grateful for his precise instructions as a huge array of questions arose later. His attention to detail and his good files would serve me well in the weeks and months after his death.

Asbestosis lung disease had claimed the life of a friend of ours. An avid believer in vitamins and numerous other remedies for a host of ailments, our friend tried many things to stay alive. Awaking at 4:00 a.m., he drank a special expensive cancer-killing tea. He was told by the supplier that doctors did not want anyone to know about the cure as it would adversely affect their volume of cancer patients.

Mike had many well-meaning friends. They, at times, tried to help, suggesting some off-the-wall cures. We received pamphlets in the mail with suggestions of how to kill cancer. One was a cure concerning peach pits from Brazil. Another friend suggested that Mike try the coffee-enema cure. Apparently, a coffee enema, perhaps several, would cleanse away the disease. I could not make eye contact with Mike as we fought giggles, each knowing what the other was thinking. He politely told the gentleman he preferred to *drink* his coffee.

When we were alone again, I asked tongue-in-cheek when he would like his enema to start. He said, "Promise you will never let anyone do that to me." I assured him that I would look out for him.

I can appreciate clutching at any help that might be out there— wanting to stay alive. Although Mike and I were conventional people, we believed in miracles and knew the advances in medical science that were happening perhaps on a daily basis. We had, however, resigned ourselves to the situation. We prayed not for a cure but to have the strength to get through what was ahead.

Although Mike had told our family doctor he didn't think he wanted to go through chemo or whatever treatment might be recommended, he agreed to see an oncologist. Sitting in the waiting room at the hospital was heartbreaking. Many of the patients were much younger than Mike. One sad looking young woman clutched a little baby in her arms while her husband wheeled her into the waiting room. I can still see that young mother and the mournful look on her husband's face as I write this and tears fill my eyes.

Mike had been diagnosed with Small Cell Lung Cancer—the most aggressive form of lung cancer. The odds of living for any length of time were one percent. As the oncologist suggested experimental treatment, repeating several times how good our health insurance was, I asked the question Mike and I really wanted and needed to know. "Will he have any quality of life?" He'd be alive.

As the consultation with the specialist continued, he again reiterated how wonderful our health insurance was and his disbelief that Mike was not interested in seeking treatment. Mike, wanting to end the discussion, said simply and firmly, "I want my insurance dollars to go to someone who actually has a chance to live."

With that and a handshake from the doctor, we were on our way home. Many friends and family wondered why he didn't try to fight this. He was not a quitter, but he was a realist. We were never without hope. It just wasn't hope for a cure. It was a hope to continue to have the strength to handle what was coming.

Driving home, we talked about his decision. I had already told him that I would be totally supportive in whatever choice he made. Our family doctor had previously told us that if he did nothing, he would probably have three pretty good months and about two lousy weeks. With treatment Mike would give up those good months for quite possibly six months of bad. When Mike told our doctor of his decision, he said he thought it was the right choice. We were made aware that sometimes when you take treatment, you just can't die. You're not living but you're not quite dead.

Even now looking back, I believe it was without a doubt the right decision for Mike. I know there are situations where you may need to buy more time. He had believed, even as a young teenager, that when your time is up, it is over, that one's days are numbered. Working for the patrol enforced that belief even more. He would be called to an accident where the car had been smashed to smithereens, yet the people survived with hardly a scratch. Sometimes in what was a minor accident, the driver would end up with a blood clot and die, or other unforeseen problems would take his or her life.

As Mike made plans to leave, we found comfort in many things. Our children were grown. They had their own lives. We had been able to enjoy the arrival of three wonderful grandchildren. All were healthy and happy. We had cleared the land for a new home on a lake outside of town, and Mike had been able to retire at age 51. I could work or not. We were truly blessed. Marriage had given us thirty-five years together and a good life. Did we want more? Of course! We didn't want this life we had together to end. Would we have done things differently at times? Sure! We would have been smarter and better at managing things. We did the best we could at the time. When we grew smarter, we did better.

It was an odd feeling at first, and now I realize how denial sets in. Mike looked great. He had lost a little weight but just enough to make him look even better. He had a hearty appetite and food tasted good. The doctor attributed his sick feeling in Arizona to cancer moving from his lung, metastasizing to his liver. Although he ate well, he did not gain weight. On the advice of the doctor, we took a walk every day. He looked too good to be dying. Occasional weakness would consume his entire body but he bounced back quickly early in his illness.

Although he would tell me throughout his life that he thought he would live until 65, he did not seem to dwell on dying. I have read about the stages discussed in the death process. He seemed to move right on to acceptance. He did not ask, "Why Me?" I didn't see any bargaining or anger. If he was depressed, he hid it well. He may have gone through some of that while we were in Arizona where we had two months of worry. A person knows one's own body, and he said often when we were in Arizona that he had been sicker in his life but had never felt quite like this.

Julie came to stay with us for the last month of Mike's life. She arrived in a hurry after hearing her dad on the phone. His usually strong voice had disappeared in the night. I, too, was worried when I heard his voice in the morning. He could barely talk in a whisper. I asked if he felt as bad as he sounded. He assured me it was just from talking so much the night before. A friend we hadn't seen for a long time had come to visit. David was a good friend of each of ours. He had grown up in my hometown of Watson and also became a friend of Mike's in his high school years. Mike was having a good night, and we had many things to talk over. Reminiscing about old times late into the night made us laugh and wish we were young again. We could almost forget about the cancer lurking in Mike's body...at least for a few hours.

David had flown in from Montana. I was walking out to the car to bring him to the airport when Julie drove in. She would stay with us until the end. Mike had talked a lot the night before but that was not the reason for his *laryngitis*. Although his voice did get a little stronger, it never really came back.

Julie and I had not been together for an extended period of time since she was a teenager. Her presence that last month was an enormous blessing. It proved to be good for all of us. She was a wonderful nurse, a comfort to us both, and a constant companion for her dad. I was exhausted and would go to bed totally worn out though I had done very little physical work.

Mike handled his pain by taking an Aleve in the morning and one at night. He had a high tolerance for pain and did not complain about any of the symptoms of the cancer that was now ravaging his body. Julie and I gave him our total attention, and he loved the massages that we would give him in the evening. He would lie on the floor while Julie rubbed his legs and I his shoulders, arms, head, and face. It seemed to calm and relax him before he took Ambien for sleep.

We would giggle quietly at the bright yellow shorts he put on for the massage. Mike's idea of bold color usually would be some kind of off white or beige. He had picked out these shorts because they were cheap. The condo we had rented in Florida had a pool but he hadn't brought swim trunks so had to buy some. The swimming trunks were $20.00 and the yellow shorts only $10.00. The warm, wonderful pool was full of men and women enjoying a perfect sunny day in beautiful Florida. I soon felt Mike's hands on my shoulder. As I turned around he said in a very serious tone, "Can you see through these shorts?" I held my smile back as much as I could but could not stop it from it extending wide across my face. "Yes...I can see all of you!" He was horrified, and I hate to admit it but...I loved the look on his face. I whispered into to his ear. "That's what you get for being so cheap." Mike stayed in the deep end, treading water until he was exhausted. He would at times go to the edge and hang on but most of the time he was moving to stay afloat. Finally, the other swimmers began leaving the pool, a few at a time. They were, however, not necessarily leaving the area; they were getting into the hot tub just a few feet away. I stayed in the pool with Mike, and we were both shriveled prunes when the last person finally left the pool area. He still wouldn't come out until I had a towel ready to cover him.

I was so grateful that Julie could be with us in Mike's last weeks. There needed to be two of us as he became weaker and someone had to be close to him at all times. We can try to imagine what certain situations will be like. However, when we actually face things, real life is different than we anticipate.

He did not want to be in his bedroom except to sleep. He liked to sit at the dining room table. There he could look out at what had become the perfect place—the home of our dreams.

We had talked of a lake home when the decision to move to the area was made. The thought of living outside of town did not interest me. I knew I would be the driver in the family when the kids needed to get to school functions, and I also wanted a job.

I have read we find comfort in familiar things when we feel our life is in chaos. I was a senior in high school when my parents went to Arizona to look for a business to buy. They had sold their oil business in the small town where we lived and were looking for new horizons. My sister and her husband had found teaching positions in Tucson and wanted my parents to give the west a chance. Another sister and two brothers were only seven and eight and of course would go with Mom and Dad.

I was seventeen and had only four months until graduation. I would stay with my grandmother until I graduated. My aunt bought me an electric blanket to chase away the cold in the unheated second story of Grandma's little house. She also bought me a box of Chantilly Bath Powder. That fragrance gave me a sense of comfort and warm feelings because I missed my parents and siblings horribly. I had not bought or even thought about Chantilly Bath Powder in years, but when Mike was sick, I found it and had that same feeling again—I was safe in a warm home surrounded with love.

When I heard the words "lung cancer" from the doctor, I prayed to God, "Please don't make me listen to Mike gasp for every breath." My prayers were answered. Mike never coughed or had trouble breathing. Shortly before his death the Hospice Nurse checked Mike's lungs as well as Julie's and mine. The nurse commented that his sounded the best.

Mike never lost his sense of humor. It would see us through some really dark and scary times. We laughed whenever we could. That kept us going. We were both down at times but never at the same time. When one of us was particularly sad, the other would be their cheerleader.

"You never knew how strong you are… until being strong is the only choice you have."

–Cayla Mills

CHAPTER 50

KNOCKIN' ON HEAVEN'S DOOR

When Mike was first diagnosed, we talked for hours. As our initial shock and frantic feelings subsided, we reminisced and, throughout the next days and weeks, made plans for what needed to be done before he died, when I'd be left alone. Our talks were open and honest as our emotions spilled out. By the last few weeks of Mike's life, we had said about all there was to say. I thought about the Pete Seeger song, *"You gotta walk that lonesome valley. You gotta walk it by yourself."*

Mike was withdrawing, and *Hospice Care: The Little Blue Book*, also called *Gone from My Sight: The Dying Experience* by Barbara Karnes, was a comfort to me. It talked of withdrawing from life—of one foot in each world, of waning interest in the world, television, news of the day, opening the mail—the realization and acceptance of the coming end of life.

Four days before his death, Mike's mother was coming to visit. He needed a shave and made his way into the bathroom. I followed him. He seemed especially weak that morning. As I walked in, I could see that he was holding onto the corner of the medicine cabinet. He steadied himself as he got things ready for his shave. He still used a straight edge razor, and before he started, I wondered if he could handle it. He had taken care of himself in every way and didn't want me doing things for him. "Can I help?" I asked, trying not to sound bossy.

"Do you think I want you, with a razor in your hand, this close to my throat?" he asked with a wink. I just sat down on the stool and watched him. I held back the tears as this once strong man's hands trembled, as he spread the shaving cream on his face. It took him awhile, and he seemed to look especially careful at his face. It was gaunt and orange now. He seemed surprised. I think he realized how different he looked.

Two long-time friends had come to visit the week before. They had been our neighbors years ago. The woman had been battling pancreatic cancer about the same amount of time as Mike had been dealing with lung cancer, although neither had known what their actual ailment was for a long time.

"Do you think she'll die before me?" Mike asked after they left.

"She's more orange than you are," I said.

Our friend would live three weeks longer than Mike.

Mike's mom was shocked to see how Mike had deteriorated since her last visit. I can't say that I noticed it as much, for I had seen him every day of his illness. I had not noticed the subtle day-to-day changes. I sensed the end was close, but I had no idea how extremely near it was.

His mother fixed breakfast for him the next morning: eggs and bacon, his favorite. Without chemo, he had not lost his appetite. She fixed the best eggs—just the way he liked them: over easy. He had difficulty holding the fork and even more difficulty cutting the white around the egg. They were not tough; it's just that he had so little strength. I reached for the fork to help him, but he shook his head. The food sat there and got cold.

That night he awoke. *He's up,* I thought, as I heard Mike's bed bump against the bedroom wall. It was the middle of the night. He was standing next to his bed, agitated and disoriented. I talked softly, asking if he was in pain and encouraging him to get back into bed. Not easily redirected, blinking his eyes, and staring at me with a look of confusion had me unnerved. I suddenly felt as if I couldn't trust him. Continuing to urge and cajole finally worked, and he lay down and settled in.

We had talked at great length about the coming end—his last days. He had asked only three things of me: he wanted as few people as possible involved in his care (that was easy as Julie came to stay the last month of his life); he wanted to be kept as pain free as possible; and he wanted to die at home.

My usual routine was to wake him in the morning to give him his bump of morphine, a tiny pill that dissolved quickly under his tongue. It only lasted a short time, just long enough for him to swallow the longer lasting more powerful pain pill that would hold him for about four hours. I did not let him sleep past a certain time because I didn't want the effects to wear off totally. The pain would be severe, and it would take a long time to bring it back under control.

Although weak at times, he could still exert tremendous strength. Suddenly I doubted my ability to handle him. I feared he would not understand what I wanted him to do. As he put the morning pill in his mouth and took a sip of water, he told me he couldn't swallow. I gently rubbed my hand up and down his throat, hoping to stimulate the action of swallowing. It wasn't working, and he had to spit the water and the pill out. I had asked the hospice nurses many questions; however, what to do if he couldn't swallow was not one of them. Crushing morphine was not an option. That would take away the effectiveness of the drug.

The next morning his mom and I took a walk, and Julie called the ambulance. It was a difficult task for her, but I knew that he could push my buttons easier than hers, and the hospital is where he needed to be. When his mom and I returned, I told her that we would find one of two things: Either he would be on his way to the hospital, or the ambulance drivers would be tied up, he'd have taken the ambulance, and be on the run.

Although he was now extremely weak, at times he could also still find the strength that he had enjoyed over all those years. We walked in to find Mike and Julie gone. We quickly went to the hospital. Since he was enrolled in Hospice, Julie had called to let them know he would be coming.

Mike was already settled into a room when we arrived. As soon as I walked in, he asked me to take him home. I ignored the request and asked how he was feeling. I knew that when the decision was made to take him to the hospital, he was never coming back home. The doctor had tried a shot of morphine, but his veins collapsed. A morphine patch on his chest perhaps stung because he tore it off. Eventually a morphine patch on his back worked.

Mike's days, perhaps hours, were numbered, but, despite this, perhaps because of this, I took time away from him to take care of two important matters.

His check from the state arrived. I took it into the bank to deposit it. (Mike didn't like direct deposit.) I signed his name and then mine, which I had done a few times in the past.

I handed the check to her to the cashier. She informed me that they don't want anyone else signing their name on the check now. But, since it's for deposit only, it should be okay.

We had banked in that small bank for twenty-one years. I told her Mike was sick. She had heard. She wondered if I had his Power-of-Attorney?

"Yes," I said, impatiently.

The cashier told me to bring it along next month, and there'll be no problem.

"He won't be alive," I replied, angry about everything that was happening and would happen because he wouldn't be here. Little did I know that he would die in nine hours.

I walked across the street to the funeral home. My stepfather was a funeral director in the area where I grew up. I wanted services in each town: The first one in the town we were now living. That's where we had lived for the past 21 years, and the second where he grew up. Mike had been baptized and confirmed at the church in his home town. His mother was a loyal church member and worker.

I had already called my stepfather to ask him where the funeral plans should originate. I didn't know who should be taking care of Mike's body, as he would eventually be buried in my family cemetery. My stepfather said it should begin with a funeral home where we now live.

Mike knew the funeral director. I only knew *of* him and had attended some of the funerals he had taken care of. I introduced myself and told him that Mike was ill. He already knew. When I told him that I wanted two funerals—one here, another funeral and burial 250 miles away, he assured me that he could handle that. The only problem might be, he went on to say, that inclement weather could pose a problem if Mike died in the winter. I told him weather would not be a problem and that I believed Mike would die within the next few days.

I can still see the look on the funeral director's face as I write. That look of surprise or disbelief, perhaps because I was calm and so controlled.

Later I wondered why and how could I sit in that funeral home feeling so peaceful.

I told the director that, unlike Mike, I would not bargain with him about the price. I said facetiously, but meaning every word, that if the situation were reversed, if *I* were about to die, Mike would probably be busy making the coffin for me. Mike had asked me if I thought I could just haul him and his casket in the back of the pickup. He would have wanted to bargain for the best price as well. The director laughed a little at my comment for he knew Mike liked to save money.

Mike's Mom, our daughter Julie, and our son John, who had arrived from Hawaii the day before, and I went to the hospital to be with Mike. He was quiet, and seemingly his pain was under control. We went back home. I had paper work from the hospital to fill out. However, I felt different about leaving him. An uneasy feeling stayed with me. Julie and I went back to the hospital as soon as I finished. Arriving, we were told by a nurse that his blood pressure had been dropping and death was not far away.

We sat quietly. The day before, our presence had made him restless. He wanted to sit up, get up, and, of course, go home. That evening, he was in a semiconscious state, his eyes partly closed, just slits showing, his breathing labored. We heard the snoring sound—respiratory tract secretions—associated with death. Suddenly his eyes opened and he looked at us. Julie and I leaped from our seats and stood on each side of the bed. He felt cool to my touch.

We assured him he could leave us, that we would be okay without him. His breathing slowed; there was a long pause between breaths. "He's dying," Julie said softly.

"Right now?" I asked, laying my head on his chest. He was quiet; but before I raised my head up, another deep gasp came from his lungs, startling me. It was quiet again, then over. Julie called John; he and

Mike's mom immediately came to the hospital. The funeral director would soon be there too, expressing his sympathy and disbelief that Mike's death had come so soon after our meeting.

We were subdued when we arrived home. I took the DNR (Do Not Resuscitate) order off the front door and laid down on the loveseat, staying there until morning. Surprisingly, restful sleep engulfed all of us.

"Sorrow," begins a French proverb, "comes swiftly on horseback, but leaves slowly on foot."

CHAPTER 51

IF TOMORROW STARTS WITHOUT ME

The morning after Mike's death, Julie was on the phone making calls to friends and family. John was communicating with his wife in Hawaii, arranging their flight back to the Main Land. I called the church to discuss day, time, and food for the funeral. After that had been established, my mother-in-law called her pastor and had that same discussion about the funeral. Later Julie and I went to the funeral home to finalize plans. We discussed visitation, chose a casket, memorial brochures, flowers—all the arrangements needed for saying our last goodbye.

Several hundred people came through the visitation line at the funeral home. Hugs and words of sympathy filled my world. We had never talked about cremation, although I had asked him if he wanted to be viewed after he died. "Yes," he said without hesitation, "this is what dying from cancer looks like."

Earlier in the day, I got a call from a friend who had been at the funeral home. "Have you seen him," she asked. I said "No, is something wrong?" "Well," she said, "not really I guess." I went early to have a look. I took a deep breath and walked up to the coffin. It was certainly not the first time I had done that but this was different. It was Mike. He was quite orange but he really didn't look a lot different than the last time I had seen him. Several who had not seen him those last ten days or two weeks talked of how he had changed. A cousin of mine told me she would not have known it was him but she had not seen him for many months. I can't say for sure how much he had changed, although he was probably at least 60 pounds lighter. I had been with him every day for the last many months and the changes in his appearance, although perhaps not exactly subtle, I had not noticed them much. Talking to my daughter now about that day, she said she wished we had closed the casket.

As I write this, I can picture the dress I wore for the visitation. I know I started off with my shoes on but had soon taken them off, my bare feet hidden by the long hemline. I probably stood for three hours, mostly in the same spot. "It was a relief," I remember saying to someone as he hugged me and said, "You have my sympathy." That feeling of peace had come over me almost the moment Mike took his last breath. I had several months to think about what my life would be like after he was gone. I had thought about what I might be doing months later, but I hadn't thought much about the first day or the first weeks after he died.

Mike died late on a Tuesday night, September 7, 1999. His first funeral was on Saturday, September 11, 1999. Our church had a magnificent singer who also played the piano. I asked him to play some upbeat music before the service started. One of my friends said later that as she listened to the music, and thought, *There's a little zip in those songs.* He also sang Amazing Grace, Precious Memories, and The Lord's Prayer during the service. Friends spoke about Mike; the Clerk of Court spoke; and the pastor's sermon asked the question, "Who's to say what a long life is?"

We chose the Bible verses from Ecclesiastes: 3, 1-8 for the In-Memoriam.

> *To everything there is a season, and a time for every purpose under the heaven:*
> *A time to be born, and a time to die; a time to plant, and a time to pluck up that which is planted;*

> *A time to kill and a time to heal; a time to break down, and*
> *a time to build up;*
> *A time to weep, and a time to laugh; a time to mourn, and*
> *a time to dance;*
> *A time to cast away stones, and a time to gather stones*
> *together; a time to embrace, and a time to refrain from*
> *embracing;*
> *A time to get, and a time to lose; a time to keep, and a time*
> *to cast away;*
> *A time to rend, and a time to sew; a time to keep silent, and*
> *a time to speak;*
> *A time to love, and a time to hate; a time of war and a time*
> *of peace*

Many friends and family came to pay their respects. One section of the sanctuary was filled with law enforcement, firefighters, and EMTs.

I remember feeling especially strong that day, and if tears came, they were few. I wanted to be calm for my children, grandchildren, Mike's mom, and ultimately for myself. And it wasn't over. There would be another funeral on the following Tuesday. I walked behind the casket outside to the hearse. My sister, recalling that day, said she remembers me standing there all alone. If I was, I don't remember. My memory is of my dear uncle, saluting and crying as the casket was loaded into the back of the hearse.

My aunt and uncle had a cabin on a lake not far from us. We spent many wonderful times there, and they dearly loved Mike. We helped them, at times, with things at the cabin. Sometimes we helped with their dock and boatlift and other chores. I remember one particular day we went out in the dead of winter. My uncle had called and expressed concern about the deep snow that was on the roof. Mike and I went to the cabin with a ladder, a roof rake, and a couple of shovels. Mike went up on the roof and shoveled as much as he could to the end of the roof. The snow was very deep and soon I heard a scream from the opposite side of the roof. My heart almost stopped, and I knew he had fallen off. I ran around to the back thinking the worst and how I was going to get him to the hospital. Actually, he had jumped off into the deep snow. When I arrived with my eyes as big as saucers and filled with fear, he was lying on the top of the snow bank making a snow angel with a grin on his face. What a relief!

I continued to be surrounded by family and friends on Saturday night. Sunday I was ready to have some time alone. A second funeral for Mike would be on Tuesday, September 14, a week after his death. When we had talked about a funeral, Mike had suggested there be just a graveside service at the cemetery. As we talked about it, I told him that I thought there should be a funeral in the church where he had been baptized and confirmed and also where his mother had spent many hours volunteering and helping with funerals, weddings, and anything that went on in the church. He had decided yes, that that might be a good idea, but he also said, "But maybe I'll stink." I assured him that I had talked to my stepfather, who was a funeral director and who assured me that a second funeral, a few days later, would be just fine. There would be no problem.

I was finally alone Sunday night. I packed a suitcase and planned to stay for a few days. My drive on Monday was uneventful. I visited with my mom and stepdad but stayed overnight with Mike's mom. Tuesday morning felt different. This truly would be the end. Mike would be buried, and all would be over. Several of the pallbearers had come for the second funeral. However, it was a five-hour drive and some could not be a part of the second funeral. So we picked other friends from around the area to be part of this last goodbye. A huge replica of a Minnesota State Trooper's badge sat in the front of the church along with flowers. High school classmates came to say goodbye to Mike. My stepbrother and sister-in-law sang Amazing Grace, Precious Memories, and The Lord's Prayer. I rode to the cemetery, about 10 miles away, with my son John, his wife, and their children. I saw a trooper salute us as we turned onto the road that led to the cemetery. It reminded me of the day of Mike's dad's funeral when another trooper saluted us as Mike drove his mother and me to the cemetery.

The funeral director didn't know they could drive along the side of the graveyard to be close to Mike's grave. So they parked in the front part of the church parking lot; it was a long walk to his resting place. I walked along the rows of headstones where I had walked many times. My mother later asked me how I could walk behind Mike's casket and be so brave. "I was among friends as I walked to his gravesite," I had answered.

When I got to the gravesite, I stood close to the casket. Soon my niece was standing on one side and my great niece on the other. They each held my hands. They were ten and eleven. Law enforcement who attended stayed a distance away from the casket. I remember a deputy, a close friend of Mike's, sobbing as the pastor said the words "dust to dust." A man who had been in our Sunday School played "Taps," which is the name of that final call, the eerie melancholy sound signifying the end of day that had always made me cry. Tears came. We were soon returning to the church for lunch and visiting. Julie stayed at the cemetery and watched the actual burial. She came to the church for a brief time but was emotionally drained and ready for it all to be over.

I stayed with my mother-in-law that night, and the next day, my daughter Julie, Mike's mom, and I read sympathy cards and wrote thank you notes. The next morning my mother-in-law and I drank coffee and talked. She had been alone for ten years. Always seeming like a capable, independent person, she expressed how lonesome she was at times. She told me if she had it to do over, she would have someone to be with, and that I was too young to be alone. She went on to say she may have never married again but would have had someone to go to dinner, a movie, or travel with.

I left for home on Friday. I went to visit my mom and stepdad for a few hours then stopped at the cemetery. Black dirt stood out like a sore thumb on the still green grass of September. Without a doubt there was a fresh grave. As youngsters, we had seen many new graves. We attended church there on Sundays, and during the school year, we were in Sunday School also. We often wandered around the cemetery between Sunday School and church. A new grave with no grass on it was somewhat fascinating and spooky at the same time.

I thought of the Poem "If Tomorrow Starts Without Me," as I walked toward Mike's grave. *If tomorrow starts without me, and I'm not here to see. If the sun should rise you find your eyes all filled with tears for me...*

I spent some time there sitting by Mike's grave and walking around where other relatives were buried. My dad was not far from Mike. I knew they would be talking about old times. They were great friends and took several trips together when Dad was about 55 and Mike 30. Dad had an old VW bus, and they toured around the Western United States. They would switch drivers; however, Mike drove most often. It was the early 70s and the Hippy era was not quite over. Mike loved to tell of hitchhikers seeing the VW coming down the road and how they would grab their stuff and come running, assuming the driver would stop for them. What a surprise when Dad just drove on by. My dad liked Mike the minute he met him. He warned Mike when he said, "Susan is a spirited young lady." Dad often said that his children were spirited. My family also liked Mike. They saw the twinkle in eye but didn't know the extent of the prankster side of him until they came for his retirement party.

I talked to my sister as I was writing about the cemetery and she and reminded me of the many times she stopped there to visit Mike after his death. She was in a battle with breast cancer and taking chemo and radiation. Our mother was in a nursing home in that area and coming to visit her was a monthly ritual. My sister would stop at Dad's grave, then at Mike's. She would share what was going on in her life with them.

It is a comfort for me to know that Mike's body is there in that pretty cemetery on the hill. The wind rustles through the trees, corn stalks sway in the breeze, birds sing, and geese fly overhead, honking their song on the way to the Lac qui Parle Reserve. Mike was a frustrated farmer and loved to hunt. I believe he is right where he should be.

The front of our grave stone.

The back of the stone.

Our picture on the front.

It was strange to walk in the door of the home we had carefully planned and worked so hard to have exactly as we wanted. I then felt alone. Thoughts about the last weeks and that final day scrolled through my head. I called Mike's mom and my mom to tell them I was safely home and also talked to my children. I had been alone so many times, but this of course was different. This was permanent. Mike was not coming home from work, from a hunting or fishing trip—he was gone forever.

The only way to get over a death is by seeing it as a life completed, instead of a life interrupted.

—Anonymous

CHAPTER 52

IF I NEEDED YOU, WOULD YOU COME TO ME

I have believed in God for as long as I can remember. Church services, Bible school, Sunday school, morning devotions, and evening prayers were a part of my upbringing. And, yes, I believe in angels. We could call them spirits, angels, even ghosts that come in and out of our lives. Mike said many times, "If you need me, I'll be there." I needed him, and he *was* there.

I had often been home alone. Mike worked nights, weekends, holidays and on his days off often went hunting or fishing. Sometimes that took him into Canada to fish and other times he was off to Colorado to hunt elk. I didn't mind being alone. I was used to it and actually liked my own company. And, of course, for many years our children were home with me. There is a definitely different feeling to know he was never coming home again—never walking into the house ever again. There is definitely a strange feeling to know you are alone and that that will continue. After his death I begin to hear what I considered strange noises. It didn't take me long to realize that they were sounds of the house that have been going on since the day we moved in. I was hearing the furnace cutting on, a softener running, refrigerator defrosting, the simple basic noises of a home.

The first few weeks after his death, I had trouble sleeping. Sleep has always been so important for me. I cherish my eight hours' worth.

Nothing had ever kept me from sleeping. But those first days after Mike's death were different. I had never locked doors when Mike was gone, not even when he was off hunting for several days or weeks. Now it was my responsibility. There was no one to share that. It was me... me alone. There was also a part of me that felt almost afraid to sleep.

I had never felt alone. Now, overnight, my mind had changed. I didn't feel safe and secure. I awoke in the middle of the night almost every night the first several weeks. Maybe I thought I heard something or a scary dream woke me. Often, I was being chased, I ran, and I fell. I was disgusted with myself for being afraid.

Mike talked often during his illness that I had to be more careful, more aware of my surroundings. "People will know I'm dead," he would say so matter-of-factly and without emotion. We had only locked our garage door when we left town. He encouraged me to begin locking the garage during the day even when I was home. A friend put up a motion detector so that when I drove up I had light between the garage and house. It would irritate me to walk to the garage, find it locked, and I'd be without keys. I hated all the changes.

Mike came to me in my dreams. He looked good, maybe about 40. He brought calm and peace back into my life. He sat at the table, his hands folded, telling me I was going to be fine. "You're not going to be scared for very long." He told me to be patient with myself and he was right. My fear didn't last long.

I took a few steps to feel more secure about my safety. I called my neighbors to tell them when or if I was going to be on a ladder in the basement replacing light bulbs. I let them know when I was going away and when I expected to be back. I also told them when I was cleaning the gutters on the back of the garage.

Writing thank you notes and making calls to insurance companies, the State of Minnesota, and others, asking what they needed from me and getting the paperwork from them to fill out kept me busy. It was amazing how many copies of the death certificate I needed.

About a week after Mike's burial, I was sitting at our dining room table with a stack of papers containing phone numbers and information. I was preparing to call the Minnesota State Retirement office. Mike put the letters I would need from the different agencies in a folder. He had made a few notes on some of them. I looked at the note he had left on the letter from the state. *Don't let them screw you out of your money and don't be afraid to sue them.*

I called the number for the State of Minnesota Retirement Board. I assumed they would need a copy of Mike's death certificate before they would send his monthly checks in my name. The letter I had in front of me clearly stated how much I would receive in the event of Mike's death. After telling the woman on the phone that Mike had passed away and gave her my name and the other information, she returned to me with the information she had found. She declared in a monotone voice, that Mike had chosen the option that in the case of his death I would get nothing.

"Well, I'll tell you what, I'm looking at a letter dated (such and such), and this is what it says."

Just a minute. She would check again. She was looking at the wrong file. I was right and would receive the check when they received the death certificate and paperwork that she would send me to fill out.

I was on a roll. Next, I called a life insurance company. With Mike's name, my name, and the policy number, I got this response from the woman who answered the phone. She asked me if I knew why he would have left this policy to someone named...?"

"No, I do not. Better check his file a little closer."

Oops! They had put in a new computer system and that was the name of the programmer entering the information.

I hung up the phone and was angry at first, but then had to laugh. I did wonder how I would have handled that had I been older. I may have taken them at their word and not asked questions.

We had bought a computer the year before Mike died. Neither of us knew much about running it, but we could send an email and used it occasionally for research. It was in the basement, and after Mike's death, my son moved it to the main floor. There was only one problem. I couldn't remember the password. I called a friend and we talked. I tried to get into the computer but nothing I tried worked. The friend offered to come over to help, but I was frustrated and having a hot flash. I had a good cry and went to bed.

The password was also written on a paper in an envelope. I had looked for it and could not find it. I am a thrower and had gone through papers I no longer needed and many were already gone.

Mike came in the night. He was sitting at the table again and said, "You know the password. Just think about it. You have it written down too, you'll find it."

I called our Internet provider the next morning, telling her about Mike's death and my problem with the computer. She asked if I had any idea what it might be but also said that the account was in Mike's name and she wasn't at liberty to help me. She told me to just think about it, using the same words Mike had the night before.

I said it might be this...as a word popped into my head. "But," I told her, "it's the same one I tried last night, and it didn't work."

Yes, I was right. She would stay on the line with me while I turned on my computer and make sure I could get it to work. This time it worked. She said I may have spelled it wrong or touched the wrong key the night before. Whatever I had done wrong was now right. I would also soon find the envelope with the password inside.

I had no trouble going through Mike's clothes. He was not a clotheshorse and wore only what was necessary. Coming across some of his hunting things, his Carhart bibs and heavy winter jackets, sent a tear rolling down my cheek. The rest of his clothes were easy to dispose of.

Seeing some of the machines and things he loved, sold, given away, or hauled away made me sad—not because *I* cared about them but because *he* did. A friend hauled his expensive John Deere lawn tractor with all its attachments to the implement dealer where it had been purchased. They quickly sold it. Another friend drove his truck to the car dealership where that had been purchased, and again it was quickly sold. A neighbor put our pick-up camper on his pick-up and took it to a camper sale where they sold it for me. There was still a garage full of things to deal with but seeing all the stuff still sitting in our garage helped me feel closer to him.

I had put Mike's wallet in his dresser drawer the day he died and left it there for several months. One day I decided it was time to look through it. In it I found our children's baby pictures, their graduation pictures, and many licenses and identification cards for different organizations. I also found money. I felt sad going through all those things and a little guilty taking the money out. The billfold was old and falling apart. I threw it away.

That night he again came to me. It was so real that I felt like I could touch him. "I can stay with you a little while," he said. "My clothes are gone and that's OK, but I can't find my wallet."

I quickly explained that I had just taken it out of the dresser that afternoon and would give it back. "No," he said, "It's yours now."

I still dream of him but not as often. He now seems to be more in the far end of a room or in an area where he is still watching but, on the outskirts—perhaps on the outskirts of my life as I am now blessed to have a wonderful man sharing my life. That's exactly what Mike had wanted for me and with the man he thought would be perfect for me.

"Come back. Even as a shadow, even as a dream."

—Euripides

CHAPTER 53

JUST LIKE STARTING OVER

Mike had advice for me on every front. His words, "Do what you need to do to be okay and move on. Life is for the living. Don't waste a day. If you think of someone, call them. If you want something, buy it. If you want to go someplace, go. Don't spend your time feeling sad."

On a rainy day in June 1999, Mike brought up the subject of having another man in my life. We had agreed to talk about anything the other wanted to discuss. Sitting on the couch that day I was uncomfortable.

"I don't want to talk about the next person I might have in my life," I said.

"We promised we would talk about anything the other wanted to discuss," he said, reminding me of our promise to each other. He went on to say that this is what we needed to talk about. "You're too young to be alone; you have too many years left. You'll be old someday. I can picture you getting old."

There were several single men that we knew. He named a few, saying this person might call you but we know he drinks too much, or that person likes to chase women, or another person we knew couldn't handle money.

When he mentioned Ken, he always said, "I just think he's a really nice guy."

Mike had an uncanny knack of sizing up a person. I don't think it was necessarily his police training. He had it as a young man. If he said, "The guy is a phony," he was eventually proven right. I was much easier taken in by a smile, or small talk. I believed people were mostly nice.

"You're not going to tell me whom I will have next," I said, half kidding but half irritated that he would want to be in charge of that also. (Law enforcement officers do have control issues.)

"Well, just give Ken a call. Have lunch with him. What would be wrong with that?"

Eventually, I did just that. I had known Ken for about six years. He had come into the lumberyard and asked for me. His cousin had a resort and I waited on many customers that had resorts. Ken introduced himself, and told me he had heard I was the only one that knew anything. "I don't know everything," I had said with a smile, "but I *think* I do, and that's what counts."

Ken was remodeling his cabin into a year-round home. I had seen him off and on at Christmas and retirement parties. I would normally have seen him at the lumberyard in the summer after Mike passed away, but decided not to go back to work.

The secretary at work called to tell me a man had been asking about me. She described him as that handsome white-haired man. I called Ken and asked him to join me for lunch. He was working for the Fire Center, dispatching aircraft. He didn't have much time for lunch, but there was a restaurant at the airport. He could meet me there. So, we had that lunch Mike had suggested.

Ken has a smile that welcomes you in and a soft, comforting voice. I thought to myself that his mellow voice must sound good to a pilot on the other end of the radio. It has a reassuring quality that gives you the feeling that everything will be all right. We decided to have lunch again and then eventually dinner.

The first time he came to my house he wondered if I had a cat or a pet. "No," I said, "Do you?" Thinking to myself *if you do, I'm crossing you off.*

I had written a list of qualities that a man would have to have should I decide to let him into my life. It filled one entire legal page and half of the other side. The beginning was superficial: no facial hair, no earrings, no tattoos that showed, no long hair. Then, there were other things: no camping (my idea of roughing it would be a motel without a pool), no garden, and absolutely no animals.

The dogs that came in and out of our lives were a joy to Mike and the kids, but they were not a particular joy to me. I took care of them. Our dogs were not small and every one of them shed. I ate dog hair, wore dog hair, and slept in dog hair for years.

"How come our dogs are always sitting in your lap in pictures," my daughter asked, as we looked at old photos years later. I answered, "Because I kept them alive, fed them, and took them to the vet. I took care of all the dogs while the rest of you just enjoyed them." I had my share of dogs from the time I was married until 1983 when I took our Springer Spaniel to the veterinary clinic. Our dog Duke bit our son. They were best buddies and Duke always slept in our son's room. The dog had fallen into a Chemical Hot Pond, and, as the vet stated, *lost his mind.* The dogcatcher had saved him from drowning but he had to be put to sleep. I took him to the vet. Mike could not.

I then decided that Duke would be the last animal to enter our home. I had put my life on hold many times to care for a dog while the others went on enjoying theirs.

When I asked Ken the question about animals, I would not have changed my thinking nor would I ever expect someone to give up an animal for me. I know that would cause bitterness down the road. As we age, we may all have a list of things we won't do anymore.

The rest of my list had things like social skills. I didn't want a shy man. I wanted to enjoy the years that I had left being involved with people, going places, and making new friends. I didn't want to take care of anyone at a party or social gathering who might say, "Don't leave me alone. I don't know anyone here." No whiners for me, thank you very much.

Mike and I had grown up in the same area and went to school in the same high school. Although he was two years older, I knew everyone in his class and he, mine. At class reunions, we didn't have to babysit each other. I did, however, remember classmates bringing their spouses and the spouses hanging on tightly or looking particularly bored because they didn't know anyone.

Our neighborhood was having a block party, and I was going to help my neighbor get things ready. I had asked Ken if he would be interested in coming. Yes, he would. As I helped the hostess, I watched Ken through the window. He pulled up a chair and was soon engaged with the people around him. He looked quite comfortable as he interacted with strangers. I would later truly realize that he can indeed talk to anyone. Okay, I thought, he's passed another test with flying colors.

We would see each other often and enjoyed each other's company. He invited me to go to northern Minnesota, for a wedding reception where I would meet more of his family. He was close to his cousins, and as I watched him mingling with family and friends, I liked the importance he placed on family. I looked at him and thought, *I want this guy.*

We would travel to Arizona for the winter. Ken had a place near my rental. We rode many miles on motorcycle and I met new friends along with many retired troopers and their wives. I had not been on a cycle for about seventeen years until I started seeing Ken. The first time I went riding with him, tears ran down my face as I heard the engine of his Honda Goldwing start up. Memories of the 20 years Mike and I rode came flooding back.

Ken and I would marry in the fall of 2001. Our wedding guests were family and friends we had each had in our lives for so many years—about 180 guests joined in our celebration. We have been blessed to have found each other—to have a second chance for love and companionship. We make a good team. Our lives have been filled with adventure, traveling thousands of miles on motorcycle and in our respective vehicles.

Ken and Sue's wedding.

Besides the extensive travel that we have enjoyed in the western states, we have seen the fabulous EAA Air Venture Fly-In Convention at

Oshkosh, Wisconsin. We cycled into New York State, Maine, Nova Scotia, and Prince Edward Island where we also enjoyed being passengers on four different ferries. We spent a night in a quaint Bed and Breakfast in Bar Harbor, Maine. We had intended to roam the shops and trendy restaurants downtown, but Ken's WeatherBug told him we had better get out quick. The remains of a hurricane that had hit Florida would come roaring in with wind and rain soon. We hustled to pack our cycle and put on our rain gear. As we drove out of town, the first raindrops began. It wasn't long until we had to pull into a gas station and stayed for about an hour while the rain poured down. Later, heading west, we would run out of the storm.

Four wheeling in Arizona, Minnesota, Wisconsin, and South Dakota has kept excitement and adventure in our lives. Family is important to each of us. Together we have five children, two sons-in-law, a daughter-in-law, and seven grandchildren. I have thought often of my discussion with Mike and his urging to call Ken to have lunch with him. It was Mike's advice that would change my life and has given me happiness beyond belief. He looked out for me until the very end.

"All we have to decide is what to do with the time that is given us."

—The Lord of the Rings.

CHAPTER 54

FUNNY HOW TIME SLIPS AWAY

It's New Year's Eve 2019. I've enjoyed a delicious dinner, the company of friends, and my husband Ken. I managed to stay awake until midnight—an oddity as I get older. I couldn't go right to sleep as memories scrolled through my mind.

I thought of my first New Year's Eve without Mike. It was January 31,1999. People were talking of the doomsday that was certain to befall us. Newspapers and television had advice on what to do, how to survive. It was said that the change from 1999 to 2000 could be plagued with dire consequences—perhaps even the end of the world. At the very least, our computers would fail. Terrible disruptive things would surely happen. We could be forced to live without heat, electricity, and running water. People were stocking up on food and water much like they did when the Cold War was raging, when bomb shelters were being built, and the fear that "The Russians are coming...The Russians are coming."

I had spent the time between Christmas and New Year's with my sisters in Arizona. Calling the airlines from my sister's in Minneapolis for a flight back to home, I was told there would not be time for my ticket to arrive in the mail. I was given my travel number over the phone with instructions to come early and to please be patient as the airline wasn't sure what was going to occur. Although it was the day of New Year's Eve, they weren't sure what would happen should their electronics fail.

The flight home, a shuttle airplane from Minneapolis, arrived safely. Friends Sharon and Dave picked me up and invited me to spend New Year's Eve with them. Over the years we had spent many New Year's Eves together. I thanked them for their offer but declined. I was okay with spending my first New Year's Eve alone. I had also rung in the New Year many times by myself. Mike often worked holidays and New Year's Eve was no exception. I usually took the tree down and packed the Christmas decorations away while ringing in the New Year alone.

When asked by my friends what I would do if the power went out, if I had no heat, if things turned bad, I assured them that I would be fine. I wanted to be alone with my thoughts and memories.

I watched the New Year come in, first overseas, then in New York. At the stroke of midnight, the year 2000 arrived in Minnesota and nothing had gone wrong. The electricity stayed on, my television did not go black, and the world still existed. I still existed and had to begin a new life. I had been loved and cared for the past 35 years. I had been an immature young woman when that life began. As I started my life alone, although I felt strong and confident, I still felt so sad.

I remember thinking at one time that Mike might die someday in a car crash because of the many roads conditions he drove in and the miles he traveled—but never cancer. After he retired, knowing that women usually outlive their husbands, I had played a scenario in my mind. We would be old. I hadn't decided on an age. I would bring him coffee while he worked on a machine in the garage or on a project in his workshop and find he had died of a heart attack. I can't say why I had decided on a heart attack, maybe because that is the way his father died, and it seemed to be a fast and easy way to leave this earth.

New Year's Eve of 2019, I thought of that night nineteen years ago. The world had felt uncertainty for the year 2000 with Y2K arriving and the prediction of dire consequences as the world waited for the stroke of midnight. But nothing happened.

Years later, with a controversial election in 2016, an unprecedented prior election season, and a President-elect that was not a politician— certainly not cut from the same cloth we were used to—*again* there was uncertainty in our world. Several people had weighed in on the election saying that Trump would never be president. Numerous politicians, along with famous and infamous people gave similar assurances along with much laughter that Donald Trump would not occupy the White House. They were wrong.

Ken and I went to a Commemorative Air Force Back to the 40s Dance the winter of 2017. Many people arrived dressed in their military uniforms, and women who were dressed as Betty Grable and Rosie the Riveter also roamed the hangar. The majestic B25's gigantic nose protruded inside the large building that was filled with tables, chairs, and a large area assigned as the dance floor.

Songs made famous by Glenn Miller, Sammy Kaye, Tommy Dorsey, and many other big bands from the 40s era had us swinging to the music. I sat by a man in an Army uniform covered in medals. I asked him what all those medals meant? He went on to explain that he was a full bird colonel. "Is our nation safe?" I asked. I knew it would be interesting conversation and asked if he would answer a few questions. I told him I was writing a book about law enforcement. He seemed excited and eager to talk.

Yes. We are safe. He spoke of the elite force that takes care of our country whether it be in the Army, Air Force, Navy, Coast Guard, or Marines. They are skilled dedicated men and women. He did question how many times they had been deployed and that too many deployments hurt both the fighting military men and their families. Families are asked to endure too much also.

"Do you think we should have a draft?" I asked.

No, but he thinks every girl and boy that graduates from high school should be expected to give two years to their community or government. They should perform some type of service to help others. It would give them a sense of responsibility and would all around help them to grow up. He laments that we are not asking our young people to *grow up*.

So far, so good. I continued: "What are your feelings about police brutality?"

He believes we ask a lot of our law enforcement today. He knows a lot of people involved in police work and the majority of problems are few. The media likes to sensationalize the problems while not publicizing the difficulties of their job and the dedicated men and women who protect and take care of us every day.

He believed city police need to be out in their communities. Police should get out of their squad cars, walk around, and get to know the people. The more the officers know about the area they serve, the better they will be able to meet their needs and the more the public will trust them.

As I come to the end of this story, I am also reminded of the novels I have already written. They are fiction; still, they reflect a part of me also. Writers take bits and pieces of their own lives and adapt them into their novels. I was told by a friend who is also a writer to take situations—places in my world—and make them more exciting than they really are. We embellish, of course, when writing fiction, since most of our lives would not make truly exciting stories. Also, aspects of our true world invade our imagination, leaving some pieces of our real lives in the story.

My first novel, "A Small Pile of Bones," is set in Minnesota. The first lines of the synopsis say, *"It is an intricate web, spun from mistaken identities and long-buried, life-changing secrets. Romance and discreet passion, scandal, love, and loyalty trap the painful past, that ultimately evolves into tearful reunions and heartwarming joy. Were all seven of Claire and Andy Van Buren's Rh factor infants buried at Hillside Cemetery? Did Victoria's uncle, Dr. Robert Wheeler, save any of them? His recently opened notes—part of a file that was entrusted with his attorney until his death— lead a band of self-appointed and professional detectives to the truth. Along the way, the sound of a backhoe, slamming the hard ground of the cemetery, make the grave robbers' stomachs churn. What they find, a dying nurse's delivery of an old rusty metal box, her confession—all contribute to secrets revealed, identities untangled, and hearts reunited."* In the story I write about the graveyard that is close to town and plants that need to be watered often in order to survive the wind blowing through the cemetery. I write, *"The wind howled across the prairie, blowing flowerpots into the woods if not loaded down with rocks or held sturdily in place with spikes."* That's true, and when I put flowers on graves in that cemetery on Memorial Day, that's exactly what I do to keep them from blowing away.

My second novel, "Stay For The Sunset" is set in Arizona. The first words of the synopsis say: *"In the rugged mountains surrounding Northern Arizona, the wealthy owner of Apache Tears Ranch wipes tears from his old eyes. Cancer roars through his body with no regard for his plans for the rest of his life or the plans for his heirs. The letter, telling young Kate Mitchell of her grandfather's death, launches a journey that will take her to meet the estranged family of her mother and father. Agreeing to the requirement that she stay at the beautiful Garrison ranch for a minimum of nine days, she boards the amazing Gulfstream 650 jet. Excitement and apprehension fill her mind as she travels to Arizona for the reading of her grandfather's Will and his Memorial Service. Breathtaking sunsets, deception, murder, kidnapping,* and romance entrap the young Kate. Family secrets and a gathering storm of violence from drug and human smugglers will soon bring danger and test Kate's courage and the bravery of others."

Cycling with friends throughout Arizona over the last seventeen years, Ken and I have amassed over 250,000 miles on four different motor cycles. The beauty of the desert and mountainous landscapes soon encouraged me to write the story that scrolled through my mind. Many readers have wanted to find the Apache Tears ranch, the expansive and opulent ranch between Mesa and Payson. I tell them it doesn't exist but they want to find it.

Letters Never Sent takes place in my home area and is set in the imaginary town of Slow Creek and on the shores of Lac qui Parle Lake.

I write: *"In the dark, dank cellar, under the abandoned Slow Creek Post Office, letters and postcards lay waiting to be mailed. They harbor silent voices with long-buried secrets. Rodents have chewed on the envelopes and scattered them around the dirt floor. The foster sister's return to Slow Creek, just to plan their Aunt Diane's burial, is interrupted by the discovery of the lost mail. However, finding the misplaced correspondence takes them on a quest...with disturbing results. Unable to resist the temptation to open the letters, they discover information that will change the course of several peoples' lives. Deception creates turmoil in what had seemed to be tranquil lives. Confessions of murder shock the sisters and require them to take action. They agonize over opening and delivering the letters—or simply handing them over to the authorities. Renewing old friendships and long-lost loves bring the sentimental sisters' excitement, anxiety, and thought-provoking decision-making".*

My fourth novel, *Blood Moon*, is set in northern Minnesota.

I wrote: *As a full moon rolls slowly across a star-studded sky, thrill seeking marauders await their next prey. A lonely woman gets caught up in tantalizing thoughts of taking on the role of another's persona. It's a netherworld where even the most abhorrent satisfaction is found. Emily Blake arrives at Stonebridge Resort on beautiful Lake Pokegama to attend an all-school reunion. Troubling memories lie deeply buried. Estrangement from her brother and a strained relationship with her father weigh heavily on her mind. Her abduction after the reunion has her struggling to quiet fears and reconnect with her family. A hoarder, an aging Hollywood actress, the beautiful Judge Chantal McAllister, and the owners of the prestigious Stonebridge Resort join together in this fascinating story of erased memories, horrifying visions, romance, and subsequent forgiveness.*

We've all had uncertainty in our lives for many different reasons. I had been a widow for just four months when 2000 arrived. I had ambiguous thoughts as to what my life would be with the loss of Mike. I wasn't sure, nor was I totally confident that I would know what to do in every situation that might arise. Still, I did have confidence in my ability to cope. I had faith in God and faith in myself.

I found my way. It was at times a frightening journey but also a learning expedition. I am confident that we, the resilient, tough American people, will find our way through this new storm of politics. As we struggle to find common ground, let's remember that good will overcome bad, that together—first as a community, then as a state, and lastly as a resilient and confident nation—we will overcome anything that stands in our way. We can and will be strong enough for whatever challenges come. Also, we *need* unending faith in ourselves and in others.

With the array of television shows on satellite TV, I have been able to enjoy a favorite television show from long ago. "The Twilight Zone" offers life lessons that can do more than just save us from being eaten by aliens.

Some of the titles are culture blessings: "Don't Live in the Past," "Be Your Own Person." Those were engaging episodes, telling stories of fantasy and science fiction. Most of them were dramatic but often had humor mixed in with their teachings. Those lessons continue to wear well today. It enlightens us to several inescapable truths. It also helps us with the realization that this life we cherish will not last forever.

Mike's grandmother lived to be 90 and told me that if you live to be old, you will have endured many heartaches. She had buried her parents, all but one sibling, her husband, and two sons. Tremendous faith in God and acceptance in His strength to help her through the dark days brought her peace.

Mike was blessed to have that same feeling of peace. His unfailing belief that death comes when it is supposed to, that God's planning is perfect, gave him comfort and helped us, his loved ones, accept and find that peace as well.

We will all be confronted by death at some time. Many have already faced that with the death of their grandparents, parents, other family members, or friends. I have already buried my grandparents, my parents, my husband, my sister Carolyn, and many close friends. It is not odd at my age to have experienced life and all its happiness, sadness, challenges, and the loss of loved ones.

How will I feel when I am ready to die? Or maybe not ready to die but know that I'm going to? I have asked myself those questions many times; but I still don't know the answer. I don't fear death, but I'm not looking forward to it at this point of my life either. I have had what I consider a good life. I think as we age, we come to realize more gradually that change is a natural part of our lifecycle. If we like something, it will eventually change. If we dislike something, it will eventually change.

I like to think I will be resolved—at peace—ready to meet my Maker when my time comes. I would hope to be brave for my children, but I can't say for sure that I will be. I can't exactly trust how I might react. Of course, that too depends on how old I am. Perhaps the old die a bit better—more resolved at taking that last breath while suffering with painful joints, failed health, and an effort to continue living day by day. At that time, it may be easier to die than to stay alive.

Having said goodbye to most of our family and friends by the time we are old, may make giving up this life easier. I think, as we age, we become aware and at peace about our own mortality. As I write this, I have few regrets and still love life.

I continue to be in awe of Mike's response to the doctor's dreadful diagnosis. Just fifty-four years old when he heard the diagnosis in May, when he turned fifty-five in July, and when certain death was eminent in September did not seem a long time, but it was long enough. We didn't need the extra time the oncologist offered with the experimental treatments he had suggested; those not-quite-living not-quite-dead last months.

Why would Mike want to seek treatment? Our family doctor didn't actually ask the question, although in certain ways he did. When he told Mike about the prognosis and the time he might have for living, it was almost as if he had asked, *Do you want some pretty good months and a few rough weeks, or do you want to be in agony for six months and die anyway.*

A trooper's wife, had planned a birthday party for Mike. It was a tentative plan as Mike would often have bouts of weakness and his legs wouldn't hold him up. He was, however, feeling good on that sunny day July 18, 1999, and the afternoon was perfect. Old friends, most of who had been or still were in the law enforcement arena, joined in the celebration of their friend Mike's birthday, eating cake and ice cream, reminiscing, and saying goodbye.

If I am blessed to have a sane mind before I die, I hope to have the conviction, the total faith in God, that Mike had.

"The world is a fine place and worth fighting for and I hate very much to leave it," writes Robert Jordan in *For Whom the Bell Tolls*. I will have heard the bell toll for many of my loved ones, and eventually that day will come when the bell will toll for me.

"Promise to kiss me on my brow when I am dead. I will feel it."

—Victor Hugo, Les Misérables

CHAPTER 55

THE MIDNIGHT HOUR

He's a quiet man—shy until he gets to know you and not used to sharing his feelings. He can tease and banter back and forth with his cohorts, but he rarely truly shares his feelings.

The night shift has ended, his squad car is parked in the driveway. He opens the door to exit, and gently closes the car door. He slowly opens the entrance door to his home and walks up the stairs, taking his gun belt off and putting it on the top shelf of the closet. Even though he does it quietly, his daughter hears the clunk of the gun hitting the shelf and the keys on the ring attached make a jingling sound as they land. He snaps off his tie, unbuttons his shirt, and hangs it on a hanger. Pulling his Tee shirt out of his pants, he lights a cigarette and walks out on the deck. It's a warm summer, still dark, early morning.

His family is asleep, but they have each, in a sub-conscience state, heard the subtle noises that tell them he is home. His sleeping family will be up soon—children off to school and his wife to work. He's been a worrier for as long as he can remember. Wishing he could share those worries, open up emotionally, share his fears, he has tried but he cannot.

There's so much he wishes he could talk about. The sights, sounds, and smells that have been a part of his life all these patrol years swirl through his mind. He wonders how to tell someone about pulling a teenager from a mangled automobile. He remembers the lie he told, saying "You're going to be okay. Just hang on; the ambulance is coming. There were a few last breaths and then she was gone. He thinks of high-speed chases. When he was young, he liked them. They were exhilarating and fun, but not anymore—not as the big city chases became fatal for the bad and the innocent. He's given people breaks and come down hard on a few. He's been in those dark places, feeling overwhelmed. He can't find the right words to explain the look on the parents' faces when they open the door and find a policeman standing there. Blaring lights and sirens have their own special eerie sound. It's something he never quite gets used to, but he doesn't really remember that they're there either—not until the crisis has passed and his mind is quiet.

There are times when he feels satisfied, content that he has helped make a difference, that he's been there in time of crisis and created order from chaos. He is pleased with himself, with the times he has talked to a teenager, explained that the trooper's goal is not to write tickets, but to try and keep a fast-driving, bullet-proof young man from killing himself and others. He smiles as he thinks about the comments from motorists. He has heard so many, but one sticks in his mind: "They must have a quota." His grin continues as he thinks to himself, *No, we do not have a quota.*

Putting his hands behind his head as he lies on the bed, he muses: He's soon to retire and memories of his last 30 years scroll through his head. He thinks about the late-night callouts.

When he was young, he was up in an instant, pulling his pants on, grabbing his shirt off the hanger. Three steps down the hallway, he quickly pulled his gun belt down from the shelf of the closet. His boots were on in a minute, and he was out the door. Even in the dead of winter, the cold car hadn't bothered him. He could flop back in bed after investigating an accident or roaring down the road on a blood run. *That was the clue,* he thought. *He was young and police work is a young man's job.*

There might be a stalled car in the ditch—maybe an accident or somebody walking down the highway. He'd be down the road a few miles before he felt totally awake. He has wondered these last years of working, with the change in today's society if this is a real call, if someone is actually in distress? Or will he have to fight for his life? There's no help from anyone in the middle of the night on the desolate highway. He may be 40 miles from a town.

He also reflects on the physical, emotional, and mental drain of lost sleep, forgone social activities, and the missed times with his children. He did make it to their Christmas programs a few times, as well as to one broom ball game; but most of the time he was working or, at the very least, on call. His mind conjures up the smells of an accident scene, the distinct smell of gasoline, sometimes a burning car, screams, pandemonium, and the unforgettable stench of death.

His reverie continues, as does his insomnia. He remembers a day off one summer day. He was at a picnic. A man fell to the ground, and somebody hollered at him for help expecting he would do something. He ran over and gave the man CPR, although he knew it was already too late, a little color came back into the dead man's face. He was probably breaking his ribs as he pumped his chest; but he had done something—people expected him to do *something*.

He recalls his wife's words. "I wish you would let others see you as I do." His reply would be, if he was in a particular mood, "You're the only person who can hurt me. You know me so well."

His children would never understand. He was a worrier and couldn't change. Maybe he was like that at least a little when he was younger but his career in law enforcement most certainly had exacerbated his existing fears for his loved ones.

Ordinary. That word could describe him and the world he and his family lived in for some of his life. The other part of his life—his career—is anything but ordinary for anyone but him. He carries with him emotional damage. There is even physical damage with the occasional knockdown, drag-out fight with a drunk. Dead bodies are hard to get used to—mangled bodies dismembered from the violence of a crash—but become ordinary. Perhaps at one point he would call it an ordinary life. He's watched people take their last breaths, trying to calm them, and he believes to this day that being with them has given them a sense of peace in their last moments. Bright red blood becomes ordinary. At one time, it had made him cringe, but not anymore. When it's over, he walks into a restaurant, orders a burger, talks shop with other law enforcement, and acts like the sight he just saw is not still laboring in his mind. It's ordinary.

One minute you're driving down the road the next minute you're going a hundred miles an hour. Working weekends, holidays, birthdays, and anniversaries has taken a toll not only on his life but the life of his spouse, children, friends, siblings and parents.

As sleep eludes him, he remembers that he is fortunate to have a few friends that are not in the law enforcement community. There's so much value in those friends.

He thinks of all the others in the law enforcement arena. Deputies and local police see even more of the seamy side of human beings and their life. Working for too many years, one cannot help but become cynical. Forget trusting people. The worst in people is what seems to come to the surface and it is more difficult to find something good in them.

Although always planning to come home, he's not truly sure that he will. The things he's seen today scroll through his head like a horror movie. Someone is counting on him for help. He has memories of discussions with other law enforcement, when their defenses are down, when they are at a party with fellow officers and their guard is compromised. They talk more about their feelings when a party atmosphere has taken over. They talk of the need to be there for each other and of the public that sometimes hates them. No one knows that they could be dealing with their own personal problems.

He's always cautious, acutely aware of what's going on around him. His wife has given him a bad time: "Do you trust anyone? Are you always suspicious?" Yes, he has to admit. He has stopped trusting the public and is beginning to dislike all people in general.

Maybe it's time to get out, but he can't see himself in any other profession. Retirement is in his mind more as each day goes by. He doesn't share the ugly part of work, but it is still there. He doesn't rush home to tell his spouse what he just saw or what he experienced. It's easier to say it was fine or I just don't want to talk about it when asked about the day. He has, without realizing it, become numb to the daily troubles of others but it still lurks. He has also at times become numb to his family, to his friends. He's shut off his feelings for so long.

Some officers say they've had enough and get out before they are ready for retirement, but most of them feel compelled to be in that line of work. It does take the attributes of an ordinary person, since much of their work is mundane, especially for the local police officer. Some of their day is filled with 911 hang ups, animal complaints, welfare checks, gas drive offs, suspicious activity. The officer, man or woman, must be someone who isn't always ordinary. They must be someone who will step up, be ready and willing when required—to be *extra*ordinary.

> "*Tomorrow is the most important thing in life. Comes into us at midnight very clean. It's perfect when it arrives and it puts itself in our hands. It hopes we have learned something from yesterday.*"
>
> —John Wayne

"Forever on the Job"

Once you receive your shield it never comes off, whether they can see it, or not. It fuses to the soul through adversity, fear, and adrenaline and whoever has worn it with pride, integrity, and guts can sleep through the "call of the wild" that waifs through bedroom windows in the deep of the night. When police retire: When a good police person leaves the "Job" and retires to a better life, many are jealous, some are pleased and yet others, who may have already retired, wonder.

We wonder if he knows what he is leaving behind, because we already know. We know, for example, that after a lifetime of camaraderie that few experience, it will remain as a longing for those past times. We know in the law enforcement life there is a fellowship which lasts long after the uniforms are hung up in the back of the closet. We know even if he throws them away, they will be on him with every step and breath that remains in his life. We also know how the very bearing of the man speaks of what he was and, in his heart, still is. These are the burdens of the job.

You will still look at people suspiciously, still see what others do not see or choose to ignore and always will look at the rest of the law-enforcement world with a respect for what they do; only grown in a lifetime of knowing. Never think for one moment you are escaping from that life. You are only escaping the "job" and; merely being allowed to leave "active" duty. So, what I wish for you is that whenever you ease into retirement, in your heart you never forget that "Blessed are the Peacemakers" for they shall be called children of God, and you are still a member of the greatest fraternity the world has ever known.

—Unknown

SP 280
10-7
Off Duty

Printed in the United States
By Bookmasters